RACE AND HUMAN RIGHTS

RACE AND HUMAN RIGHTS

EDITED BY
Curtis Stokes

MICHIGAN STATE UNIVERSITY PRESS • EAST LANSING

♾ The paper used in this publication meets the minimum requirements of ANSI/NISO
Z39.48-1992 (R 1997) (Permanence of Paper).

Michigan State University Press
East Lansing, Michigan 48823-5245

Printed and bound in the United States of America.

15 14 13 12 11 10 09   1 2 3 4 5 6 7 8 9 10

LIBRARY OF CONGRESS CATALOGING-IN-PUBLICATION DATA
Race and human rights / edited by Curtis Stokes.
p. cm.
Includes bibliographical references.
ISBN 978-0-87013-750-1 (pbk. : alk. paper) 1. Racism—United States. 2. Human
rights—United States. 3. Discrimination—United States. 4. War on Terrorism,
2001– 5. Minorities—United States—Social conditions. 6. United States—Race
relations. 7. United States—Politics and government—2001– I. Stokes, Curtis.
E184.A1R223 2008
305.800973—dc22
2008017057

Book and cover design by Sharp Des!gns, Inc., Lansing, Michigan

Michigan State University Press is a member of the Green Press Initiative and is
committed to developing and encouraging ecologically responsible publishing
practices. For more information about the Green Press Initiative and the use of
recycled paper in book publishing, please visit *www.greenpressinitiative.org.*

Visit Michigan State University Press on the World Wide Web at *www.msupress.msu.edu*

For Josiah Roy F. Tibay
and all the children of the world,
and my wife, Julie, for her understanding
and patience with me.

Contents

Acknowledgments

This book is the product of contributions from many people, especially the ten scholars whose chapters constitute the core of the anthology. The chapters are selected and revised papers that were originally delivered at three recent conferences sponsored by Michigan State University's (MSU) Race in 21st Century America conference project. We also thank everyone else who participated in these conferences, either as invited speakers or panelists, or from the general public.

The following MSU faculty and staff are thanked for their long-standing commitment toward the Race in 21st Century America conference project: Murray Edwards (Office of Cultural and Academic Transitions), Danny Layne (Julian Samora Research Institute), Joe T. Darden (Department of Geography), Geneva Smitherman (Department of English), George Cornell (Native American Institute), Dorothy Harper Jones (African American and African Studies Program), Francisco Villarruel (Julian Samora Research Institute), Theresa Melendez (Chicano/Latino Studies Program), Ronald E. Hall (School of Social Work), and Gloria Smith (African American and African Studies Program). Additionally, I thank MSU faculty for either encouraging or requiring their students to participate in the race conferences, as well as students who have participated in these conferences.

For the past eight years, James Madison College faculty, staff, and students have provided the core support for whatever success the Race in 21st Century

America conference project has had. I thank especially the following faculty and staff: Norman A. Graham, Jonas Zoninsein, Louise A. Jezierski, Anna Pegler Gordon, Andaluna C. Borcilia, Lisa D. Cook, Austin D. Jackson, Lori Lancour, Pamela J. Martinez, Peter J. Murray, Kim N. Allan, Grant B. Littke, Jeffrey A. Judge, Rocky R. Beckett, Carolyn Koenigsknecht, Gabriel G. Tanner, and Danielle E. Johnson.

The following MSU units have made it possible to sustain the Race in 21st Century America conference project: Office of the President, Office of the Provost, James Madison College, Office of the Vice President for Student Affairs and Services, Office for Inclusion and Intercultural Initiatives, and College of Arts and Letters. Long-standing and impressive individual support from MSU has come from Lou Anna K. Simon, former provost and now president; Lee N. June, associate provost and vice president for Student Affairs and Services; Paulette Granberry Russell, director of the Office for Inclusion and Intercultural Initiatives; Sherman Garnett, dean of James Madison College; Patrick J. McConegy, former acting dean of the College of Arts and Letters; and especially Robert F. Banks, former and now retired associate provost and vice president for Academic Human Resources.

Finally, I thank the Michigan State University Press, especially Julie Loehr, assistant director and editor-in-chief, for supporting this project.

Preface

This volume is the third in a book series resulting from Michigan State University's (MSU) Race in 21st Century America conference project. Occurring biennially since 1999 and typically drawing between 1,000 and 1,500 pre-registrants, there are two central components of the race conference idea. Our racially and ethnically diverse planning committee brings to campus scholars, community activists, and ordinary residents, representing significant racial, ethnic, and ideological diversity, to participate in thoughtful conversations with the MSU community about the contentious and stubborn problem of race in America. Our conversations aim to generate ideas to equip conference attendees when organizing and mobilizing their communities, as well as when challenging public officials and legislators on the importance of working toward closing the persistent racial gap in life chances separating whites from other racial groups in the United States. To this end, anthologies comprising selected papers presented at various race conferences are published. The current anthology brings together selected and revised papers from race conferences occurring between 2003 and 2007, as well as a couple of essays from invited contributors, on the theme of race and human rights.

Introduction

CURTIS STOKES

HUMAN RIGHTS, COMPETING CONCEPTIONS

The current worldwide discussion of human rights has its immediate origins in the implications of the terrorist attacks on the World Trade Center, Pentagon, and United Airlines flight 93 on September 11, 2001, and the domestic and international consequences of the U.S.-led invasions of Afghanistan (October 2001) and Iraq (March 2003). A quick glance at publications by respected organizations like Human Rights Watch and Amnesty International in the decades immediately preceding September 11 reveals that governments and political organizations of diverse ideological orientations engaged in political assassinations, torture, and inhumane treatment of individuals and targeted groups. What was new after September 11 was the intensity of the discussion about human rights, both in the United States and internationally. The truly remarkable side of the conversation in the United States was the ease with which many American policy makers and political elites designed ways to reconcile liberal democracy with the use of torture in the name of national security, however much this was at odds with U.S.-supported international covenants and even American law.[1]

Yet what do we mean by human rights? Jack Donnelly writes: "If human rights are the rights that one has simply as a human being, then only human beings have human rights; if one is not a human being, then by definition one can not have human rights. Because only individual persons are human beings, it would seem obvious that only individuals can have human rights."[2]

In fact, the belief in human rights is an old idea that is not specific to any historical period, nationality, or ethnicity; interpretations of what constitutes a right, or even an obligation, are as varied as the peoples and cultures that constitute humanity.[3] However, with the rise of capitalism, bourgeois revolutions, and liberal political philosophy on both sides of the Atlantic, the first major debates on the meaning and core elements of what constitutes human rights occurred. This was especially so during the English Civil Wars of the mid-seventeenth century and their immediate aftermath and, of course, the French Revolution; both an individualistic and communitarian or group-based view of rights appeared in this era.

In 1646 Richard Overton, a Leveller philosopher, summed up the emerging and soon to be dominant individualistic strain of the Western view of rights: "To every individual in nature is given an individual property by nature not to be invaded or usurped by any. For every one . . . has a self-propriety, else could he not be himself; and this no second may presume to deprive any of without manifest violation and affront to the very principles of nature and of the rules of equity and justice between man and man." Or as John Locke would later put it, "every man has a property in his own person."[4] The idea of "self-propriety" would evolve into demands for a growing list of natural or human rights, including universal suffrage, private property, religious toleration, and freedom of press and association as extensions of one's person. Alongside this view of human rights in civil and political terms advanced by English liberals such as Overton and Locke, which was narrowly applied to individuals and often linked to a defense of existing and increasing inequality in private property, there appeared a more group-oriented conception of rights associated with the Diggers (a movement of poor and landless farmers seeking to till in common portions of traditional English common lands, which were increasingly being expropriated by government and wealthy landowners). Preceding Karl Marx by two centuries, Gerrard Winstanley, the leading Digger philosopher, argued that genuine freedom is possible only with the existence of common ownership of property, and he offered a powerful critique of the effects of rising agrarian capitalism on poor and middling farmers. Winstanley writes: "Buying and selling is the great cheat that robs and steals the earth one from another. It is that which makes some lords, and others beggars, some rulers, others to be ruled; and makes great murderers and thieves to be imprisoners and hangers of little ones."[5]

The French Revolution provided an even sharper contrasting of these competing views of human rights, one placing an emphasis upon "individual" civil and political rights and especially securing private property (these were often presented as inseparable) and the other conception understanding individualism and human development in large measure as being mediated through "society," thus validating the idea of social responsibility and in some sense the necessity of common or social ownership of property.[6] Ishay correctly summarizes the relationship between the two competing human rights poles in the West. The Enlightenment, he says, "represented the formative age of our modern conception of human rights. . . . [T]he rights to life, civil liberty, and property became the credo of the new age. To promote these liberties, Enlightenment thinkers envisioned the spread of commercial enterprises and republican institutions." Over the next two centuries, this was to become the dominant Western understanding of human rights, especially so in the United States. On the other side of the ledger was, Ishay appropriately notes, the developing socialist movement, first articulating, in embryonic form, its human rights perspective during the English Civil Wars and later in its critical assessment of the political economy limits of the French Revolution. According to Ishay, "Despite its important contribution to human rights discourse, the human rights legacy of the socialist—and especially the Marxist—tradition is today widely dismissed. Bearing in mind the atrocities that have been committed by communist regimes in the name of human rights, the historical record still needs to show that the struggle for universal suffrage, social justice, and worker's rights . . . was strongly influenced by socialist thought."[7] Even as they embraced a human rights project in principle, whether a group-oriented model or individualistic model, atrocities were (and continue to be) committed by both Communist and liberal democratic regimes; consider, for example, the strong similarities between the racialized history of the United States and Joseph Stalin's Soviet Gulag.[8]

Given its origins, culture, and history, the United States generally has a narrower understanding of human rights than many other economically developed Western nations. Therefore it is not surprising that the United States typically celebrates those sections of the United Nations Universal Declaration of Human Rights (1948) focusing on civil and political rights while downplaying those highlighting the importance of social and economic rights. For example, the U.S. State Department's Web site indicates that its "2006 Country Reports on Human Rights Practices" (released on March 6, 2007) "cover recognized individual, civil, political and worker rights, as set forth in the Universal Declaration of Human Rights." The State Department, however, is silent on Article 25, which speaks to social and economic rights.[9] A case in point is that the extraordinary gains of the Cuban Revolution in health care and education for all Cubans can be essentially dismissed in the country report for Cuba by asserting that Cuba is a "totalitarian state," where, we are told, "prison conditions continued to be harsh and life threatening"—this is said about Cuba even though arguably far worse human rights abuses in Cuba are occurring at the Guantanamo Bay detention center, run by the United States in connection with its "war on terrorism."[10] Not only does the United States artificially distinguish between civil and political rights and social and economic rights, often leading the nation to align itself with repressive regimes supposedly in the name of national security interests, but it, as can be seen in Iraq, Afghanistan, and Guantanamo Bay, frequently violates those very human rights principles it claims to embrace.

This discrepancy between the United States' claimed principles and its practice (even when focusing narrowly on civil and political rights), at home and abroad, led Amnesty International to conclude, already in 1998: "The USA was founded in the name of democracy, political and legal equality, and individual freedom. However, despite its claims to international leadership in the field of human rights, and its many institutions to protect individual liberties, the USA is failing to deliver the fundamental promise of rights for all."[11]

RACIALIZING HUMAN RIGHTS

With the above debates on individual and group-based conceptions of human rights as background, as well as the question of professed principles versus actual practice in national human rights projects, the contributors to this volume examine the meaning of human rights in the United States, historically and in the post–September 11 era. Particular attention is given to exploring the racial dimensions of human rights. In our view, human rights undoubtedly include the fight for civil and political rights but are far more than these, and thus our understanding of human rights suggests the need for a more expansive framework, especially so if historically excluded racial groups in the United States, like blacks and American Indians, are ever to substantively eliminate the centuries-old and deep racial gap in life chances separating them from white Americans.[12] Collectively, the ten chapters in this book point in the direction of the need for a more expansive American view of human rights, with this introductory chapter providing the context for a new conversation and practice on the intersection of racial inequality and human rights concerns.

Chapters 1 through 3 examine the racial implications of the "war on terrorism." In chapter 1, Natsu Taylor Saito, with America's "war on terrorism" as backdrop, provides a broad overview of the extensive historical and contemporary interrelationship between racial oppression and the national security state. Noting that the attacks on human rights, even as that concept is narrowly understood and implemented by the United States, had their origins at the very founding of the nation but have worsened since the events of September 11, 2001, she calls for a progressive movement to challenge the status quo if the racially repressive security state is to be overcome. Ward Churchill, in chapter 2, focuses more narrowly on the birth and evolution of the Pinkerton detective agency, presenting it as an early forerunner of the Federal Bureau of Investigation (FBI), which has played a central role in the suppression of civil and political rights since its birth. In chapter 3, Darryl C. Thomas examines the role of Africa in post–World War II American foreign policy ambitions and the United States' more recent attempts at empire building. Thomas finds that some African leaders, even at the expense of their own countries, have been complicit with America's national security state in eroding rights across the African continent.

Chapters 4 through 6 examine the relationship between immigration and race. Robert Aponte, in chapter 4, in an examination of the difficult social and economic conditions facing blacks and Latinos, provides a statistical and comparative analysis of the level of exploitation faced by Latinos, especially Mexican-descended Latinos. Noting the recent emergence of Latinos as the largest minority group in the United States, he argues that their social and economic conditions today are worse than those faced by black Americans. He suggests that any human rights debate today not addressing this new reality will need to be reconstituted. In chapter 5, H. L. T. Quan examines the role of immigration as a human rights issue, especially when linked to the problem of citizenship in the United States. With an analysis of both the 2005 Katrina disaster and consequent displacement of largely black New Orleans, as well as the more recent and massive immigration rights rallies across the country, Quan considers the work of political scientist Samuel P. Huntington as pivotal in her call for a new conception of citizenship rights. Robert C. Smith, in chapter 6, examines the weak response of African American leadership to the rise and challenge of Latinos, as well as the negative implications of unrestricted immigration upon black life chances. He notes that Latinos, like earlier ethnic immigrants from Western Europe, may be on a path toward whiteness and that this outcome could be bleak for the future of blacks in the United States.

Chapters 7 through 10 examine affirmative action as a human rights tool. Providing a historical analysis of the origins and development of affirmative action, especially in Michigan, Pero Gaglo Dagbovie, in chapter 7, utilizes the writings of Ira I. Katznelson and Philip F. Rubio to present his argument that affirmative action, even if not explicitly stated in public policy, historically has primarily benefited white Americans. He argues that affirmative action, as we know it today, was originally conceived out of the 1960s black protest movement to address the historical and contemporary racial gap in life chances separating black and white Americans. In chapter 8, George A. Yancey analyzes the white Religious Right and suggests the need for outreach activity from both the black community and the white Religious Right if progress is to be made on addressing the problem of race in America. Acknowledging that this would be a very difficult project, Yancey believes common ground on some specific issues can be reached between the white Religious Right and the black community. Observing that existing race advancement strategies by black leaders are going nowhere, he thinks his recommended approach can do no worse. With the United Nations Universal Declaration of Human Rights and its annual human development reports as backdrop, Jonas Zoninsein, in chapter 9, examines the place of affirmative action policy in Brazil and more generally Latin America. Noting the large gap in life chances separating dark-skinned and light-skinned Latin Americans, Zoninsein argues that affirmative action should be viewed as a human rights issue, with all of the implications this argument has for the problem of race in the United States. J. Angelo Corlett, in the final chapter, provides a philosophical overview and analysis of the problem of affirmative action in the United States, arguing that affirmative action as presently understood and implemented in the United States, primarily benefiting white women and to some extent ethnic and racial groups other than blacks and American Indians, needs to be reconfigured and its benefits applied to the nation's worse-off groups, especially blacks and American Indians. Though not optimistic about the outcome, he directly appeals to white women, in the name of human rights, to abandon self-interest and publicly support the application of a reconstituted affirmative action policy toward people of color, especially blacks and American Indians.

CONCLUSION

At its origins in early modern Western Europe and the United States, the now dominant liberal view of human rights as essentially civil and political rights was not applied to dark-skinned peoples in Africa, Asia, and the Americas. Today, racial inequality is in principle a human rights question, as can be seen in United Nations documents and publications. But reality is another matter. The so-called war on terrorism is but the most recent example of how the application of a human rights agenda, even one narrowly focused on civil and political rights, can be turned against dark-skinned peoples across the globe, including in the United States.

NOTES

1. See, for example, the United Nations "Convention Against Torture and Other Cruel, Inhuman or Degrading Treatment or Punishment" adopted in 1984, and the "International Covenant on Civil and Political Rights," adopted in 1966 (Office of the High Commissioner for Human Rights http://www.ohchr.org/EN/Pages/WelcomePage.aspx). Both treaties were ratified by the U.S. Senate and are now American law. While the U.S. government has been attempting, with strong resistance from human rights groups, to redefine what constitutes torture, U.S. non-government organizations have been increasingly charging the United States with clear violations of its obligations under the "torture" treaty. See "U.S. Fails to Uphold Torture Treaty Abroad and at Home" (American Civil Liberties Union http://www.aclu.org/intlhumanrights/gen/25446prs20060504.html).

2. Donnelly, *Universal Human Rights,* 20. To his credit, Donnelly does go on to say that "individuals are members of communities" and thus these latter must be factored into any human rights equation; but it is not altogether clear how this enriches his individualist claim.

3. For an African interpretation of the intersection of human values, religion, and society, see "The Zulu Personal Declaration" (1825), in Asante and Abarry, *African Intellectual Heritage,* 371–78. Also, Johansen, *Forgotten Founders,* provides a fine analysis on the importance of rights in the political thought of American Indians.

4. Richard Overton, "An Arrow against all Tyrants" (1646) in Sharp, *English Levellers,* 54–72; and Locke, *Two Treatises of Government,* 287. Levellers (small shopkeepers and independent tradesmen) were among the earliest liberal democrats, though sometimes mistakenly and even deliberately charged by their more conservative critics with wanting to "level" private property. Theirs was a commitment to a kind of political democracy rather than economic democracy.

5. Gerrard Winstanley, "A Declaration from the Poor Oppressed People of England" (1649), and "The True Levellers' Standard Advanced," in Hill, *Winstanley*, 101. Diggers considered themselves to be the "true" Levellers, and indeed they were. See David W. Petegorsky, *Left-Wing Democracy in the English Civil War*, for an excellent overview and analysis of Digger political philosophy.

6. Lynn Hunt provides a useful overview of the centrality of France for the modern human rights debate. See Hunt, *French Revolution and Human Rights*.

7. Ishay, *Human Rights Reader*, xxiv–xxv, 93. A sharply critical analysis of the role of democratic rights in the socialist, including Marxist, tradition, is provided by F. A. Hayek, economist and Nobel laureate. He writes, "One of the most influential political movements of our time, socialism, is based on demonstrably false premises, and despite being inspired by good intentions and led by some of the most intelligent representatives of our time, endangers the standard of living and the life itself of a large proportion of our existing population" (*The Fatal Conceit: The Errors of Socialism*, 9). In an unpublished 1933 essay linking the Nazi political party to Marxism, Hayek says:

> The persecution of the Marxists, and of democrats in general, tends to obscure the fundamental fact that National Socialism is a genuine socialist movement, whose leading ideas are the final fruit of the anti-liberal tendencies which have been steadily gaining ground in Germany since the later part of the Bismarckian era, and which led the majority of the German intelligentsia first to 'socialism of the chair' and later to Marxism in its social democratic or communist form ("Nazi-Socialism," *The Road To Serfdom*, 245).

Contrary to critics like Hayek, how did Marx and Engels understand the modern origins of the human rights debate and its significance for the laboring population? According to Marx and Engels, the birth and early development of a modern human rights agenda from the seventeenth century onward was, at bottom, historically and materially determined rather than having derived from an appeal to nature, God, laws or some other seemingly timeless, free-floating ideological phenomena. In their view the "liberty, equality and fraternity" of the French Revolution, as well as Thomas Jefferson's "self-evident" truths referenced in the Declaration of Independence, were ultimately the product of class conflict in an era of rising agrarian and industrial capitalism. Whatever their origins, civil and political rights were highly valued by Marx and Engels because such hard-won democratic rights, wrested by workers from the ruling classes, led to improvement in the well-being of the working class, even if this improvement was severely limited under bourgeois conditions because of pervasive economic inequality inherent to the capitalist economic system. More important, they argued that these very limited forms of freedom and equality, which nevertheless must always be defended by the working class, provide an environment for workers to move freely, agitate and organize in their struggles to satisfy everyday needs and to eventually overturn the capitalist economic system and possibly usher in a socialist era of human development, bringing with it genuine freedom and equality, including economically, for the working class and all humanity. Affirming his commitment to civil and political rights, and not just social and economic rights, Marx's observation on political developments in pre-1850 Germany is typical of his perspective: "Of all political elements the people is by far the most dangerous for a king. . . . The real people, the proletarians, the small peasants and plebs . . . would above all else extort from His Majesty [Frederick Williams] a constitution, together with a universal franchise, freedom of association, freedom of the press and other unpleasant things" ("The Communism of the Rheinischer Beobachter," *Collected Works,* vol. 6, 233). Similarly in 1865 Engels writes: "As distinct from the old Estates, distinguished by birth, it [the bourgeoisie] must proclaim human rights. . . . To be consistent, it must therefore demand universal, direct suffrage, freedom of the press, association and assembly and the suspension of all special laws directed against individual classes of the population. And there is nothing else that the proletariat needs to demand from it. It [the proletariat] cannot require that the bourgeoisie should cease to be a bourgeoisie, but it certainly can require that it [the bourgeoisie] practices its own principles consistently" ("The Prussian Military Question and the German Workers' Party," *Collected Works,* vol. 20, 77). Nowhere in their voluminous writings did either Marx or Engels say the aforementioned freedoms they embraced in bourgeois society would cease to exist following the creation of the post-capitalist society—only that the freedoms won under bourgeois conditions would finally be placed on a firm and genuinely equal social and economic foundation in the revolutionary socialist era. That the former Soviet Union and other contemporary self-styled socialist governments went in a different political direction is incontestable. Yet how much responsibility, if any, should accrue to Marx and Engels for the historic defects and essential failure of the former Soviet Union? Though they did not produce a single book that systematically and explicitly focuses on democracy and democratic rights, the following writings by Marx and Engels point in that direction: Marx, "On Freedom of the Press and Censorship," "On the Jewish Question," "Economic and Philosophical Manuscripts of 1844," "The Civil War in France," and "Critique of the Gotha Program" (*On Freedom of the Press and Censorship; Karl Marx: Selected Writings*) and Engels, "Morality and Law" (*Anti-Duhring*). Generally balanced and insightful analyses of their views on democracy and democratic rights can be found in Hal Draper, *Karl Marx's Theory of Revolution,* Richard N. Hunt, *The*

Political Ideas of Marx and Engels, and August H. Nimtz Jr., *Marx and Engels: Their Contribution to the Democratic Breakthrough.*

8. On the seamy side of American history, see Zinn, *People's History of the United States;* Adams and Sanders, *Alienable Rights;* and Stannard, *American Holocaust.* On modern Europe, see Palmer and Colton, *History of Modern Europe;* and Tucker, *Stalin in Power.*

9. Article 25 says that "everyone has the right to a standard of living adequate for the health and well-being of himself and of his family, including food, clothing, housing and medical care and necessary social services, and the right to security in the event of unemployment, sickness, disability, widowhood, old age or other lack of livelihood in circumstances beyond his control." Ishay, *Human Rights Reader,* 493–97. One need not agree with Jeremy Bentham's claim that "natural rights is simple nonsense . . . nonsense upon stilts" (Waldron, *Nonsense upon Stilts,* 53) to recognize that even improving upon the list of items constituting human rights, though an advance over the traditional list in either the Declaration of Independence (1776) or Declaration of the Rights of Man and the Citizen (1789), does not prevent the careful observer from seeing the limits of the contemporary liberal view of human rights. Offering what appears to be a welfare or charity-like approach to human rights, Article 25 of the United Nations Universal Declaration of Human Rights, similar to the above eighteenth-century documents, directly links human rights to the "individual," with potentially a kind of Hobbesean competition, if not egoism, resulting from this approach. Where is the idea of community or society in this twentieth-century updating of the human rights agenda? What about racial and class inequality tied to the existing ownership of society's basic economic resources, which remain in private hands under a liberalism-driven charity model of human rights promoted by the United Nations and Western governments? What is the significance of these modest, however important, United Nations human rights advances having occurred under the post–World War II hegemony of the United States? See Jeremy Waldron, *Nonsense Upon Stilts,* and Tony Evans, *The Politics of Human Rights,* for good discussions of some of these issues. Also, Allen Buchanan, *Marx and Justice,* provides useful comments on Marx's contribution to the current rights debate.

10. United Nations, *Human Development Report 2006,* and U.S. State Department's Web site: http://www.state.gov. Having published numerous reports on the use of torture and general inhumane treatment of prisoners held by the U.S. government at Guantanamo, Human Rights Watch released a statement, "US: Mark Five Years of Guantanamo by Closing It" (January 5, 2007), on its Web site. In part, the statement reads, "As the fifth anniversary of the Guantanamo Bay detention center approaches, Human Rights Watch denounced the ongoing detentions there as a shameful blight on U.S.

respect for human rights. Human Rights Watch called on the Bush Administration to bring criminal charges or release the nearly 400 detainees, and restore their access to federal court." See http://www.hrw.org.

11. *United States of America: Rights for All* (1998 report by Amnesty International), http://www.amnesty.org.

12. For an overview of the depth of this racial gap, see Mishel et al., *State of Working America;* and Muhammad, et al., *State of the Dream 2004.*

REFERENCES

Adams, Francis D., and Barry Sanders. *Alienable Rights: The Exclusion of African Americans in a White Man's Land, 1619–2000.* New York: HarperCollins, 2003.

Asante, Molefi Kete, and Abu S. Abarry, eds. *African Intellectual Heritage: A Book of Sources.* Philadelphia: Temple University Press, 1996.

Buchanan, Allen E. *Marx and Justice: The Radical Critique of Liberalism.* Totowa, N.J.: Rowman and Littlefield, 1982.

Donnelly, Jack. *Universal Human Rights in Theory and Practice.* Ithaca, N.Y.: Cornell University Press, 1989.

Draper, Hal. *Karl Marx's Theory of Revolution.* New York: Monthly Review Press, 1977. Four Volumes.

Engels, Frederick. *Anti-Duhring: Herr Eugen Duhring's Revolution in Science.* Moscow: Progress Publishers, 1969.

Evans, Tony. *The Politics of Human Rights: A Global Perspective.* London: Croom, 1985.

Hayek, F. A. *The Fatal Conceit: The Errors of Socialism.* Chicago: The University of Chicago Press, 1988.

———. *The Road to Serfdom: Text and Documents.* Edited by Bruce Caldwell. Chicago: The University of Chicago Press, 2007.

Hill, Christopher, ed. *Winstanley: The Law of Freedom and Other Writings.* Baltimore: Penguin Books, 1973.

Hunt, Lynn, ed. *The French Revolution and Human Rights: A Brief Introduction.* Boston: Bedford Books, 1996.

Hunt, Richard N. *The Political Ideas of Marx and Engels: Marxism and Totalitarian Democracy, 1818–1850* [1]. Pittsburgh: University of Pittsburgh Press, 1974.

Hunt, Richard N. *The Political Ideas of Marx and Engels: Classical Marxism, 1850–1895* [2]. Pittsburgh: University of Pittsburgh Press, 1984.

Ishay, Micheline R., ed. *The Human Rights Reader: Major Political Essays, Speeches, and Documents from Ancient Times to the Present.* 2nd ed. New York: Routledge, 2007.

Johansen, Bruce E. *Debating Democracy: Native American Legacy of Freedom.* Santa Fe, N.M.: Clear Light, 1998.

———. *Forgotten Founders: How the American Indian Helped Shape Democracy.* Boston: Harvard Common Press, 1982.

Locke, John. *Two Treatises of Government.* New York: Cambridge University Press, 1996.

Marx, Karl. *Karl Marx: Selected Writings.* 2nd ed. Edited by David McLellan Oxford: Oxford University Press, 2005.

———. *On Freedom of the Press and Censorship.* Edited and translated by Saul K. Padover. New York: McGraw-Hill Book Company, 1974.

Marx, Karl, and Frederick Engels. *Collected Works.* Volumes 6 and 20. New York: International Publishers, 1985.

Mishel, Lawrence, Jared Bernstein, and Sylvia Allegretto. *The State of Working America 2006/2007.* Ithaca, N.Y.: Cornell University Press, 2007.

Muhammad, Dedrick, et al., *The State of the Dream 2004: Enduring Disparities in Black and White.* United For a Fair Economy, January 15, 2004: http://www.faireconomy.org.

Nimtz, August H. Jr. Marx and Engels: Their Contribution to the Democratic Breakthrough. Albany, New York: State University of New York Press, 2000.

Palmer, R. R., and Joel Colton. *A History of Modern Europe.* New York: Alfred A. Knopf, 1978.

Petegorsky, David W. *Left-Wing Democracy in the English Civil War: Gerrard Winstanley and the Digger Movement.* London: Alan Sutton, 1995.

Sharp, Andrew, ed. *The English Levellers.* New York: Cambridge University Press, 1998.

Stannard, David E. *American Holocaust: Columbus and the Conquest of the New World.* New York: Oxford University Press, 1992.

Tucker, Robert C. *Stalin in Power: The Revolution from Above, 1928–1941.* New York: W. W. Norton, 1990.

United Nations. *Human Development Report 2006.* New York: Palgrave, 2006. Kevin Watkins, director and lead author.

Waldron, Jeremy, ed. *Nonsense upon Stilts: Bentham, Burke and Marx on the Rights of Man.* New York: Methuen, 1987.

Zinn, Howard. *A People's History of the United States.* New York: HarperPerennial Modern Classic, 2003.

PART 1

Racial Implications of the War on Terrorism

Enhancing Whose Security? People of Color and the Post–September 11 Expansion of Law Enforcement and Intelligence Powers

Natsu Taylor Saito

Since September 11, 2001, the George W. Bush administration has unilaterally assumed the power to detain thousands of people, mostly immigrant men from Muslim or Middle Eastern countries, holding them indefinitely and incommunicado, denying them access to the courts, and interrogating them; and it has deported thousands more.[1] It has convinced Congress to pass hundreds of new laws that give the executive branch dramatically expanded powers.[2] In early 2003 the Justice Department's draft "Domestic Security Enhancement Act of 2003" was leaked to the press.[3] More commonly known as "PATRIOT II," it proposed expanding the already impressive list of powers given law enforcement and intelligence agencies by the Uniting and Strengthening America by Providing Appropriate Tools Required to Intercept and Obstruct Terrorism (USA PATRIOT) Act,[4] which was hurriedly enacted by Congress in the weeks following the attacks on the Pentagon and the World Trade Center.

These bills dramatically curtailed the civil liberties of U.S. citizens as well as immigrants, in many cases legitimizing measures long sought and/or illegally used by law enforcement agencies to suppress political dissent.[5] Particularly striking was a provision of PATRIOT II that, if passed, would have allowed the government to "expatriate" U.S. citizens, that is, strip them of their citizenship, for becoming members of or providing material support to any group deemed a "terrorist organization . . . engaged in hostilities against the United States."[6] The terms "material support" and "terrorist organization" were defined very broadly, and "hostilities" was left undefined.[7] This proposal forces us to consider just who is an "American" under these circumstances. We are told that all of these measures are necessary to protect the American people, and the most basic "American values" of freedom and democracy.[8] Yet the United States has a long history of race-based exclusion from citizenship, denial of constitutional protections to large groups of people identified as "Other," and repression of movements for social change and racial justice in the name of "national security." To understand just who and what are being protected by the "war on terror" today, we need to look at these measures in the context of the United States' long history of conflating race, "foreignness," and disfavored ideologies; its more general use of the criminal justice system to maintain social control; and its consistent use of law enforcement and intelligence powers to suppress movements of political dissent. This is a large subject, of course, and this essay provides only a brief sketch of some of the issues to be considered in such an analysis.

WHO IS AN AMERICAN?

The United States is commonly described as a "nation of immigrants,"[9] a phrase evoking images of the Statue of Liberty holding out her beacon of freedom and opportunity to the "huddled masses" oppressed elsewhere in the world.[10] In the aftermath of September 11, this image was invoked by President George W. Bush, who attempted to explain away the attacks on the grounds that "they" hate "us" because of our freedom and prosperity.[11] It is also the image used to explain increasingly restrictive immigration policies because, according to this portrayal, everyone wants to come and partake of our freedoms, and we clearly cannot accommodate them all.

In reality, the United States has been anything but hospitable to immigrants since September 11. Both temporary visitors and permanent residents have been subjected to a variety of harsh measures, including thousands of expedited deportations,[12] the "disappearance" and detention of at least 1,200 people,[13] interrogations in the form of "voluntary interviews" with officials from the Federal Bureau of Investigation (FBI) and Immigration and Naturalization Service

(INS)[14]—now under the Department of Homeland Security[15]—and a cumbersome new National Security Entry/Exit Registration System.[16]

Most of these measures have targeted men from Middle Eastern or predominantly Muslim countries, and appear to violate fundamental constitutional protections (such as the right to due process and equal protection),[17] which, at least in theory, apply to all persons in the United States, not just citizens.[18] However, the government's actions are largely immune from constitutional challenge thanks to a long history of Supreme Court cases that have said that the "political branches" of government, that is, the executive and the legislature, have essentially unfettered power with respect to immigration. Called the "plenary power doctrine," this refusal to enforce otherwise applicable provisions of the Constitution in immigration matters dates back to the Chinese Exclusion Cases of the 1880s and 1890s,[19] and has been invoked since then to allow, among other things, exclusions without hearings, deportations on the basis of secret evidence, and indefinite imprisonment when those deemed deportable have no country to accept them.[20] The measures targeting immigrants since September 11 have been particularly severe, but are nonetheless quite consistent with the government's exercise of its plenary power over immigrants since the first federal immigration laws were enacted in 1875.[21]

What does it mean, then, to call the United States a "nation of immigrants"? It is certainly not a call to the huddled masses, who have been effectively excluded by policies including national origin quotas and country caps, requirements of immediate family ties or employment, and evidence of economic support.[22] It is accurate, however, insofar as it refers to the fact that most of those who consider themselves Americans today descend from peoples not indigenous to this land. In other words, this is a settler-colonial state,[23] and the "nation of immigrants" descriptor is, perhaps, most accurately seen as a call for unity among the settler population, an opportunity to identify with the privileged "we" who claim a share of the disproportionate wealth controlled by the United States and to distance ourselves from the "they" who envy our well-being.[24]

Describing the United States as a "nation of immigrants" sanitizes its history by focusing on those who immigrated voluntarily, initially from northern and western Europe and later from other parts of the world.[25] It excludes American Indians as members of the polity, conveniently reinforcing the notion that they are "extinct,"[26] rendering invisible the genocidal practices that have accompanied the colonization of the continent since 1492,[27] and justifying an occupation that even U.S. government lawyers have conceded is not, for the most part, justified by anything resembling valid title to the land.[28] It is a characterization that disregards or, more accurately, attempts to eradicate the history of African Americans, brought to this land involuntarily—those who survived the journey forced into chattel slavery and excluded from all constitutional protection until after the Civil War.[29] Likewise, the emphasis on "immigrants" obscures the forced annexation of the northern half of Mexico[30] and the illegal overthrow and occupation of the Kingdom of Hawai'i,[31] as well as the ongoing occupation of Puerto Rico and other "unincorporated territories."[32] The history of most people of color now living in this country having thus been erased, we are left with the myth that this was an essentially uninhabited land made prosperous by the hard work of freedom-seeking European settlers.

The determinants of citizenship have both reflected and reinforced this myth. African Americans were not U.S. citizens until passage of the Fourteenth Amendment in 1868. As Supreme Court chief justice Roger Taney stated forthrightly in the *Dred Scott* case, until then persons of African descent, whether "free" or enslaved, were not only *not* citizens, but not even "persons" under the Constitution.[33] Most American Indians only became U.S. citizens in 1924 when Congress, in an attempt to undermine Native sovereignty, unilaterally imposed citizenship on them,[34] and the government continues to treat them as members of "domestic dependent" nations,[35] sovereign only to the extent it is convenient to the "larger" interests of the United States.[36]

The Constitution as originally drafted did not specify who was to be a citizen, but it did direct Congress to "establish a uniform Rule of Naturalization."[37] The first Congress, meeting in 1790, did so by limiting naturalized citizenship to "free white persons."[38] Although modified after the Civil War to include "persons of African descent,"[39] the racial restriction on citizenship was not completely eliminated until 1952.[40] Interpreting the law in 1923 to find a "high-caste Hindu" ineligible for naturalization, the Supreme Court summarized the initial understanding of who was to be an American:

> The words of familiar speech, which were used by the original framers of the law, were intended to include only the type of man whom they knew as white. The immigration of the day was almost exclusively from the British Isles and Northwestern Europe, whence they and their forebears had come. When they extended the privilege of American citizenship to "any alien being a free white person" it was these immigrants—bone of their bone and flesh of their flesh—and their kind whom they must have had affirmatively in mind.[41]

As a result of this initial construction of who was truly "American" and the related racially restrictive immigration and naturalization policies, "foreignness" has become part of the racialized identity of Asian Americans, Latinos and Latinas, and those of Middle Eastern descent.[42] One of the more obvious results of this imputed foreignness was the World War II internment of 120,000 Japanese Americans, two-thirds of whom were U.S. citizens. The U.S. military's justification for indefinitely incarcerating all persons of Japanese ancestry on the West Coast, U.S. citizens and noncitizens, men and women, children and old people, was that it could not distinguish the "loyal" from the "disloyal."[43] This rationale, upheld by the Supreme Court in the *Hirabayashi*, *Yasui*, and *Korematsu* cases on the basis of "military necessity,"[44] presumes that disloyalty is a crime for which one can be imprisoned with no semblance of due process; that certain groups can be presumed disloyal on the basis of race or national origin (that is, persons of Japanese but not German or Italian descent); and that, at least for those groups, "blood is thicker than water," making citizenship irrelevant.[45]

The perception that only Euro-derivative settlers are "real" Americans persists in many ways, despite the elimination of racial restrictions on the acquisition of citizenship. For African Americans, this is reflected in what is often called "second-class citizenship," though more accurately described as the consequences of internal colonialism—disparate treatment by the criminal justice system, persisting segregation in all aspects of life, and growing disparities in income, wealth, and access to education, housing, and health care. For other peoples of color, also plagued by these disparities, there is often a more straightforward presumption of "foreignness." Asian Americans and Latino/as are still commonly treated as "aliens" regardless of how long their families have lived in the United States.[46] Arab Americans and South Asians have been subjected to a dramatic increase in hate crimes since September 11,[47] as they have been "raced"[48] in popular consciousness as not only foreign but as having terrorist sympathies as well.[49] Ironically, even those truly native to this land are perceived as foreign, as illustrated by the murder of twenty-one-year-old Kimberly Lowe, a Creek woman killed in Oklahoma in September 2001, by young white men in a pickup truck who yelled, "Go back to your own country!" and proceeded to run her over.[50]

While the examples are endless, we can see the significance that race, ethnicity, and national origin still have today in the social and legal determination of who is a "real American" by briefly comparing the treatment of John Walker Lindh and Yaser Esam Hamdi. Soon after September 11, the United States was engaged in an undeclared, if very real, war in Afghanistan, claiming that the country's ruling Taliban government was harboring Osama bin Laden and the al Quaida network believed to be responsible for the attacks on the Pentagon and World Trade Center.[51] After a massive bombing campaign, the United States succeeded in replacing the Taliban with a more U.S.-friendly government,[52] in the process capturing over 600 men and boys of several dozen nationalities and transporting them to the U.S. naval base in Guantánamo, Cuba, where most of them continue to be detained and interrogated.[53] Two of those captured, Lindh and Hamdi, turned out to be U.S. citizens.

John Walker Lindh was immediately taken to Alexandria, Virginia, and charged with conspiring to kill Americans.[54] As White House spokesman Ari Fleischer said, "the great strength of America is he will now have his day in court."[55] And, in fact, he appeared in a civilian criminal court where, represented by counsel and supported by his family, he pleaded to reduced charges of supplying services to the Taliban and carrying an explosive during the commission of a felony, and received a twenty-year prison sentence.[56] Yaser Esam Hamdi, on the other hand, was first taken to Guantánamo Bay, where it was discovered that he was a U.S. citizen, having been born in Louisiana.[57] He was transferred not to a U.S. civilian court, but to a naval brig in Norfolk, Virginia, where he was held incommunicado for well over a year, labeled an "enemy combatant" by the government, and denied access to counsel and the courts.[58] What distinguished Hamdi from Lindh? The only apparent difference in their cases was that Lindh is a Euroamerican and Hamdi of Middle Eastern descent. Tellingly, the media immediately began referring to Lindh as "the *American* Taliban,"[59] a moniker that has never been applied to Hamdi.[60]

Maintaining Social Control through Law Enforcement

As briefly outlined above, race has played a very significant role in the definition of who is an "American." The restrictions on who receives the benefits of political participation and legal protection—available initially to "citizens" and, after the lifting of explicitly racial restrictions on citizenship, to those deemed "truly American"—have served not only the end of social exclusion but also a larger goal of preserving the economic and racial status quo. As illustrated by the use of racial repression to occupy the land and exploit the labor of people of color throughout U.S. history, racism is deeply intertwined with economic exploitation, and it is no accident that the poor are disproportionately people of color and people of color are disproportionately poor. In addition to restrictions on citizenship, another particularly significant way in which the legal system has maintained racial hierarchy and the concentrated control of wealth and resources has been through its enactment and enforcement of criminal laws. Drawing on examples from the "war on crime" and its subsidiary "war on drugs," this section focuses on how the law and law enforcement powers have been used to preserve the particular racial, economic, and political status quo that has been defined as "American," setting the stage for much of what is happening today in the "war on terror."

The law has long been used to maintain social control and racial hegemony in the United States, as illustrated by the Constitution's protection of the institution of slavery,[61] the slave codes adopted by many states,[62] the scalp bounties on American Indians once found in virtually every state or territory,[63] and the exclusionary provisions of the immigration laws. The use of the "criminal justice" system for this purpose, however, increased dramatically following the abolition of slavery. Until that time, people of African descent had been subjected to essentially unlimited control by those who claimed to own them, if enslaved, and to harsh and discriminatory laws regulating their behavior even when "free."[64] The Thirteenth Amendment, adopted in 1866, prohibited slavery or involuntary servitude *except* as punishment for crime, and in short order most of the former slave states enacted "Black codes" providing harsh penalties for a wide range of crimes such as petty theft, vagrancy, idleness, and "disrespectful" behavior toward white persons. At the same time, most southern states instituted convict lease systems, which provided large pools of virtually free and almost exclusively black labor to the owners of railroads, mines, and plantations.[65] Although the Fourteenth Amendment made persons of African descent U.S. citizens and prohibited the states from denying anyone due process or equal protection under the law on account of race, the Supreme Court consistently upheld legalized apartheid, both as manifest in criminal law and the burgeoning body of law enforcing social segregation.[66] During the 1950s, the U.S. government was confronted not only by a growing civil rights movement at home but also by international pressure, intensified by the Cold War, to conform its domestic practices to the position it had taken not only in condemning Hitler's racism but in supporting the United Nations Charter, which explicitly prohibits racial discrimination.[67] However, by the time the U.S. Supreme Court held that segregation was no longer constitutionally acceptable[68] and began putting some teeth into the Fourth, Fifth, and Sixth Amendments' protections of the rights of criminal defendants,[69] a racially bifurcated system of justice was well entrenched.

During the 1960s, the United States faced massive challenges to the status quo, not only from organized social and political forces—such as the civil rights movement, the women's movement, massive antiwar mobilizations, and the re-surgence of organized labor[70]—but also from the hundreds of urban rebellions that rocked every major U.S. city.[71] In 1967, following "riots" in Newark, Detroit, Cleveland, and nearly 150 other cities, President Lyndon Johnson convened the National Advisory Commission on Civil Disorders (commonly referred to as the Kerner Commission after its chair, Illinois governor Otto Kerner) to determine what had happened, why the "riots" happened, and what could be done to pre-vent them from happening again.[72] The Kerner Commission concluded that the primary cause of the rebellions was "pervasive discrimination and segregation in employment, education and housing" and the resulting "frustrations of power-lessness," which permeated the "ghettos."[73] It made extensive recommendations for federal programs to improve employment, education, the welfare system, and housing in poor communities, viewing these as the only viable long-term responses to its most basic conclusion that "our nation is moving toward two societies, one black, one white—separate and unequal."[74] While noting that "al-most invariably the incident that ignites disorder arises from police action," the report did not conclude that more police or harsher laws were needed; rather, it recommended improved police-community relations.[75]

Nonetheless, despite the commission's stated awareness of the underlying causes of and solutions for "social disorder," the government's primary response since 1968 has been to wage an ever-intensifying "war on crime."[76] As Richard Nixon said in campaigning for president, "doubling the conviction rate in this country would do more to cure crime in America than quadrupling the funds for Humphrey's war on poverty."[77] In the war on crime, the people—at least those residing in poor communities of color—quickly became the enemy. As Christian Parenti says, "Crime meant urban, urban meant Black, and the war on crime meant a bulwark built against the increasingly political and vocal racial 'other' by the predominately white state."[78] Or, as H. R. Haldeman bluntly noted, "[Presi-dent Nixon] emphasized that you have to face the fact that the whole problem is really the blacks. The key is to devise a system that recognizes this while not appearing to."[79] A national survey taken in the summer of 1968 found that over 80 percent of those polled believed that law and order had broken down and placed the blame on "Communists" and "Negroes who start riots."[80]

Nixon had assumed office on a "law and order" platform and, perhaps because he soon discovered that there was little federal jurisdiction over most criminal activity, rapidly declared war on drugs. Claiming a "tenfold increase" in the number of addict-users between 1969 and 1971—an increase that "came not from any flood of new addicts reported to federal authorities in 1970 or

1971 but from a statistical reworking of the 1969 data"[81]—Nixon announced to Congress in June 1971 that "the problem has assumed the dimensions of a national emergency."[82] In the meantime, the 1968 Omnibus Crime Control and Safe Streets Act had weakened *Miranda* protections, authorized more telephone taps and bugs, and allowed police forty-eight hours of unwarranted wiretapping in "emergencies,"[83] and the Comprehensive Drug Abuse Prevention and Control Act of 1970 had dramatically expanded the budgets of drug and law enforcement agencies.[84] The 1970 Organized Crime Control Act, which contained the Racketeer Influenced and Corrupt Organizations (RICO) Act, loosened the rules on admissible evidence, allowed seizures of the assets of any organization deemed a criminal conspiracy, imposed twenty-five-year sentences for "dangerous adult offenders," and empowered secret "special grand juries" with broad subpoena authority.[85] While purportedly aimed at organized crime, these tools were immediately used against organizations such as the Black Panther Party and the Puerto Rican independence activists.[86]

Nixon created the special Office of Drug Abuse Law Enforcement (ODALE) directly accountable to the White House, with interagency "strike forces" whose "extraordinary procedures [such as no-knock entrances] . . . were necessary because the nation was engaged in an all-out war against drugs and that the very survival of the American people was at stake."[87] With massive federal subsidies available for weapons, training, prison construction, and automated information, many states followed the federal lead.[88] For example, New York governor Nelson Rockefeller implemented draconian drug laws with mandatory life sentences, even for sixteen-year-olds, and asked President Nixon and New York City mayor John Lindsay to set up "emergency camps" for detaining New York City's drug addicts.[89]

Under the Reagan administration, the drug war's focus on "foreign" enemies was intensified. This set the stage for heightened military involvement, which was facilitated by amending the Posse Comitatus Act[90] and welcomed as a way of maintaining military budgets in peacetime.[91] Federal police powers continued to be strengthened, as the 1984 Comprehensive Crime Control Act allowed federal preventive detention, established mandatory minimum sentences, eliminated federal parole, scaled back the insanity defense, increased penalties for acts of "terrorism," and expanded asset forfeiture provisions.[92] The Bail Reform Act, also passed in 1984, greatly extended the use of preventive detention.[93] While purportedly designed to keep "drug kingpins, violent offenders and other obvious threats to the community" incarcerated while awaiting trial, it was immediately used to keep political resisters incarcerated.[94]

The 1986 Anti-Drug Abuse Act provided new mandatory minimum sentences without possibility of parole, including the requirement of a five-year minimum for possession of 500 grams of powdered cocaine but only 5 grams of crack cocaine, a notorious disparity in light of the fact that powdered cocaine is used much more frequently by white Americans and crack cocaine by African Americans.[95] The 1988 Anti-Drug Abuse Act expanded use of the federal death penalty; created a "drug czar" to coordinate between law enforcement, military, and intelligence agencies; allocated funds to the Department of Defense to train law enforcement officers; again expanded forfeiture laws; increased the severity of mandatory minimum sentences; and enacted "user accountability" provisions, which provided for automatic eviction from public housing for tenants engaging in criminal activity in or near housing projects.[96]

As these laws were being passed, as huge sums were allocated for police and prisons, and as an increasing proportion of the population was incarcerated, President Reagan was also dismantling the social programs that the Kerner Commission had identified as the only feasible alternative to urban rebellions. "In 1982 alone Reagan cut the real value of welfare by 24 percent, slashed the budget for child nutrition by 34 percent, reduced funding for school milk programs by 78 percent, urban development action grants by 35 percent, and educational block grants by 38 percent."[97] The 1988 Commission on the Cities reported that poverty and racial disparities had, in fact, increased since the Kerner Commission's report had been issued, concluding: "'Quiet riots' are taking place in America's major cities: unemployment, poverty, social disorganization, segregation, family disintegration, housing and school deterioration, and crime. These 'quiet riots' may not be as alarming or as noticeable to outsiders . . . but they are even more destructive of human life than the violent riots of twenty years ago."[98]

Notwithstanding the emphasis given the drug war in the 1980s, national surveys indicated that, as of July 1989, only 20 percent of the American people considered drugs to be the most pressing national problem.[99] Nonetheless, in September, in his first televised speech as president, George H. W. Bush "declared a national consensus on the primacy of this issue—'All of us agree that the gravest domestic threat facing our nation today is drugs'—and then declared war, calling for 'an assault on every front.' Urging Americans to 'face this evil as a nation united,' Bush proclaimed that 'victory over drugs is our cause, a just cause.'"[100] Shortly after this speech, 64 percent of the those polled had decided that it was the nation's most pressing problem, and 62 percent were willing to give up "a few of the freedoms we have in this country" to win the war on drugs.[101]

Who was the enemy in this war? According to the president, "Everyone who uses drugs. Everyone who sells drugs. And everyone who looks the other way."[102] Those who were targeted, in fact, were predominantly poor people of color. In Noam Chomsky's words, "The so-called drug war . . . was aimed directly at the black population. None of this has anything to do with drugs. It has to do with controlling and criminalizing dangerous populations. It's kind of like a U.S. counterpart to 'social cleansing.' . . . The more you can increase the fear of drugs and crime and welfare mothers and immigrants and aliens and poverty and all sorts of things, the more you control people."[103] In 1972, just under 200,000 people were in U.S. prisons; by 1985 there were 500,000; and by 1997 there were 1,200,000, plus another 500,000 in local jails.[104] The United States now imprisons more people than any other country and has one of the world's highest per capita incarceration rates.[105] There is no evidence that drug use or crime rates have changed significantly.[106] Despite the public perception of increasing crime, the overall crime rate has remained stable since the early 1970s.[107]

The incarceration rate of African Americans is now six times that of white Americans.[108] Although all studies report virtually equal rates of drug usage among black and white Americans,[109] in 1980, 23 percent of all drug arrests were of African Americans, who comprise about 12 percent of the population, and by 1990 African Americans accounted for 40 percent of all drug arrests and over 60 percent of drug convictions.[110] Thus, although the use of the criminal justice system to control the poor and people of color is not new,[111] it seems to be intensifying. While many factors contribute to the spiraling incarceration rate, such as the soaring profitability of the prison-industrial complex and the political capital gained by appearing "tough on crime," incarceration is also a very effective mechanism for maintaining the economic and racial status quo.

DISSENT AS UN-AMERICAN

In light of the widespread injustices and systematic destruction of communities wrought by the enforcement of criminal law, the new restrictions on constitutional rights such as freedom of expression and privacy may seem relatively insignificant to people of color. Lack of due process and violations of equal protection are, after all, everyday occurrences in our communities, and the FBI's expanded ability to find out what books we check out of the library or what Internet sites we visit might reasonably be seen as the least of our worries. What is at stake, however, in the new "war on terror" is not simply increased surveillance or inconvenience, but a fundamental threat to our ability to engage in any kind of political dissent or to advocate any significant social restructuring—in other words, our ability to change the systems of inequality manifest in American society today.

We cannot understand the real significance of contemporary "antiterrorism" measures without considering the U.S. government's long and consistent history of suppressing movements for social change, particularly movements for racial and economic justice. This section provides a few examples of that history, focusing on how those who challenge economic, social, or political structures have been conflated with immigrants, labeled "un-American," and accused of being "seditious," thus justifying the employment of surveillance, infiltration, and "counterintelligence" tactics—designed to combat subversion by foreign governments—against U.S. citizens and residents exercising constitutionally guaranteed rights. Perhaps because the United States has been so effectively portrayed as a nation of immigrants, one of the first lines of attack on those perceived as threats to the status quo has been to label them as "foreign," either literally because they are immigrants or as representatives of foreign powers or ideologies. As early as 1798 the first Alien and Sedition Acts[112] were passed on the Federalists' claim that the Jeffersonians were agents of France attempting to bring the French Revolution's "Reign of Terror" to the United States.[113] Only Republicans were prosecuted under the act, and for clearly political reasons. Thus, for example, Congressman Matthew Lyon was sentenced to four months in prison for describing President John Adams as "swallowed up in a continual grasp for power, in an unbounded thirst for ridiculous pomp, foolish adulation, and selfish avarice."[114]

The institution of slavery was, of course, an essential aspect of the initial American status quo, well protected by the Constitution, and those who spoke out against its cruelties and advocated abolition were frequently charged with sedition. Using that rationale, in certain periods the postmaster general refused to allow abolitionist literature to be sent through the U.S. mail, and despite the First Amendment's explicit guarantee of the right of the people to petition the government for redress of grievances, the House of Representatives enacted a "gag rule" forbidding the discussion of slavery.[115] In other words, citizens were being forced to give up some of their liberties for the sake of national security, as embodied in the institution of slavery.

Union organizers in the late nineteenth and early twentieth centuries were labeled "communists" and "anarchists," and working-class unrest was blamed on immigrants. The labor disputes that accompanied the depression of 1873–77, particularly the fiercely contested strikes of railroad workers and miners, were consistently depicted as the work of outside agitators.[116] During the 1880s and 1890s, immigrants were frequently conflated with anarchists, and "variously referred to as 'the very scum and offal of Europe,' 'venomous reptiles,' . . . and 'that class of heartless and revolutionary agitators' who had come 'to terrorize the community and to exalt the red flag of the commune above the stars and stripes.'"[117]

Congress, which had not regulated immigration at all until 1875, passed a series of acts in the 1880s and 1890s excluding Chinese workers,[118] and soon began debating proposals to exclude and deport "alien anarchists." In 1903 Congress passed a law prohibiting immigration by anarchists, those who believe in or advocate the overthrow of government by force and violence, and anyone "who disbelieves in" organized government or is "affiliated with any organization entertaining and teaching such disbelief."[119] This was the first federal legislation to ban immigrants on the basis of their beliefs or associations. As Robert Justin Goldstein notes,

> The anarchist laws were the first sedition laws in American history since 1798, and the first laws in American history to provide penalties for simply belonging to a group (what later became known as "guilt by association"). They became the models for later legislation directed at other targets—for example, the criminal syndicalism laws passed by many states in 1917–20 to outlaw the Industrial Workers of the World [IWW] and again in 1947–54 to outlaw the Communist Party [CP]; the 1917–18 Federal wartime Espionage and Sedition Acts, which virtually outlawed all criticism of the government and were used to harass the Socialist Party; the 1917, 1918, 1920, 1940, 1950, and 1952 immigration laws used to exclude and deport members of the IWW and CP; and the 1940 Smith Act, outlawing advocating or belonging to groups advocating overthrow of the government, for all citizens, even in peacetime.[120]

Particularly in periods of war, people identified as "Other" by virtue of race, national origin, or political views have been deemed "un-American"—a term implying more about one's "loyalty" than nationality—in a variety of ways. A brutal four-year campaign was fought to "pacify" the Philippines after that country was ceded to the United States by Spain in 1898, during which U.S. troops burned hundreds of villages to the ground, killed perhaps a million Filipinos, herded thousands into concentration camps, and engaged in systematic raping, looting, and torture. Such tactics were described as "necessary," for the enemy was not a "civilized" people; Filipinos were routinely referred to as "savages" and "niggers" and the fighting as "Indian warfare."[121] Those who opposed the war were dismissed as "liars and traitors." General Douglas MacArthur had a lawyer on the Philippine Commission draft "Treason Laws," which defined treason "as joining any secret political organization or even as 'the advocacy of independence or separation of the islands from the United States by forcible or peaceful means.'"[122]

During World War I, the Justice Department urged President Woodrow Wilson to try civilians accused of interfering with the war effort before military courts.[123] Although that effort failed, Wilson did sign the Espionage Act, which made it a crime to "willfully utter, print, write, or publish any disloyal, profane, scurrilous, or abusive language" about the United States, and allowed the post office to exclude from the mails any material advocating "treason, insurrection or resistance to any law of the U.S."[124] The following year the Sedition Act was passed, prohibiting virtually all criticism of the war or the government.[125] According to Goldstein, "Altogether, over twenty-one hundred [persons] were indicted under the Espionage and Sedition laws, invariably for statements of opposition to the war rather than for any overt acts, and over one thousand persons were convicted. Over one hundred persons were sentenced to jail terms of ten years or more. Not a single person was ever convicted for actual spy activities."[126] African Americans were particularly targeted in the hunt for subversives and draft evaders, apparently because of "the widespread suspicion among whites that . . . enemy agents were actively subverting the loyalties of African Americans, who were believed to be uniquely susceptible to those who would manipulate them for sinister purposes."[127]

As noted above, during World War II Japanese Americans were interned as "potentially disloyal" despite the fact that both the FBI and military intelligence found there was no evidence that the community posed a threat to national security, and, in fact, there were no instances of sabotage or espionage by a Japanese American.[128] The "Cold War" that followed World War II illustrated that the pursuit of those considered "disloyal" was not to be limited to periods of actual warfare, but extended indefinitely. In 1947 President Truman issued Executive Order 9835, authorizing the Justice Department to seek out "infiltration of disloyal persons" within the U.S. government and to create a list of organizations that were "totalitarian, fascist, communist or subversive . . . or seeking to alter the government of the United States by unconstitutional means."[129] By 1954 the Justice Department had created a list of hundreds of organizations, including groups such as the Committee for Negro Arts, the Committee for the Protection of the Bill of Rights, and the Nature Friends of America, and "sympathetic association," as well as membership, was considered evidence of disloyalty.[130]

The Internal Security (McCarran) Act of 1950 required all members of "Communist-front" organizations to register with the federal government and authorized a plan, not rescinded until 1968, to establish special "detention centers" for incarcerating those so registered, without trial, at any time the president chose to declare an "internal security emergency."[131] Between 1945 and 1957, the House Un-American Activities Committee (HUAC) subpoenaed thousands of Americans to hundreds of congressional hearings, requiring them to testify about their political associations and their knowledge of the activities of their friends, neighbors, and coworkers, and those who refused were jailed for contempt.[132] Those who spoke most eloquently about the oppression of African Americans, such as Richard Wright and Paul Robeson, were labeled as communist threats and subjected to extensive government surveillance. Robeson's passport was revoked, and he was forbidden from leaving the continental United States from 1950 to 1957.[133] "Communism," like anarchism, became a catchall, a vaguely defined "enemy" against whom an undeclared "war" could be fought and increasingly restrictive measures imposed on the U.S. population.[134]

Between 1947 and 1952, the FBI placed hundreds of informants within social and labor organizations and conducted "security investigations" of approximately 6.6 million Americans,[135] setting the stage for a massive program aimed squarely at suppressing all movements for social change in the United States. Between 1956 and 1971, the FBI conducted over 2,000 domestic "counterintelligence" operations, called COINTELPROS (a term derived from Counter Intelligence Program), in what a Senate investigatory committee called "a secret war against those citizens it considers threats to the established order."[136] The Senate Select Committee to Study Government Operations with Respect to Intelligence Activities (known as the Church Committee after its chair, Senator Frank Church) produced a massive four-volume Final Report in 1976 that documented thousands of illegal and unconstitutional operations conducted by the FBI, the Central Intelligence Agency, the National Security Agency, the Defense Intelligence Agency, Army Intelligence, and numerous other federal agencies over several decades, with the explicit intent of destroying social and political movements considered threats to the status quo.[137] In the committee's words, these were part of "a sophisticated vigilante operation aimed squarely at preventing the exercise of First Amendment rights of speech and association, on the theory that preventing the growth of dangerous groups and the propagation of dangerous ideas would protect the national security and deter violence."[138]

Because the Church Committee's investigation was both constricted in scope and abruptly terminated in midstream,[139] there is much we do not know about

COINTELPRO-type operations. Nonetheless, between the committee's official report and thousands of documents obtained since then under the Freedom of Information Act, we know that virtually every organization in the country that was perceived by intelligence or law enforcement agencies as advocating social change in any manner was targeted. These included all organizations composed primarily of people of color, from African American civil rights and church groups to the Black Panther Party, the American Indian Movement (AIM), the Chicano Brown Berets, and advocates of Puerto Rican independence; the "New Left" in general, including antiwar activists, student organizations, environmentalists, feminists, and gay rights advocates; and all communist or socialist groups.[140]

While numerous federal agencies engaged in similar programs, the FBI's COINTELPRO operations are the best documented and will be used here to illustrate the methods employed.[141] The best-known—and least egregious—category of their operations involved acquiring information through illegal means, including mail interception, wiretaps, bugs, live "tails," break-ins and burglaries, and the use of informants.[142] Clearly identified by the Church Committee as both illegal and unconstitutional, these are the tactics the government is currently attempting to "legalize" in the surveillance provisions of the PATRIOT acts. These means were employed not merely to obtain information, but were explicitly intended to induce "paranoia" in movements for social change. As FBI director J. Edgar Hoover stated, he wanted his targets to believe there was "an FBI agent behind every mailbox"[143]—in other words, they were used precisely because of the chilling effect they would have on speech and associational activities, not because they were yielding evidence of criminal activity.[144] The government, however, was not simply "spying" on these organizations. The stated objective of FBI COINTELPROs was to "neutralize," that is, disrupt and destroy, the targeted group and, to quote the committee's Final Report, "The techniques were adopted wholesale from wartime counterintelligence, and ranged from the trivial . . . to the degrading . . . and the dangerous."[145] Thus, for example, a tape compiled from bugs of Martin Luther King Jr.'s hotel room, allegedly documenting sexual misconduct, was used to try to blackmail King into committing suicide.[146]

A second level of tactics employed was the dissemination of information known to be false. One version, sometimes called "gray propaganda," involved the use of "confidential sources" and "friendly" media sources to leak derogatory information about individuals and publish unfavorable articles and fabricated "documentaries" about targeted groups, such as the Nation of Islam and the Poor People's Campaign.[147] Another form, known as "black propaganda," involved the fabrication of communications purporting to come from the targeted individuals or organizations.[148] In one case, the FBI had an infiltrator in the Sacramento chapter of the Black Panther Party produce a coloring book for children that promoted racism and violence. Although the Panther leadership immediately ordered it destroyed, the FBI mailed copies to companies that had been contributing food to the Panthers' Breakfast for Children program to get them to withdraw their support.[149]

A third level involved attempts to destroy organizations by creating internal dissension and by setting up groups to attack each other. As reported by the Church Committee, "approximately 28% of the Bureau's COINTELPRO efforts were designed to weaken groups by setting members against each other, or to separate groups which might otherwise be allies, and convert them into mutual enemies."[150] Thus, for example, fabricated cartoons contributed to a lethal confrontation between the Black Panther Party and the US organization,[151] and nearly a hundred instances of fabricated correspondence between Black Panther Party leaders Eldridge Cleaver and Huey Newton were instrumental in fostering intraparty violence and ensuring the 1971 split in the party.[152]

A fourth level of COINTELPRO operations involved the deliberate misuse of the criminal justice system. Working with local police departments, the FBI had activists repeatedly arrested, not because it anticipated convictions, but "to simply harass, increase paranoia, tie up activists in a series of pre-arraignment incarcerations and preliminary courtroom procedures, and deplete their resources through the postings of numerous bail bonds (as well as the retention of attorneys)."[153] Using this tactic, the Revolutionary Action Movement in Philadelphia was effectively destroyed without the government ever obtaining a criminal conviction against its members.[154] Similarly, the government made 562 arrests in the wake of the 1973 occupation of Wounded Knee by members of the American Indian Movement (AIM). Although these arrests resulted in only fifteen convictions, they succeeded in depleting AIM's resources and keeping its leaders tied up in court for years.[155]

As most of its surveillance and infiltration revealed that the targeted groups were engaging in entirely lawful activity, the FBI resorted to placing agents provocateurs in organizations to advocate violence or illegal activities. When that failed, government agents obtained convictions by using fabricated evidence or perjured testimony and by framing people for crimes they had not committed. Thus, for example, after spending twenty-seven and nineteen years, respectively, in prison for murders they did not commit, the convictions of former Black Panthers Geronimo ji Jaga (Pratt) and Dhoruba bin Wahad (Richard Moore) were overturned because of overwhelming evidence that the FBI had framed them.[156] AIM activist Leonard Peltier is still incarcerated after thirty-one years, despite acknowledgment that his conviction for the deaths of two FBI agents on the Pine Ridge Reservation in South Dakota in 1975 was obtained by using perjured testimony and falsified ballistics evidence.[157]

Finally, when all other avenues of "neutralization" failed, law enforcement agents resorted to participation in direct physical assaults and assassinations, the best known of which are the 1969 murders of Chicago Black Panthers Fred Hampton and Mark Clark.[158] As part of its concerted program to destroy AIM, in 1973 the FBI led a paramilitary invasion against AIM activists gathered for a symbolic protest at the site of the 1890 Wounded Knee massacre. The siege, which lasted for seventy-one days, involved over 100 FBI agents, nearly 300 federal marshals, 250 Bureau of Indian Affairs police, U.S. Army warfare experts, and local vigilantes.[159] The FBI also provided direct support to paramilitary groups on the Pine Ridge Reservation who have been implicated in the "unsolved" deaths of at least seventy individuals associated with AIM.[160]

What is important to note about COINTELPRO and similar "intelligence" operations in this context is that by declaring groups that advocated social change to be threats to the national security, techniques that had been developed for use against "enemy agents" who, presumably, were not protected by the Constitution were now turned on U.S. citizens and residents. The result was law enforcement practices that violated U.S. law, constitutional mandates, and fundamental human rights, not to suppress criminal activity or terrorist threats but to suppress those who challenged the status quo. As the Senate Select Committee on Intelligence Activities concluded, "The unexpressed major premise of the programs was that a law enforcement agency has the duty to do whatever is necessary to combat perceived threats to the existing social and political order,"[161] and these programs were extremely successful in undermining virtually all movements for social, racial, or economic justice during this period. While the FBI stopped calling such operations COINTELPROs when the program was exposed in the early 1970s, there is ample evidence that such operations have continued and that each successive administration has asked Congress for legislation that would legalize many of the methods described above.[162]

The War on Terror

With all of the police powers obtained in the war on drugs firmly entrenched, the 1990s brought a gradual shift in emphasis from combating drugs to fighting terrorism, with the impetus for much legislation coming from the bombings of the World Trade Center in 1993 and the Oklahoma City federal building in 1995.[163] In 1994 Congress passed the Violent Crime Control and Law Enforcement Act,[164] fulfilling President Clinton's election-year promise to put an additional 100,000 police officers on the street, providing more funds for state prisons, adding a "three strikes" mandatory life sentence provision, enhancing sentences for "gang members," directing the sentencing commission to increase penalties for offenses committed in newly designated "drug free zones" and making those convicted of such offenses ineligible for parole, and authorizing the death penalty for numerous new categories of "terrorist activity."[165]

Even though the FBI had reported only two incidents of international terrorism in the United States between 1985 and 1996, Congress passed the Antiterrorism and Effective Death Penalty Act (AEDPA) of 1996, whose "sweeping provisions served to license almost the full range of repressive techniques which had been quietly continued after COINTELPRO was supposedly terminated."[166] The act defines "national security" as encompassing the "national defense, foreign relations, or economic interests of the United States" and gives the secretary of state broad authority to designate groups as "engaging in terrorist activity" if they threaten "the security of United States nationals or the national security of the United States,"[167] an authorization similar to President Truman's 1947 executive order. Under this act, it is a felony to provide any form of material support to designated organizations, even if the support goes directly to an entirely lawful activity of the group,[168] and noncitizens can be deported on the basis of secret evidence for belonging to "terrorist" organizations without any showing of personal involvement in terrorist or criminal activity—in other words, for engaging in what would otherwise be associations protected by the First Amendment.[169] As summarized by David Cole and James Dempsey, AEDPA "resurrected guilt by association as a principle of criminal and immigration law. It created a special court to use secret evidence to deport foreigners labeled as 'terrorists.' It made support for the peaceful humanitarian and political activities of selected foreign groups a crime. And it repealed a short-lived law forbidding the FBI from investigating First Amendment activities, opening the door once again to politically focused FBI investigations."[170]

At the same time, Congress passed the Illegal Immigration Reform and Immigrant Responsibility Act of 1996, which made it easier to deport immigrants not only for their political associations, but also for minor criminal convictions.[171] Noncitizens, already excludable or deportable for serious criminal offenses and for virtually any drug offense,[172] are now retroactively deportable for a wide range of minor crimes that have been redefined as "aggravated felonies." As a result, numerous longtime permanent residents have been deported for misdemeanor pleas or convictions entered decades ago.[173] Invoking the specter of terrorism, the Clinton administration was thus able to implement many laws that had long been on the executive branch's "wish list." George H. W. Bush, for example, had twice proposed to allow secret evidence in deportation hearings,[174] and both the first Bush and the Reagan administrations had unsuccessfully attempted to criminalize "support" for terrorism.[175]

With the September 11 attacks on the Pentagon and the World Trade Center, the stage was set for the swift passage of the next level of police and intelligence powers,[176] as Americans were informed once again that they would have to "sacrifice some liberties for their security."[177] With Attorney General John Ashcroft's dire warning that the "blood of the victims" of the next terrorist attack would be on the hands of members of Congress if they did not act quickly,[178] the USA PATRIOT Act[179] was rushed through the legislature and signed into law in just three days.[180]

The PATRIOT Act, a lengthy and complicated piece of legislation containing 158 separate provisions, dramatically expanded the government's law enforcement and intelligence-gathering powers.[181] Generally speaking, the act provides the government with enhanced surveillance powers, blurs the line between criminal and intelligence investigations, criminalizes political protest, and further curtails immigrants' rights.[182] While an in-depth analysis is not possible here, I will briefly highlight a few of its provisions, which, in the name of protecting "our" security, significantly narrow the class of those protected by law.

According to Nancy Chang of the Center for Constitutional Rights, in passing the PATRIOT Act, Congress "granted the Bush administration its long-standing wish list of enhanced surveillance tools, coupled with the right to use these tools with only minimal judicial and congressional oversight."[183] The scope and duration of authorized surveillance and physical searches have been expanded,[184] including authorization for "sneak-and-peak searches," known in COINTELPRO days as "black bag jobs," that is, searches conducted without notice of the warrant until after the search has been completed.[185] It is now easier for the government to obtain warrants for records from third parties such as telephone or utility companies, Internet providers, banks and credit card companies, and even public libraries.[186] In addition, many companies report being pressured to "turn over customer records voluntarily, in the absence of either a court order or a subpoena, 'with the idea that it is unpatriotic if the companies insist too much on legal subpoenas first.'"[187]

In many ways, the PATRIOT Act attempts to extend and legitimize the COINTELPRO-era practice of using methods initially developed for use against foreign agents against U.S. citizens and organizations. The act defines "foreign intelligence information" very broadly to include not only information relating to attacks or sabotage by foreign powers or their agents but also "information, whether or not concerning a United States person [that is, a U.S. citizen or permanent resident], with respect to a foreign power or foreign territory that relates to (i) the national defense or the security of the United States; or (ii) the conduct of the foreign affairs of the United States."[188] Under this definition, any person's opinion on any aspect of U.S. foreign policy, regardless of how theoretical, or even inane, may be considered "foreign intelligence information" and can now be disclosed "to any Federal law enforcement, intelligence, protective, immigration, national defense or national security official" to assist in the performance of his or her official duties.[189]

It has generally been assumed that the relaxed standards for warrants available under the Foreign Intelligence Surveillance Act (FISA)[190] were constitutionally acceptable because the purpose of the authorized surveillance was foreign intelligence information, not intended for use in criminal prosecutions.[191] Now, however, U.S. citizens and permanent residents can be targeted on the basis—although not solely on the basis—of First Amendment protected activities and subjected to extensive, and perhaps secret, surveillance and searches because they are involved in activities that, under the broadened definition of "foreign intelligence information," relate to U.S. foreign policy or national security.[192]

As noted above, in the late 1940s the Justice Department began keeping a list of "subversive" organizations, and it considered not only membership but "sympathetic association" with such organizations as evidence of disloyalty.[193] In 1996 the Antiterrorism and Effective Death Penalty Act authorized the secretary of state to create a list of "foreign terrorist organizations" and made it a felony to provide material aid to such organizations.[194] The PATRIOT Act now authorizes the creation of a separate "terrorist exclusion list,"[195] with increased penalties for providing material support to designated organizations.[196] Had this provision been in effect in the 1980s, it would have covered any support for South Africa's African National Congress, and, presumably, support for any antiapartheid activity could have been deemed "sympathetic association."

Immigrants are now more vulnerable than ever, for the act both broadens the definition of who is deportable and gives the attorney general expanded powers to indefinitely detain noncitizens.[197] "Terrorist activity" is now a deportable offense,[198] and the definition of "terrorism" has been amended in immigration law to include any crime involving a weapon or other dangerous device "other than for mere personal monetary gain."[199] Thus, a fight in a bar in which knives or chairs were used in a threatening manner may now be considered terrorist activity for which an immigrant can be summarily deported. "Engaging in terrorist activity" now encompasses soliciting members or funds, and providing material support or even "encouragement" to a "terrorist" organization, even if the activity is undertaken solely to support the lawful, humanitarian activities of the organization, and even if the associational activities would otherwise be protected by the First Amendment.[200] These organizations need not be on any official list, but can simply be groups that are comprised of "two or more individuals, whether organized or not," engaging in certain activities, including the use or threat of violence.[201]

The provision of the PATRIOT Act with the greatest potential for chilling the exercise of First Amendment rights and suppressing political dissent may be the section of the act that creates the new crime of "domestic terrorism," broadly defined to encompass activities that "involve acts dangerous to human life that are a violation of the criminal laws of the United States or of any State" and which appear intended to "intimidate or coerce a civilian population," "influence the policy of a government by intimidation or coercion," or "affect the conduct of a government by mass destruction, assassination, or kidnapping," and which "occur primarily within the territorial jurisdiction of the United States."[202] Again, had this been the law in the 1950s and 1960s, any civil rights protests involving civil disobedience would have qualified as "domestic terrorism." Today any serious social protest, such as demonstrations against the World Trade Organization, the war in Iraq, or police brutality, is, by definition, intended to influence government policy and could easily be interpreted as involving "coercion."[203] Such protests now become domestic terrorism if a law is broken and life is endangered, perhaps by demonstrators who fail to obey a police officer's order and block an intersection or break a window. Not only the protesters but also those who provide them with "material support," such as transportation or lodging, must now consider the fact that they could face felony charges and long prison terms. According to Chang, "[b]ecause this crime is couched in such vague and expansive terms, it is likely to be read by federal law enforcement agencies as licensing the investigation and surveillance of political activists and organizations that protest government policies, and by prosecutors as licensing the criminalization of legitimate political dissent."[204]

As noted earlier, in January 2003 a draft of the Justice Department's Domestic Security Enhancement Act of 2003 was leaked to the press. Commonly referred to as "PATRIOT II," this proposed legislation would significantly enhance the government's already extensive powers.[205] A few of its provisions that illustrate the Justice Department's intensifying effort to define even broader sectors of the U.S. public as "the enemy" and to give itself virtually unlimited power to wage war against dissent will be highlighted here.

FISA allows many of the Fourth Amendment's protections against unreasonable searches and seizures to be circumvented under the theory that the methods authorized are to be used against "foreign powers" that pose threats to the national security. The first section of PATRIOT II would expand FISA's definition of "foreign power" to include all persons who engage in "international terrorism," without any requirement of affiliation with an international organization. "Agents of a foreign power" are currently defined as those who knowingly engage in intelligence-gathering activities on behalf of a foreign power, if those activities "involve or may involve a violation" of federal criminal law,[206] but the proposed revisions would remove the requirement of a possible violation of criminal law.[207] The "wartime" authorization currently given the attorney general to engage in electronic surveillance or physical searches without prior FISA Court approval when Congress has declared war would extend to the periods immediately following a congressional authorization of the use of military force or an attack on the United States deemed to be a national emergency.[208]

The crime of "domestic terrorism," created by the PATRIOT Act, would be incorporated into the definition of "terrorist activities," including related "preparatory, material support, and criminal activities,"[209] and the definition of "material support" for both "international terrorism" and "domestic terrorism" would include "instruction or teaching designed to impart a specific skill" and providing an organization with "one or more individuals (including himself) to work in concert with it or under its direction or control."[210] All surveillance activities authorized in criminal investigations would become available in investigations of terrorist activities,[211] and "domestic security" investigations would no longer be subject to the limitations on criminal investigations provided by the Fourth Amendment.[212]

Private entities have traditionally been given greater latitude than the government to gather information on individuals, on the theory that the Fourth Amendment applies to state action and the information would not be used in a criminal prosecution. Referring to this distinction as "perverse,"[213] the Justice Department proposes to give the government "equal access" to consumer credit reports,[214] to expand the financial and communications information it can obtain from private agencies using administrative subpoenas known as "national security letters,"[215] and to protect businesses and their personnel who "voluntarily" provide information to law enforcement agencies.[216] At the same time that the government would be given this expanded access to information about citizens, the proposed legislation would amend the Freedom of Information Act[217] to allow the government to refuse to disclose information regarding detainees until it chooses to initiate criminal proceedings against them.[218]

Despite the Church Committee's 1976 exposure of widespread illegal and unconstitutional conduct by federal law enforcement and intelligence agencies, working closely with state and local police, no legislation was passed to limit such conduct and no official punished for engaging in such practices.[219] As a result, virtually the only constraint on such activity has come from court orders restraining police departments from investigating citizens without reasonable suspicion or probable cause to believe they have engaged or may engage in criminal conduct.[220] Drawing explicitly on the Prison Litigation Reform Act, which terminated many consent decrees resulting from civil suits brought over prison conditions,[221] the new PATRIOT II would prohibit, prospectively and retroactively, most consent decrees in police surveillance cases.[222]

Drawing explicitly on measures instituted in the "war on drugs," the draft act proposes to extend presumptive pretrial detention to persons accused of "offenses that are likely to be committed by terrorists."[223] Using the same rationale, it would extend the government's ability, already provided in the PATRIOT Act,[224] to subject those convicted of terrorism-related offenses to "up to lifetime postrelease supervision."[225] According to the Justice Department's analysis, this is justified because "involvement by offenders in terrorism may be the result of persistent (or lifelong) ideological commitments that will not simply disappear within a few years of release."[226]

Also expanding on measures implemented in the "war on drugs," PATRIOT II proposes eliminating the statute of limitations with respect to terrorism-related offenses,[227] expanding the list of crimes subject to the death penalty,[228] and denying federal benefits, such as grants, contracts, loans, and professional or commercial licenses, to those convicted of terrorism offenses.[229] Not surprisingly, the proposed legislation would make it even easier to exclude, imprison, and deport noncitizens. As noted earlier, the 1996 Illegal Immigration Reform and Immigrant Responsibility Act redefined "aggravated felony" to include numerous misdemeanors and made immigrants retroactively deportable on the basis of prior pleas or convictions.[230] Noting that this provision "perversely" makes immigrants subject to expedited deportation for offenses much less serious than crimes such as espionage, sabotage, draft evasion, or alien smuggling, the Justice Department proposes to expand the list of offenses triggering the expedited removal provisions and to expand the act's applicability to all aliens, including permanent residents,[231] and to provide enhanced criminal penalties for violations of immigration laws.[232]

Thus, the existing provisions of the PATRIOT Act and the proposed "enhancements" of PATRIOT II dramatically expand the definition of "terrorism-related crimes," making it much easier to prosecute people for political dissent and to impose extremely harsh penalties, including pretrial detention and up to lifetime postrelease "supervision" on them. The effect is to eliminate a large and as-yet undefined sector of "U.S. persons," citizens and permanent residents, from the "we" being protected by the measures allegedly being taken "for our security." But the draft Domestic Security Enhancement Act goes even further, proposing to allow the government to make U.S. citizens literally "Others" by stripping them of their citizenship. The Immigration and Nationality Act would be amended to allow the expatriation of a citizen who joins, serves in, or provides material support to a terrorist organization "engaged in hostilities against the United States, its people, or its national security interests."[233] Given the broadly expanded definitions of "material support," "terrorist organization," and "national security interests" and the lack of definition of "hostilities," this provision has virtually unlimited potential for rendering U.S. citizens stateless,[234] and—in light of the United States' history of disregarding international law,[235] as illustrated by the treatment of those held at Guantánamo Bay[236]—protected by no law at all.

The enemy is again amorphous, the war pervasive, and the reach of constitutional protections even more circumscribed.[237] More and more U.S. citizens and permanent residents have been and can be imprisoned, for longer periods of time and for a wider range of "crimes" on the basis of evidence obtained with virtually no First or Fourth Amendment protections. U.S. citizens are now openly subjected to measures historically limited to "agents of foreign powers" and can literally be rendered "foreign." History has shown us, from the 1798 Sedition Act through COINTELPRO, that those most likely to be targeted by such measures are not actual criminals or terrorists, for adequate laws have always existed for their apprehension, but those engaged in activities deemed "undesirable" by those in power.

WHO—OR WHAT—IS SECURED BY EXPANDED POLICE POWERS?

This chapter has focused on the question of just who is an "American" for purposes of the measures being taken in the name of "our" security. It first provided a brief overview of the role that race and national origin have played in determining citizenship, because that history helps us identify the structural origins of racial hierarchy in the United States and continues to inform public perceptions of who is "really" an American. I next considered how, by declaring crime and drugs to be threats to the national security, law enforcement agencies have been given dramatically expanded powers, with the result that a huge proportion of the population most likely to be dissatisfied with the status quo—the poor and people of color—have been or are under the immediate threat of being incarcerated. I then presented some of the ways in which political ideology, not just ethnic identity, has been a determinant of who, or what, is protected by law; how those with "un-American" beliefs have been portrayed either as foreign or as agents of foreign powers; and how the powers of the state have been used, legally or illegally, to suppress organizations and activities seen as threatening to the status quo. Finally, I summarized how these developments have come together in the current war on terrorism, which has targeted immigrants, people of color, and those who dissent politically, focusing particularly on measures that will further reduce the legal and constitutional protections available to U.S. citizens, rendering them indistinguishable from "agents of foreign powers" in the eyes of the government.

Historically, the U.S. criminal justice system and intelligence agencies have been used to shore up the institution of slavery, to crush labor movements, to protect explicitly colonial and imperialist ventures overseas, and to undermine movements for social change, all in the name of protecting national security or American interests. By creating widespread fear about the dangers inherent in anarchy, communism, drugs, crime, uncontrolled immigration, or terrorism, much of the population has been convinced to cede more and more of the rights guaranteed them by the Constitution, to "sacrifice some freedoms for the sake of security." In the name of "law and order," the police power of the state has been expanded to encompass nearly every aspect of everyday life,[238] and the United States now incarcerates more people than any other country in the world. In the name of preserving the "American values" of freedom and democracy, policies and practices have been condoned that are, in the words of the Church Committee, "abhorrent in a free society."[239] The Church Committee's 1976 conclusion about COINTELPRO and related governmental operations is equally applicable to the more recent wars on crime, drugs, and terrorism: "The unexpressed major premise . . . [is] that a law enforcement agency has the duty to do whatever is necessary to combat perceived threats to the existing social and political order."[240]

In light of this history, I return to the question originally posed: who is being protected by these dramatically expanded law enforcement and intelligence powers? It is not the poor, who comprise the bulk of those incarcerated,[241] or the communities of color, in which at least one-third of all young men are or will be in prison or on probation or parole.[242] It is not immigrants, even lawful permanent residents, who have been interrogated, detained, disappeared, and deported by the thousands, or the victims of hate crimes against those who are, or appear to be, "foreign." It is not those who struggle for civil rights and liberties, or racial justice, or the sovereignty of American Indian nations, or the independence of Puerto Rico. It is not union organizers, environmental activists, those who promote gay and lesbian rights, or those who oppose U.S. military interventions overseas or the economic policies of the World Bank or the World Trade Organization.

If the status quo, rather than the people in general, is what is protected by these measures, have we come full circle, back to the assumptions of the "founding fathers" that who and what is "American," protected by the Constitution and the powers of the state, is not "we the People" but a small subset of those people and the interests they represent? For many of us, it is not acceptable to live in a world in which untold numbers of children die of malnutrition and preventable diseases, millions of all ages die in ongoing wars, hundreds of languages and their attendant cultures are disappearing, and vast swaths of land have been rendered uninhabitable by a relentless quest for "progress." Similarly, many of us cannot sit by and watch our communities be ravaged by the incarceration of our youth, skyrocketing unemployment, and lack of access to decent health care, education, or housing, especially in a country in which the top 1 percent of the population controls nearly 40 percent of its wealth.[243] Yet this *is* the status quo being protected by law and power in the United States today. If we want to have the ability to effect change in any of these areas, or even to be able to express our opinions about such issues, we cannot allow any further suppression of dissent in the name of "fighting terror."

NOTES

This essay was initially presented at the 2003 Race in 21st Century America conference at Michigan State University. I am grateful to Curtis Stokes for organizing that event and to the Georgia State University College of Law for its research support. This essay develops my analysis in *For "Our" Security: Who Is an "American" and What Is Protected by Enhanced Law Enforcement and Intelligence Powers?* 2 Seattle J. Soc. Justice 23 (2003), and has since been updated and expanded in my book, From Chinese Exclusion to Guantánamo Bay: Plenary Power and the Prerogative State (2007).

1. I have addressed these detentions in detail in Natsu Taylor Saito, *Will Force Trump Legality after September 11? American Jurisprudence Confronts the Rule of Law*, 17 Geo. Immig. L.J. 1 (2002). See David Cole, *Enemy Aliens*, 54 Stan. L. Rev. 953 (2002); Nancy Chang, Silencing Political Dissent: How Post–September 11 Anti-Terrorism Measures Threaten Our Civil Liberties (2002); Jordan J. Paust, *Judicial Power to Determine the Status and Rights of Persons Detained without Trial*, 44 Harv. Int'l L.J. 503 (2003); Amnesty International, Amnesty International's Concerns Regarding Post September 11 Detentions in the USA (March 14, 2002), available at http://web.amnesty.org/library/Index/ENGAMR510442002. http://web.amnesty.org/ai.nsf/Index/AMR510442002?OpenDocuments&of=COUNTRIES.

2. See Legislative Information on the Internet, *Legislation Related to the Attack of September 11, 2001*, available at http://thomas.loc.gov/home/terrorleg.htm.

3. Domestic Security Enhancement Act of 2003 ("PATRIOT II"), draft of January 9, 2003, available at http://www.pbs.org/now/politics/patriot2-hi.pdf. The draft includes the proposed text of the legislation as well as a "Section-by-Section Analysis." Apparently as a result of public resistance to a further restriction of civil liberties, former attorney general John Ashcroft embarked on a national tour in August 2003 to promote the USA PATRIOT Act, apparently to help the administration implement PATRIOT II in piecemeal fashion, rather than as one comprehensive act. See *President Urging Wider U.S. Powers in Terrorism Law*, New York Times, September 11, 2001 (reporting a speech in which George W. Bush argued that the PATRIOT Act did not go far enough and proposed further expansion of powers, including "administrative subpoenas" and expansion of pretrial detention and the death penalty in terrorism-related cases).

4. Uniting and Strengthening America by Providing Appropriate Tools Required to Intercept and Obstruct Terrorism (USA PATRIOT) Act, Pub. L. No. 107-56, 115 Stat. 272 (2001). The act was signed into law on October 26, 2001, just three days after it was introduced in the House of Representatives. The history of the bill is available at http://thomas.loc.gov/cgi-bin/bdquery/z?d107:HR03162:@@@L&summ2=m&.

5. For an analysis of the USA PATRIOT Act in the context of this history, see Natsu Taylor Saito, *Whose Liberty? Whose Security? The USA PATRIOT Act in the Context of COINTELPRO and the Unlawful Repression of Political Dissent*, 81 Ore. L. Rev. 1051 (2002).

6. PATRIOT II, supra note 3, § 501: Expatriation of Terrorists. See text accompanying notes 233–236 infra.

7. See text accompanying notes 206–210 infra.

8. See, e.g., The National Security Strategy of the United States of America (2002) (a policy report prepared by the Bush administration and released to Congress on September 19, 2002): "In the war against global terrorism, we will never forget that we are ultimately fighting for our democratic values and way of life. Freedom and fear are at war." (§ 3, n.p.).

9. See, e.g., Editorial, A Constitutional Anachronism, New York Times, September 6, 2003, which begins with the statement "America is a nation of immigrants" and proceeds, using examples such as Secretaries of State Henry Kissinger and Madeline Albright, to argue that the Constitution's requirement that the president be a "natural born citizen" should be changed.

10. See, e.g., Lynne Cheney, America: A Patriotic Primer (2002), a children's book that depicts the Statue of Liberty on the page for the letter "A." In the notes, she quotes Emma Lazarus's 1883 poem "The New Colossus," which is inscribed on the statue: "Give me your tired, your poor, / Your huddled masses yearning to breathe free, / The wretched refuse of your teeming shore. / Send these, the homeless, tempest-tossed to me, / I lift my lamp beside the golden door!"

11. In his first televised address on September 11, 2001, President Bush said, "America was targeted for attack because we're the brightest beacon for freedom and opportunity in the world." On September 20 he said to Congress, "Americans are asking, why do they hate us?" and, continuing, "They hate our freedoms." Ziauddin Sardar and Merryl Wyn Davies, Why Do People Hate America? (2002), 137. Prosperity in this construction is seen as a natural outgrowth of a "free market" economy, which, in turn, has been given the status of an essential human right. See National Security Strategy, supra note 8, which consistently links "democracy, development, free markets and free trade" (Introduction, n.p.).

12. In January 2002 the Washington Post reported that the Justice Department was prioritizing the deportation of 6,000 men of Middle Eastern descent, selected by gender, age, and country of origin from the more than 300,000 deportable noncitizens in the country. Cole, supra note 1 at 975; Dan Eggen and Cheryl W. Thompson, U.S. Seeks Thousands of Fugitive Deportees; Middle Eastern Men Are Focus of Search, Washington Post, January 8, 2002.

13. See Chang, supra note 1 at 69–87, 960–65; Saito, supra note 1.

14. See Cole, supra note 1 at 975 (noting the Justice Department's November 2001 announcement that it would interview 5,000 young men, selected on the basis of their age, date of arrival, and country of origin).

15. The Homeland Security Act of 2002, Pub. L. No. 107–296, 116 Stat. 2135, abolished the INS as an agency and distributed its functions to the Bureaus of Citizenship and Immigration Services (BCIS), Customs and Border Protection (BCBP), and Immigration and Customs Enforcement (BICE) within the newly created Department of Homeland Security.

16. 67 FR 52584 (August 12, 2002). See Robert S. White, *New Post-9/11 Registration Procedures for Foreign Workers, Students, and Visitors*, 91 Ill. Bar J. 253 (2003).

17. See Cole, supra note 1 at 974–77.

18. Although noncitizens in the United States have limited constitutional rights with respect to immigration matters, federal courts have consistently held that they are "persons" protected by the Constitution. See Wong Wing v. United States, 163 U.S. 228 (1896) (noncitizens cannot be punished without a criminal trial because they are protected by the Fifth and Sixth Amendments); Yick Wo v. Hopkins, 118 U.S. 356, 369 (1886) (noncitizens in the United States are protected by the Fourteenth Amendment); Plyler v. Doe, 457 U.S. 202, 210 (1982) (even those unlawfully present are "persons" guaranteed Fifth and Fourteenth Amendment due process); Mathews v. Diaz, 426 U.S. 67, 77 (1976) ("[e]ven one whose presence in this country is unlawful, involuntary, or transitory is entitled to . . . constitutional protection"); see David A. Martin, *Graduated Application of Constitutional Protections for Aliens: The Real Meaning of* Zadvydas v. Davis, 2001 Sup. Ct. Rev. 47, 8486 (2001); Gerald L. Neuman, Strangers to the Constitution: Immigrants, Borders, and Fundamental Law (1996), 1–15.

19. Chae Chan Ping v. United States (The Chinese Exclusion Case), 130 U.S. 581 (1889).

20. See Hiroshi Motomura, *Immigration Law after a Century of Plenary Power: Phantom Constitutional Norms and Statutory Interpretation*, 100 Yale L.J. 545 (1990); Stephen H. Legomsky, *Immigration Law and the Principle of Plenary Congressional Power*, 1984 Sup. Ct. Rev. 255 (1984); Natsu Taylor Saito, *Asserting Plenary Power Over the "Other": Indians, Immigrants, Colonial Subjects, and Why U.S. Jurisprudence Needs to Incorporate International Law*, 20 Yale L. & Pol. Rev. 427 (2002); T. Alexander Aleinikoff, Semblances of Sovereignty: The Constitution, the State, and American Citizenship (2002).

21. Act of March 3, 1875, ch. 141, 18 Stat. 477 (1875).

22. For a brief overview of these policies and their evolution, see Thomas Alexander Aleinikoff, David A. Martin, and Hiroshi Motomura, Immigration and Citizenship: Process and Policy (4th ed., 1998), 152–75.

23. For a concise summary of internal colonialism as manifest in the United States, see Ward Churchill, *A Breach of Trust: The Radioactive Colonization of Native North America*, in Churchill, Acts of Rebellion: The Ward Churchill Reader (2003), 111, 114–16; see also Howard Adams, A Tortured People: The Politics of Colonization

(1995) (applying a similar analysis to indigenous nations in Canada); Michael Hector, Internal Colonialism: The Celtic Fringe in British National Politics, 1536–1966 (1975) (explicating the concept of internal colonialism).

24. The United States, which has only 5 percent of the world's population, consumes 25 to 30 percent of the world's resources and has "40 percent of industrialized-world GDP [gross domestic product], 50 percent of total world defense spending, 60 percent of the total world growth rate, 70 percent of tradable world financial wealth, and 80 percent of world military R&D [research and development]." Criton Zoakos, *Why the World Hates America: The Economic Explanation*, International Economy, March 22, 2003, at 10, 2003 WL 19419255; see also Arlie Russell Hochschild, *A Generation without Public Passion*, Atlantic Monthly, February 2001 (citing a 30 percent consumption rate); U.S. Census Bureau, 2000 Statistical Abstract of the United States, tbl. 1390, "Energy Consumption and Production by Country, 1990 and 1998" (noting that in 1998, the United States accounted for approximately 25 percent of the world's total energy consumption), available at http://www.census.gov/prod/2001pubs/statab/sec30.pdf.

25. See Aleinikoff et al., supra note 22 at 176–77 (Fig. 2.1, The Origins of U.S. Immigration, by Region, 1821–1979). See Roger Daniels, Coming to America: A History of Immigration and Ethnicity in American Life (2nd ed., 2002).

26. Jimmie Durham summarizes the standard history as follows: "When the Europeans first came to North America they found an untamed wilderness inhabited only by a few primitive but noble savages. Those savages, called Indians, lived in nature almost like animals. They melted away when confronted by civilisation, technology, and progress." Jimmie Durham, A Certain Lack of Coherence: Writings on Art and Cultural Politics (1993), 23. The alternative is to say that American Indians were simply earlier immigrants, as Lynne Cheney does in her children's primer: "N is for Native Americans, who came here first." Cheney, supra note 10. To quote Durham again, "Nothing could be more central to American reality than the relationships between Americans and American Indians, yet those relationships are of course the most invisible and the most lied about." Durham at 138.

27. See Ward Churchill, A Little Matter of Genocide: Holocaust and Denial in the Americas 1492 to the Present (1997).

28. See Ward Churchill, *Charades, Anyone? The Indian Claims Commission in Context*, in Churchill, Perversions of Justice: Indigenous Peoples and Anglo-American Law (2003), 125, 140 (noting that in 1956 the Justice Department warned Congress that the country's legal ownership of about half the area of the lower forty-eight states was subject to serious challenge, and the Interior Department's 1970 conclusion that about "one third of the nation's land" still legally belongs to native people).

29. See Lerone Bennett Jr., Before the Mayflower: A History of Black America (6th ed., 1993); Ira Berlin, Many Thousands Gone: The First Two Centuries of Slavery in North America (1998).

30. See Rodolfo Acuña, Occupied America: A History of Chicanos (3rd ed., 1988).

31. See Ward Churchill and Sharon H. Venne, eds., Islands in Captivity: The Record of the International Tribunal on the Rights of Indigenous Hawaiians (2004); Haunani-Kay Trask, From a Native Daughter: Colonialism and Sovereignty in Hawai'i (2nd ed., 1999).

32. See Christina Duffy Burnett and Burke Marshall, eds., Foreign in a Domestic Sense: Puerto Rico, American Expansion, and the Constitution (2001); Pedro A. Caban, Constructing a Colonial People: Puerto Rico and the United States, 1898–1932 (1999); Jose Trias Monge, Puerto Rico: The Trials of the Oldest Colony in the World (1997); Efren Rivera Ramos, The Legal Construction of Identity: The Judicial and Social Legacy of American Colonialism in Puerto Rico (2001).

33. Dred Scott v. Sanford, 60 U.S. (19 How.) 393, 407 (1856). Justice Taney added that those of African descent had been regarded by the country's founders as "beings of an inferior order, and altogether unfit to associate with the white race, either in social or political relations; and so far inferior, that they had no rights which the white man was bound to respect." *Id.*

34. Citizenship Act of 1924, 43 Stat. 253, 8 U.S.C. § 1401(a)(2).

35. In *Cherokee Nation v. Georgia*, Supreme Court justice John Marshall asserted that American Indian nations were neither independent foreign countries nor states of the Union, but "domestic dependent nations" whose "relation to the United States resembles that of a ward to his guardian." 30 U.S. (5 Pet.) 1, 17 (1831).

36. As the Supreme Court summarized: "The sovereignty that Indian tribes retain is of a unique and limited character. It exists only at the sufferance of Congress and is subject to complete defeasance. But until Congress acts, the tribes retain their existing sovereign powers. In sum, Indian tribes still possess those aspects of sovereignty not withdrawn by treaty or statute, or by implication as a necessary result of their dependent status." United States v. Wheeler, 435 U.S. 313, 323 (1978).

37. U.S. Const. art. I, § 8, cl. 4.

38. Naturalization Act of 1790, 1 Stat. 103 (repealed by Act of January 19, 1795, which reenacted most of its provisions, including its racial restrictions). See Ian F. Haney Lopez, White by Law: The Legal Construction of Race (1996).

39. Act of July 14, 1870, ch. 255, § 7, 17 Stat. 254.

40. Immigration and Nationality Act, ch. 477, 66 Stat. 163 (1952).

41. United States v. Bhagat Singh Thind, 261 U.S. 204, 213 (1923) (holding a "high-caste Hindu" ineligible for naturalization).

42. See Natsu Taylor Saito, *Alien and Non-Alien Alike: Citizenship, "Foreignness," and Racial Hierarchy in American Law*, 76 Ore. L. Rev. 261 (1997); Keith Aoki, *"Foreign-ness" and Asian American Identities: Yellowface, World War II Propaganda, and Bifurcated Racial Stereotypes*, 4 Asian Pac. Am. L.J. 1 (1996); Juan F. Perea, *Los Olvidados: On the Making of Invisible People*, 70 N.Y.U. L. Rev. 965 (1995); Kevin R. Johnson, *Civil Rights and Immigration: Challenges for the Latino Community in the Twenty-first Century*, 8 La Raza L.J. 42 (1995); David J. Weber, Foreigners in Their Native Land: Historical Roots of the Mexican Americans (1973); Natsu Taylor Saito, *Symbolism Under Siege: Japanese American Redress and the "Racing" of Arab Americans as "Terrorists,"* 8 Asian L.J. 1 (2001).

43. See Roger Daniels, The Decision to Relocate the Japanese Americans (1975), 33–45; Michi Weglyn, Years of Infamy: The Untold Story of America's Concentration Camps (1996); Roger Daniels, Prisoners without Trial: Japanese Americans in World War II (1993).

44. See Hirabayashi v. United States, 320 U.S. 81 (1943); Yasui v. United States, 320 U.S. 115 (1943); and Korematsu v. United States, 323 U.S. 214 (1945).

45. See Eugene V. Rostow, *The Japanese American Cases: A Disaster*, 54 Yale L.J. 489 (1945), reprinted in Eugene V. Rostow, The Sovereign Prerogative: The Supreme Court and the Quest for Law (1962), 193–266.

46. See *id.*

47. See Hussein Ibish, ed., American-Arab Anti-Discrimination Committee, Report on Hate Crimes and Discrimination against Arab Americans: The Post–September 11 Backlash (2003); United States: "We Are Not the Enemy:" Hate Crimes against Arabs, Muslims, and Those Perceived to Be Arab or Muslim after September 11, Human Rights Watch, Vol. 14, No. 6 (G), November 2002, available at http://www.hrw.org/reports/2002/usahate/.

48. See john a. powell, *The Racing of American Society: Race Functioning as a Verb Before Signifying as a Noun*, 15 Law & Ineq. 99 (1997).

49. See Saito, supra note 42.

50. *Hate in the News: Violence against Arab and Muslim Americans*, available at http://www.tolerance.org/news/article_hate.jsp?id=412 (listed with Oklahoma hate crimes).

51. See John Quigley, *The Afghanistan War and Self-Defense*, 37 Valparaiso U. L. Rev. 541 (2003); Jordan J. Paust, *Use of Armed Force against Terrorists in Afghanistan, Iraq, and Beyond*, 35 Cornell Int'l L.J. 533 (2002) (both criticizing the United States' self-defense rationale).

52. See Matthew Lippman, *Aerial Attacks on Civilians and the Humanitarian Laws of War: Technology and Terror from World War I to Afghanistan*, 33 Cal.W. Int'l L.J. 1, 56–65 (2002); Michael P. Scharf and Paul R. Williams, *Report of the Committee of Experts on*

National Building in Afghanistan, 36 New England L.R. 709 (2002); Laura A. Dickinson, *Reluctant Nation Building: Promoting the Rule of Law in Post-Taliban Afghanistan*, 17 Conn. J. Int'l L. 429 (2002).

53. See Memorandum from Amnesty International to United States Government on the rights of people in U.S. custody in Afghanistan and Guantánamo Bay (April 14, 2003), available at http://web.amnesty.orgt/ai.nsf/recent/AMR510532002; Human Rights Watch, *U.S.: Growing Problem of Guantánamo Detainees*, May 30, 2002, available at http://www.hrw.org/english/docs/2002/05/30/usdom4007.htm; Richard J. Wilson, *United States Detainees at Guantánamo Bay: The Inter-American Commission on Human Rights Responds to a "Legal Black Hole,"* 10-Spg. Human Rights 2 (2003); Erin Chlopak, *Dealing with the Detainees at Guantánamo Bay: Humanitarian and Human Rights Obligations Under the Geneva Conventions*, 9-N03 Human Rights Brief 6 (2002).

54. See United States v. Lindh, 227 F. Supp. 2d 565 (E.D. Va. 2002); Melysa H. Sperber, *John Walker Lindh and Yaser Esam Hamdi: Closing the Loophole in International Humanitarian Law for American Nationals Captured Abroad While Fighting with Enemy Forces*, 40 Am. Crim. L. Rev. 159, 160–61 (2003).

55. Katharine Q. Seelye, *Walker Is Returned to U.S. and Will Be in Court Today*, New York Times, January 24, 2002. See also Cole, supra note 1 at 953–54.

56. United States v. Lindh, 227 F. Supp. 2d at 572.

57. See Hamdi v. Rumsfeld, 296 F.3d 278, 280 (4th Cir. 2002); Alejandra Rodriguez, *Is the War on Terrorism Compromising Civil Liberties? A Discussion of Hamdi and Padilla*, 39 Cal. W. L. Rev. 379, 381–82 (2003); Sperber, supra note 54 at 162–63.

58. Following a Supreme Court ruling that Hamdi had a minimal right to challenge his "enemy combatant" classification, the United States deported him in exchange for renunciation of his U.S. citizenship. See Hamdi v. Rumsfeld, 542 U.S. 507 (2004). See Thomas J. Lepri, *Safeguarding the Enemy Within: The Need for Procedural Protections for U.S. Citizens Detained as Enemy Combatants Under* Ex Parte Quirin, 71 Fordham L. Rev. 2565, 2579–83 (2003).

59. Cole, supra note 1 at 954.

60. The treatment of Jose Padilla, aka Abdullah al-Muhajir, and Timothy McVeigh presents an even starker contrast. A U.S. citizen born in Brooklyn of Puerto Rican descent, Padilla was arrested in the United States, apparently in connection with a "dirty bomb" plot, declared an enemy combatant, and taken to a military brig. After being held for three years without charge, the Fourth Circuit ruled that he had to be charged or released. He was subsequently convicted of conspiring to support terrorism abroad, based on a 1997 phone conversation taped by the FBI. See Jay Weaver, *Jose Padilla Trial*, Miami Herald, August 24, 2007; Padilla v. Hanft, 423 F.3d 386 (4th Cir.

2005); Samantha A. Pitts-Kiefer, *Jose Padilla: Enemy Combatant or Common Criminal?* 48 Villa. L. Rev. 875 (2003). McVeigh, a white American, was charged with the 1995 bombing of the federal building in Oklahoma City, characterized at the time as the most devastating terrorist act to have taken place on U.S. soil. While he was ultimately convicted and executed, no one questioned that he would have his "day in court." See United States v. McVeigh, 153 F.3d 1166 (10th Cir. 1998); Stephen Jones and Jennifer Gideon, United States v. McVeigh: *Defending the "Most Hated Man in America,"* 51 Okla. L. Rev. 617 (1998).

61. See U.S. Const. art. II, § 8, cl. 15; art. II, § 9, cl. 1; art. IV, § 2, cl. 3; see also Paul Finkelman, Slavery and the Founders: Race and Liberty in the Age of Jefferson (1996), 1–33; Staughton Lynd, *Slavery and the Founding Fathers*, in Melvin Drimmer, ed., Black History: A Reappraisal (1968), 115.

62. See A. Leon Higginbotham Jr., In the Matter of Color: Race and the American Legal Process: The Colonial Period (1978).

63. See Ward Churchill, *"Nits Make Lice": The Extermination of North American Indians, 1607–1996*, in A Little Matter of Genocide, supra note 27 at 129, 180–88.

64. See Higginbotham, supra note 62.

65. See Matthew J. Mancini, One Dies, Get Another: Convict Leasing in the American South, 1866–1928 (1996); David M. Oshinsky, "Worse than Slavery": Parchman Farm and the Ordeal of Jim Crow Justice (1996); Alex Lichtenstein, Twice the Work of Free Labor: The Political Economy of Convict Labor in the New South (1996).

66. See Plessy v. Ferguson, 163 U.S. 537 (1896) (upholding as constitutional "separate but equal" accommodations in public transportation); see Leon F. Litwack, Trouble in Mind: Black Southerners in the Age of Jim Crow (1998); C. Vann Woodward, The Strange Career of Jim Crow (1966).

67. See Mary L. Dudziak, Cold War Civil Rights: Race and the Image of American Democracy (2000).

68. See Brown v. Board of Education, 374 U.S. 483 (1954) (holding segregated schools unconstitutional and implicitly overturning *Plessy v. Ferguson*). Congress also extended protection under the law by passing the Civil Rights Act of 1964, 42 U.S.C. § 200a (1994) and the Voting Rights Act of 1965, 42 U.S.C. § 1973bb (1994).

69. See, e.g., Mapp v. Ohio, 367 U.S. 643 (1961) (requiring states to exclude evidence obtained in violation of the Fourth Amendment); Gideon v. Wainwright, 372 U.S. 335 (1963) (holding states obligated to provide counsel for indigent criminal defendants); Miranda v. Arizona, 384 U.S. 436 (1966) (requiring those subjected to custodial interrogation to be advised of their right to remain silent and their right to counsel).

70. See Howard Zinn, A People's History of the United States 1492–Present (1995), 435–528; Robert Justin Goldstein, Political Repression in Modern America: From 1870

to 1976 (2001), 429–545; Christian Parenti, Lockdown America: Police and Prisons in the Age of Crisis (1999), 3–4, 33–35.

71. See Report of the National Advisory Commission on Civil Disorders (1968) (hereafter cited as Kerner Report).

72. *Id.* at 1. The commission was established pursuant to Executive Order 11365, issued July 29, 1967. *Id.* at xvi.

73. *Id.* at 10–11.

74. *Id.* at 1, 23–29.

75. See *id.* at 206, 299–322.

76. In March 1965 Lyndon Johnson had declared "war on crime," announcing to Congress, "We must arrest and reverse the trend toward lawlessness," despite the fact that his Crime Commission reported shortly thereafter that there was no significant increase in crime, and that "virtually every generation since the founding of the Nation . . . has felt itself threatened by the specter of rising crime and violence." Robert M. Cipes, The Crime War (1968), 3, 8. A significant question that should be asked, but which is beyond the scope of this essay, is "a war on *which* crime?" Leaving aside the even bigger question of which conduct is defined as criminal, it must be noted that in 1996, the National Institute of Justice estimated that the cost to society of "violent" crime was about one-tenth that of corporate crime, but we have seen no comparable war on white collar crime. George Winslow, *Capital Crimes: The Corporate Economy of Violence*, in Tara Herivel and Paul Wright, eds., Prison Nation: The Warehousing of America's Poor (2003), 41, 45.

77. See Parenti, supra note 70 at 8.

78. *Id.* at 7.

79. *Id.* at 12, citing H. R. Haldeman, The Haldeman Diaries: Inside the Nixon White House (1994), 53. Nixon had already directly linked the "crime problem" to the civil disobedience tactics of the civil rights movement, saying, "the deterioration [of respect for law and order] can be traced directly to the spread of the corrosive doctrine that every citizen possesses an inherent right to decide for himself which laws to obey and when to disobey them." *If Mob Rule Takes Hold in the U.S.: A Warning from Richard Nixon*, U.S. News and World Report, August 15, 1966 (quoted in Parenti, supra note 70 at 6).

80. Thomas Cronin, Tiana Conin, and Michael Milakovich, The U.S. versus Crime in the Streets (1981), 68 (cited in Parenti, supra note 70 at 7).

81. Edward Jay Epstein, Agency of Fear: Opiates and Political Power in America (rev. ed., 1990), 174. As the 1972 election approached, this was arbitrarily reduced to 150,000 addicts as evidence of success in the drug war. *Id.* at 177.

82. *Id.* at 173.

83. Omnibus Crime Control and Safe Streets Act of 1968, Pub. L. No. 90–351, 82 Stat. 197 (1968).

84. Organized Crime Control Act of 1970, tit. IX, 84 Stat. 922, 941–47 (codified as amended at 18 U.S.C.A. ch. 96).

85. The Racketeer Influenced and Corrupt Organizations (RICO) Act was a chapter of the federal criminal code created by title 9 of the Organized Crime Control Act of 1970 (OCCA), Pub. L. No. 91–452, 84 Stat. 922 (codified as amended predominantly in scattered sections of 7, 15, 18 and 49 U.S.C.).

86. Congress enacted RICO over dissenters who objected to RICO's scope extending "beyond profit-motivated organized crime. During the enactment process, Congress made clear that RICO would extend to the politically, rather than economically, driven Black Panther Party, the KKK, or the Communist Party. Moreover, Congress has rejected subsequent attempts to exclude political demonstrators from RICO's purview." R. Stephen Stigall, *Preventing Absurd Application of RICO: A Proposed Amendment to Congress's Definition of "Racketeering Activity" in the Wake of* National Organization for Women, Inc. v. Scheidler, 68 Temp. L. Rev. 223, 243 (1995).

87. See Eva Bertram, Morris Blachman, Kenneth Sharpe, and Peter Andreas, Drug War Politics: The Price of Denial (1996), 107; Epstein, supra note 81 at 19. According to Epstein, Nixon had hoped to use ODALE as a White House–controlled "counterintelligence" agency, but in the wake of Watergate, it became part of the new Drug Enforcement Agency (DEA). *Id.* at 252.

88. These funds were distributed through the Law Enforcement Assistance Administration (LEAA), created by the Omnibus Crime Control and Safe Streets Act. See Comment, *Federal Interference with Checks and Balances in State Government: A Constitutional Limit on the Spending Power*, 128 U. Penn. L. Rev. 402 (1979) (noting that by 1976, 20 percent of most state budgets came from such federal funding).

89. Epstein, supra note 81 at 43.

90. According to Kevin Fisher, "Prior to 1981, the Posse Comitatus Act of 1878 made it a felony for any member of the Army or Air Force to assist in the enforcement of civilian criminal laws. Partial repeal of the Posse Comitatus Act, insofar as it applied to civilian drug enforcement activities, was an early priority of the Reagan Administration. In response to administration proposals in this area, Congress amended the Posse Comitatus Act in 1981 to permit the use of military equipment and the extraterritorial use of military personnel in civilian law enforcement." Kevin Fisher, *Trends in Extraterritorial Narcotics Control: Slamming the Stable Door after the Horse Has Bolted*, 16 NYU J. Int'l L. & Pol. 353, 391 (1984); see also Bertram et al., supra note 87 at 112.

91. For an update on the heightened role of the military in the domestic "war on terror," see Ann Scales and Laura Spitz, *The Jurisprudence of the Military-Industrial Complex*, 1 Seattle J. for Soc. Just. 541 (2003).

92. Comprehensive Crime Control Act of 1984, Pub. L. 98–473, 98 Stat. 1989 (1984); see Parenti, supra note 70 at 50–51. Nationally, gross receipts from seizures went from approximately $100 million in 1981 to over $1 billion in 1987. Parenti, supra note 70 at 51.

93. Bail Reform Act of 1984, 18 U.S.C. §§ 3141–50, 3156.

94. Ward Churchill and Jim Vander Wall, The COINTELPRO Papers: Documents from the FBI's Secret War Against Dissent in the United States (2nd ed., 2002), il (noting that it "provid[ed] the FBI with a weapon far superior to the strategy of pretext arrests" in detaining, among others, the Puerto Rican *independentistas*, Resistance Conspiracy defendants, and IRA asylum seekers); see also Laura Whitehorn, "Preventive Detention," in Ward Churchill and J. J. Vander Wall, eds., Cages of Steel: The Politics of Imprisonment in the United States (1992), 365–77.

95. Anti-Drug Abuse Act of 1986, Pub. L. No. 99–570, 100 Stat. 3207 (1986); see Jason A. Gillmer, United States v. Clary: *Equal Protection and the Crack Statute*, 45 Am. U. L. Rev. 497 (1995); William Spade Jr., *Beyond the 100:1 Ratio: Towards a Rational Cocaine Sentencing Policy*, 38 Ariz. L. Rev. 1233 (1996).

96. Anti-Drug Abuse Act of 1988, Pub. L. No. 100–690, 102 Stat. 4181 (1988); see Christopher D. Sullivan, *User-Accountability Provisions in the Anti-Drug Abuse Act of 1988: Assaulting Civil Liberties in the War on Drugs*, 40 Hastings L.J. 1223 (1989); Jim Moye, *Can't Stop the Hustle: The Department of Housing and Urban Development's "One Strike" Eviction Policy Fails to Get Drugs Out of America's Projects*, 23 B.C. Third World L.J. 275 (2003).

97. Parenti, supra note 70 at 40–41.

98. Fred R. Harris and Roger W. Wilkins, eds., Quiet Riots: Race and Poverty in the United States (1988), 181–82.

99. Bertram et al., supra note 87 at 115.

100. *Id.* at 114.

101. *Id.* at 115–16.

102. *Id.* at 114.

103. Noam Chomsky, *Drug Policy as Social Control*, in Prison Nation, supra note 76 at 57, 58. See Graham Boyd, *Collateral Damage in the War on Drugs*, 47 Villa. L. Rev. 839 (2002).

104. Marc Mauer, Race to Incarcerate (1999), 9; see also Joel Dyer, The Perpetual Prisoner Machine: How America Profits from Crime (2000), 1–2. According to a December 1999 report of the General Accounting Office, the number of women in prison

increased fivefold from 13,400 in 1980 to 84,400 in 1998, with 72 percent of all women in federal prison serving time for drug offenses. Nell Bernstein, *Swept Away*, in Prison Nation, supra note 76 at 66, 67.

105. As of 1997, the United States was incarcerating 1 out of every 155 Americans, second only to Russia among the fifty-nine nations in Europe, Asia, and North America for which data are available. Mauer, supra note 104 at 19–23.

106. Parenti, supra note 70 at 59.

107. According to the FBI's Uniform Crime Rate (based on reported crimes), the rate per 100,000 population was at about 6,000 in 1980, dropped somewhat in the mid-1980s, and was again at about 6,000 in 1991. The National Crime Survey (based on surveys to assess victimization, and generally assumed to be more accurate) reported a drop from nearly 12,000 in the early 1980s to about 9,000 in 1991. See Jerome G. Miller, Search and Destroy: African-American Males in the Criminal Justice System (1996), 26–30.

108. In addition, 80 percent of all persons facing felony charges are indigent. Stephen B. Bright, *The Accused Get What the System Doesn't Pay For*, in Prison Nation, supra note 76 at 6.

109. See David D. Cole, *Formalism, Realism, and the War on Drugs*, 35 Suffolk U. L. Rev. 241, 247–48 (2001); Kenneth B. Nunn, *Race, Crime and the Pool of Surplus Criminality: Or Why the "War on Drugs" Was a "War on Blacks,"* 6 J. Gender, Race & Justice 381, 395 (2002).

110. Parenti, supra note 70 at 57. See Nunn, supra note 109.

111. See John K. Alexander, Render Them Submissive: Responses to Poverty in Philadelphia, 1760–1800 (1980); Charshee C. L. McIntyre, Criminalizing a Race: Free Blacks during Slavery (1993); Neil Websdale, Policing the Poor: From Slave Plantation to Public Housing (2001); Scott Christianson, With Liberty for Some: 500 Years of Imprisonment in America (1998).

112. Alien Act, ch. 58, 1 Stat. 570 (1798), amended at 41 Stat. 1008 (1920) (current version at 8 U.S.C. § 1424 [2001]); Sedition Act, ch. 74, 1 Stat. 596 (1798) (expired 1801).

113. Richard O. Curry, *Introduction*, in Richard O. Curry, ed., Freedom at Risk: Secrecy, Censorship, and Repression in the 1980s (1988), 3, 5; William Preston Jr., Aliens and Dissenters: Federal Suppression of Radicals, 1903–1933 (2nd ed., 1994), 21–22.

114. Chang, supra note 1 at 22.

115. Michael Kent Curtis, *The Crisis Over the Impending Crisis: Free Speech, Slavery, and the Fourteenth Amendment*, in Paul Finkelman, ed., Slavery and the Law (1987), 161–205; see also Winthrop D. Jordan, White Over Black: American Attitudes toward the Negro, 1550–1812 (1968), 329–30.

116. William Preston Jr. says, "A narrow focus on the Irish in the Molly Maguires [who organized dramatic strikes in the Pennsylvania coal mines], on the few union leaders

of alien birth, and on the scattered radicals among foreign-born strikers encouraged the idea broadcast by the New York *Herald* that 'the railroad riots were instigated by men incapable of understanding our ideas and principles.'" Preston, supra note 113 at 24–25; see also Goldstein, supra note 70 at 3–101.

117. Goldstein, supra note 70 at 41.

118. See Act of May 6, 1882, ch. 126, 22 Stat. 58 (suspending the immigration of all Chinese laborers for ten years); additional Chinese exclusion laws were passed in 1884, 1888, and 1892. See Sucheng Chan, ed., Entry Denied: Exclusion and the Chinese Community in America, 1882–1943 (1991); Lucy Salyer, Laws Harsh as Tigers: Chinese Immigrants and the Shaping of Modern Immigration Law (1995).

119. Act of March 3, 1903, ch. 1012, § 2, 32 Stat. 1219. See Turner v. Williams, 194 U.S. 279 (1904) (holding that the act did not violate the First Amendment). While portrayed as a response to the 1901 assassination of President McKinley by Leon Czolgosz, Czolgosz was a U.S.-born citizen with only vague anarchist connections. See Preston, supra note 113 at 27–33; Aleinikoff et al., supra note 22 at 695–96.

120. Goldstein, supra note 70 at 69.

121. See Daniel B. Schirmer and Stephen Rosskamm Shalom, eds., The Philippines Reader: A History of Colonialism, Neocolonialism, Dictatorship, and Resistance (1987), 5–33; Stuart Creighton Miller, "Benevolent Assimilation": The American Conquest of the Philippines, 1899–1903 (1984).

122. Miller, supra note 121 at 156–66.

123. Sanford J. Unger, FBI (1976), 41–42.

124. Espionage Act of 1917, ch. 30, 40 Stat. 217 (1918).

125. Sedition Act, ch. 75, 40 Stat. 553 (1918).

126. Goldstein, supra note 70 at 113; see also Michael Linfield, Freedom Under Fire: U.S. Civil Liberties in Times of War (1990), 33–67.

127. Theodore Kornweibel Jr., "Investigate Everything": Federal Efforts to Compel Black Loyalty during World War I (2002), 3.

128. See Daniels, supra note 43 at 6; Weglyn, supra note 43 at 45 (noting State Department representative Curtis Munson's 1941 report, which stated not only that "there is no Japanese 'problem' on the Coast," but that the *nisei* [second generation] "show a pathetic eagerness to be Americans.")

129. Ward Churchill and Jim Vander Wall, Agents of Repression: The FBI's Secret Wars Against the Black Panther Party and the American Indian Movement, 2nd ed., 2002, 32.

130. *Id.* at 32–36.

131. *Id.* at 33; Zinn, supra note 70 at 423–24. See Mari Matsuda, *McCarthyism: The Intern-ment and the Contradictions of Power*, 40 B.C. L. Rev. 9, 19 B.C. Third World L.J. 9 (1998) (joint issue).

132. See Alan Bigel, *The First Amendment and National Security: The Court Responds to Governmental Harassment of Alleged Communist Sympathizers*, 19 Ohio N.U. L. Rev. 885, 890 (1993); see Corliss Lamont, Freedom Is as Freedom Does (4th ed., 1990); Frank Wilkinson, *Revisiting the "McCarthy Era": Looking at* Wilkinson v. United States *in light of* Wilkinson v. Federal Bureau of Investigation, 33 Loy. L.A. L. Rev. 681 (2000) (discussing his conviction for refusing to testify to HUAC in light of documents the FBI was later forced to produce).

133. See Addison Gayle, Richard Wright: Ordeal of a Native Son (1980), 219–21, 262–63, 277–86; Philip S. Foner, ed., Paul Robeson Speaks (1978), 4.

134. See Ellen Schrecker, Many Are the Crimes: McCarthyism in America (1998). Her title is taken from Supreme Court justice (and Nuremberg prosecutor) Robert Jackson's statement, "Security is like liberty in that many are the crimes committed in its name." United States *ex rel.* Knauff v. Shaughnessy, 338 U.S. 537, 551 (1950) (Jackson, J., dissenting). For an analysis of parallels between the Cold War and the war on terrorism, see David Cole, *The New McCarthyism: Repeating History in the War on Terrorism*, 38 Harv. C.R.-C.L. L. Rev. 1 (2003).

135. Churchill and Vander Wall, supra note 129 at 36.

136. Senate Select Committee to Study Government Operations with Respect to Intelligence Activities, Final Report: Intelligence Activities and the Rights of Americans, S. Rep. No. 755, Bk. III, 94th Cong., 2nd Sess (1976) at 77. See Churchill and Vander Wall, supra note 94; Churchill and Vander Wall, supra note 129; Saito, supra note 5; Brian Glick, War at Home: Covert Action against U.S. Activists and What We Can Do About It (1989); Cathy Perkus, ed., COINTELPRO: The FBI's Secret War on Political Freedom (1975).

137. See Senate Select Committee, Final Report, supra note 136.

138. *Id.* at 3.

139. See Peter Mathiessen, In the Spirit of Crazy Horse (1991), 125–26.

140. See Senate Select Committee, Final Report, supra note 136; Churchill and Vander Wall, supra note 129; Churchill and Vander Wall, supra note 94; Glick, supra note 136; Perkus, supra note 136. "White hate" groups such as the Ku Klux Klan were also targeted, but the FBI's aim appears to have been more to control than to destroy these organizations.

141. The categorization of COINTELPRO methods used here is based on the cogent summary of illegal practices found in Churchill and Vander Wall, supra note 129 at 39–53; and in Ward Churchill, *"To Disrupt, Discredit and Destroy": The FBI's Secret*

War Against the Black Panther Party, in Kathleen Cleaver and George Katsiaficas, eds., Liberation, Imagination and the Black Panther Party (2001), 78–117.

142. Churchill and Vander Wall, supra note 129 at 39. See Clifford S. Zimmerman, *Toward a New Vision of Informants: A History of Abuses and Suggestions for Reform*, 22 Hastings Const. L.Q. 81 (1994).

143. Churchill and Vander Wall, supra note 129 at 39–40.

144. To give just one example, after fifteen years of litigation, the Socialist Workers Party (SWP) and its youth organization, the Young Socialist Alliance (YSA), won a lawsuit against the FBI for surveillance that began in 1936 and entailed 20,000 days of wiretaps, 12,000 days of listening "bugs," 208 burglaries of offices and homes, and the employment of thousands of informants. According to the opinion of the District Court for the Southern District of New York, "Presumably the principal purpose of an FBI informant in a domestic security investigation would be to gather information about planned or actual espionage, violence, terrorism or other illegal activities designed to subvert the governmental structure of the United States. In the case of the SWP, however, there is no evidence that *any* FBI informant *ever* reported an instance of planned or actual espionage, violence, terrorism or efforts to subvert the governmental structure of the United States." Socialist Workers Party v. United States, 642 F. Supp. 1357, 1379–80 (S.D.N.Y. 1986) (emphasis added); see Margaret Jayko, ed., FBI on Trial: The Victory in the Socialist Workers Party Suit against Government Spying (1988).

145. Senate Select Committee, Final Report, supra note 136 at 3.

146. *Id.* at 82; Churchill and Vander Wall, supra note 129 at 55, 57.

147. Senate Select Committee, Final Report, supra note 136 at 35–36.

148. Churchill and Vander Wall, supra note 129 at 43–44; Senate Select Committee, Final Report, supra note 136 at 35–36.

149. Churchill and Vander Wall, supra note 94 at 159.

150. Senate Select Committee, Final Report, supra note 136 at 40.

151. With such help from the FBI, tensions escalated to the point that two US members, widely believed to be informants, shot and killed Black Panther Party members Jon Huggins and Bunchy Carter at a meeting on the UCLA campus in January 1969. Churchill and Vander Wall, supra note 129 at 42–43; some of the leaflets and related FBI memoranda are reproduced in Churchill and Vander Wall, supra note 94 at 130–33.

152. Churchill and Vander Wall, supra note 129 at 40–42.

153. *Id.* at 44.

154. *Id.* at 47.

155. *Id.* at 176; see John William Sayer, Ghost Dancing the Law: The Wounded Knee Trials (1997).

156. See Wahad v. City of New York, 1999 WL 608772 (S.D.N.Y. 1999) (suit for damages); Dhoruba Bin Wahad, Mumia Abu-Jamal, and Assata Shakur, Still Black, Still Strong; Survivors of the U.S. War against Black Revolutionaries (1993); Jack Olsen, Last Man Standing: The Tragedy and Triumph of Geronimo Pratt (2000); Churchill and Vander Wall, supra note 129 at 77–94.

157. See Jim Messerschmidt, The Trial of Leonard Peltier (1983); Mathiessen, supra note 139.

158. See Hampton v. Hanrahan, 600 F. 2d 600 (7th Cir. 1979); rev'd in part, 446 U.S. 754 (1980), remanded to 499 F. Supp. 640 (1980) (holding that gross negligence in the raids resulting in the deaths of Hampton and Clark was actionable); Roy Wilkins and Ramsey Clark, Search and Destroy: A Report by the Commission of Inquiry into the Black Panthers and the Police (1973); Nikhil Pal Singh, The Black Panthers and the "Undeveloped Country" of the Left, in Charles E. Jones, ed., The Black Panther Party Reconsidered (1998), 57, 79–80; Churchill and Vander Wall, supra note 129 at 64–77; Goldstein, supra note 70 at xvi.

159. See Ward Churchill, Civil Rights, Red Power and the FBI: Rise and Repression of the American Indian Movement (on file with author); Churchill and Vander Wall, supra note 129 at 141–70.

160. See Churchill and Vander Wall, supra note 129 at 164–97. For the FBI's report on these deaths, see Report of the Federal Bureau of Investigation, Minneapolis Division: Accounting for Native American Deaths, Pine Ridge Indian Reservation, South Dakota, Department of Justice (May 2000); for a detailed response, see Ward Churchill, The FBI's "Accounting" of AIM Fatalities on Pine Ridge, 1973–1976 (both available at www.freepeltier.org).

161. Senate Select Committee, Final Report, supra note 136 at 3.

162. See, e.g., id. at 13–14 (noting operations that continued after Hoover's official "termination" of COINTELPROs); Churchill and Vander Wall, supra note 129 at 370–76 (noting operations in the 1980s against groups opposed to U.S. policy in Latin America and antiwar and antinuclear activists); Brian Glick, Preface: The Face of COINTELPRO, in Churchill and Vander Wall, supra note 94 at xiv–xv (noting FBI operations directed at environmental activists and advocates of Puerto Rican independence); Bernard P. Haggerty, "Fruhmenschen": German for COINTELPRO, 1 How. Scroll, 36, 38 (1993) (detailing recent campaigns of harassment of black elected officials).

163. See Jennifer A. Beall, Are We Burning Only Witches? The Antiterrorism and Effective Death Penalty Act of 1996's Answer to Terrorism, 73 Ind. L.J. 693, 694–95 (1998).

164. Violent Crime Control and Law Enforcement Act of 1994, Pub. L. 103-322, 108 Stat. 1796 (1994) (amending the Omnibus Crime Control and Safe Streets Act of 1968, and therefore also referred to as the 1994 Omnibus Crime Control Act).

165. Parenti, supra note 70 at 63. It also allocated an additional $25 million per year for the FBI's "counterterrorism" budget and $25 million per year for training state and local SWAT teams. Churchill and Vander Wall, supra note 94 at 1 (citing 18 U.S.C. § 2339B (1994).

166. Churchill and Vander Wall, supra note 94 at li. See also David B. Kopel and Joseph Olson, *Preventing a Reign of Terror: Civil Liberties Implications of Terrorism Legislation*, 21 Okla. City U. L. Rev. 247 (1996) (noting the dangers of the antiterrorism bills subsequently enacted as AEDPA); Michael J. Whidden, Note, *Unequal Justice: Arabs in America and United States Antiterrorism Legislation*, 69 Fordham L. Rev. 2825 (2001) (noting the discriminatory application of AEDPA).

167. David Cole and James X. Dempsey, Terrorism and the Constitution: Sacrificing Civil Liberties in the Name of National Security (2nd ed., 2002), 119.

168. *Id.* at 121–23.

169. William C. Banks and M. E. Bowman, *Executive Authority for National Security Surveillance*, 50 Am. U. L. Rev. 1, 267 (2000).

170. Cole and Dempsey, supra note 167 at 2–3.

171. Illegal Immigration Reform and Immigration Responsibility Act of 1996, Pub. L. No. 104–208, 110 Stat. 3009 (1996).

172. See Immigration Act of 1990, Pub. L. No. 101–649, 104 Stat. 4978 (rewriting exclusion and deportation grounds and adopting provisions to ensure removal of criminal aliens); see also Aleinikoff et al., supra note 22 at 173, 425–30.

173. See Cole and Dempsey, supra note 167 at 117–26; see David Cole, *Hanging with the Wrong Crowd: Of Gangs, Terrorists, and the Right of Association*, 1999 S.Ct. Rev. 203 (1999); Kevin R. Johnson, *The Antiterrorism Act, the Immigration Reform Act, and Ideological Regulation in the Immigration Laws: Important Lessons for Citizens and Noncitizens*, 28 St. Mary's L.J. 833 (1997).

174. Cole and Dempsey, supra note 167 at 109. Despite the lack of congressional authorization and several federal court decisions rejecting the practice, the INS had nonetheless been deporting people on the basis of secret evidence during this period. See Statement of Professor David Cole, Georgetown University Law Center, On the Use of Secret Evidence in Immigration Proceedings and H.R. 2121, Before the House Judiciary Committee, Subcommittee on Immigration and Claims (February 10, 2000), available at http://www.house.gov/judiciary/c010210.htm; see Susan M. Akram, *Scheherezade Meets Kafka: Two Dozen Sordid Tales of Ideological Exclusion*, 14 Geo. Immig. L.J. 51 (1999).

175. Cole and Dempsey, supra note 167 at 108–9.

176. See Chang, supra note 1 at 48. See also Sharon H. Rackow, Comment, *How the USA PATRIOT Act Will Permit Governmental Infringement Upon the Privacy of Americans*

in the Name of "Intelligence" Investigations, 150 U. Pa. L. Rev. 1651 (2002) (noting that the new powers are unnecessary, violate civil liberties, and go beyond the stated goal of fighting terrorism).

177. As in the war on drugs, see text accompanying notes 100–101 supra, apparently the public has once again agreed, with a 2002 survey indicating that "49 percent of the public now thinks that the First Amendment 'goes too far,' up from . . . 22 percent in 2000." Diane P. Wood, *The Rule of Law in Times of Stress*, 70 U. Chi. L. Rev. 455, n.1 (2003) (citing Richard Morin and Claudia Deane, *The Ideas Industry*, Washington Post, September 3, 2002).

178. Cole and Dempsey, supra note 167 at 151. Within weeks of the September 11 attacks, Attorney General Ashcroft had testified to Congress that the Justice Department's mission had been redefined from focusing on criminal activity to detecting and halting terrorism, both in the United States and in other countries, and that its emphasis would forthwith be on prevention rather than prosecution. John W. Whitehead and Steven H. Aden, *Forfeiting "Enduring Freedom" for "Homeland Security": A Constitutional Analysis of the USA Patriot Act and the Justice Department's Anti-Terrorism Initiatives*, 51 Am. U. L. Rev. 1086–87 (2002).

179. USA PATRIOT Act, supra note 4.

180. The history of the bill is available at http://thomas.loc.gov/cgi-bin/bdquery/z?d107:HR03162:@@@L&summ2=m&.

181. See Chang, supra note 1; Whitehead and Aden, supra note 178; Jennifer C. Evans, Comment, *Hijacking Civil Liberties: The USA PATRIOT Act of 2001*, 33 Loy. U. Chi. L.J. 933 (2002); Michael T. McCarthy, *USA PATRIOT Act*, 39 Harv. J. on Legis. 435 (2002).

182. For a comprehensive consideration of the constitutional impact of the act, see Whitehead and Aden, supra note 178.

183. Chang, supra note 1 at 48; see Evans, supra note 181; Rackow, supra note 176.

184. See, e.g., USA PATRIOT Act, §§ 207 and 216; Chang, supra note 1 at 49.

185. USA PATRIOT Act, § 213; see also Chang, supra note 1 at 51–52; Whitehead and Aden, supra note 178 at 1110–13. After-the-fact notification may be delayed where it "may have an adverse result," and in the cases of seizures if "reasonably necessary," with the result that a person or organization subjected to a covert search or seizure may never be informed, or may learn about it only when the evidence obtained is used against them in court.

186. See Title II and Title III; see also Whitehead and Aden, supra note 178 at 1131–32; Mark Sommer, *Big Brother at the Library: FBI's Right to Data Raises Privacy Issue*, Buffalo (N.Y.) News, November 11, 2002.

187. Chang, supra note 1 at 49–50 (quoting Ohio State University law professor Peter Swire).

188. USA PATRIOT Act, § 203(a).

189. USA PATRIOT Act, § 203(a)(1).

190. Foreign Intelligence Surveillance Act, Pub. L. No. 95–115, codified at 50 U.S.C. §§ 1801–62 (originally enacted in 1978).

191. Banks and Bowman, supra note 169 at 5–10, 90–92.

192. On the USA PATRIOT Act's expansion of FISA searches and seizures, see Whitehead and Aden, supra note 178 at 1103–7.

193. See text accompanying notes 129–130 supra.

194. See text accompanying notes 166–167 supra. The criteria for such designation are found at 8 U.S.C. § 1189(a)(1)(A)–(C) (2003), and the list is published periodically in the *Federal Register.* See, e.g., Designation of Foreign Terrorist Organizations, 67 Fed. Reg. 14761 (March 27, 2002).

195. USA PATRIOT Act, § 805. See Designation of 39 "Terrorist Organizations" Under the "USA PATRIOT ACT," 66 Fed. Reg. 63620 (December 7, 2001). The criteria for this list are much broader than for the list created under AEDPA. See 8 U.S.C. § 1189(a)(3)(B)(iv)(I)–(III) (2003).

196. USA PATRIOT Act, § 810(d).

197. See Kevin R. Johnson, *September 11 and Mexican Immigrants: Collateral Damage Comes Home*, 52 DePaul L. Rev. 849 (2003) (noting the additional hardships imposed on Mexican immigrants by recent "antiterrorism" legislation).

198. USA PATRIOT Act, § 411.

199. Immigration and Nationality Act, 8 U.S.C. § 1182(a)(3)(B)(lil)(V)(b) (2003). This definition should be contrasted with the State Department's usual definition of terrorism as "premeditated, politically motivated violence perpetrated against noncombatant targets by subnational groups or clandestine agents, usually intended to influence an audience." U.S. State Department, Patterns of Global Terrorism 2001 (May 2002), available at http://www.state.gov.s/ct/rls/pgtrpt/2001/html/10220.htm.

200. USA PATRIOT Act, § 411(a); see also Whitehead and Aden, supra note 178 at 1098–99.

201. USA PATRIOT Act, § 411(a). The activities are listed at 8 U.S.C. § 1182(a)(3)(B)(vi)(III) (2003). If the attorney general certifies that he or she has "reasonable grounds to believe" that an immigrant is engaged in terrorist activities, as broadly defined above, or in other activities threatening to the national security, the immigrant must be detained until deportation. There is no requirement that the immigrant be given a hearing or shown the evidence on which the certification is based. USA PATRIOT Act, § 412; see also Cole and Dempsey, supra note 167 at 156; Regina Germain, *Rushing*

to Judgment: The Unintended Consequences of the USA PATRIOT Act for Bona Fide Refugees, 16 Geo. Immig. L.J. 505 (2002) (noting the likely effect of the 2001 act on political asylum adjudications).

202. USA PATRIOT Act, § 802(a).

203. See Whitehead and Aden, supra note 178 at 1093: "Conceivably, these extensions of the definition of 'terrorist' could bring within their sweep diverse domestic political groups, which have been accused of acts of intimidation or property damage such as Act Up, People for the Ethical Treatment of Animals (PETA), Operation Rescue, and the Vieques demonstrators."

204. Chang, supra note 1 at 44. She goes on to note: "Experience has taught us that when prosecutors are entrusted with the discretion to file trumped-up charges for minor crimes, politically motivated prosecutions and the exertion of undue pressure on activists who have been arrested to turn state's witness against their associates, or to serve as confidential informants for the government, are not far behind." *Id.* at 113.

205. As noted above, it appears that, due to popular resistance, this proposed legislation has been/is being introduced piecemeal, rather than in the draft form proposed. I have included this critique of the initially proposed version, however, because it is important to track the origins of each of these proposals.

206. PATRIOT II, § 101, Analysis at 1; § 107 also removes the distinction between U.S. persons and foreign persons with respect to the use of pen registers.

207. PATRIOT II, § 102, Analysis at 1.

208. PATRIOT II, § 103, Analysis at 1–2.

209. PATRIOT II, § 121.

210. PATRIOT II, § 402, Analysis at 21.

211. PATRIOT II, § 121, Analysis at 5.

212. PATRIOT II, § 123, Analysis at 6–8 (noting an explicit exception under "*Katz* and progeny" for activities directed at foreign powers, and the Supreme Court's statement in *United States v. United States District Court* ["*Keith*"], 407 U.S. 297 [1972] that "domestic security surveillance may involve different policy and practical considerations from the surveillance of 'ordinary crime.'")

213. PATRIOT II, Analysis at 9.

214. PATRIOT II, § 126, Analysis at 9.

215. PATRIOT II, § 129, Analysis at 11–13.

216. PATRIOT II, § 313, Analysis at 19.

217. Freedom of Information Act (FOIA), Pub. L. No. 93–79, 88 Stat. 1896 (1974) (codified as amended at 5 U.S.C. § 552a [1994]). For developments concerning FOIA, see Wendy Goldberg, Recent Decisions, *Freedom of Information Act*, 68 Geo. Wash. L. Rev. 748

(2000). The detainee exemption would be specifically added to FOIA's Exemption 3. See Analysis at 14.

218. PATRIOT II, § 201, Analysis at 13–14. This is a direct attempt to prevent courts from mandating the release of information about detainees, as happened in *North Jersey Media Group, Inc. v. Ashcroft*, 308 F.3d 198, 217–19 (3rd Cir. 2002) and *Center for National Security Studies v. United States Department of Justice*, 215 F. Supp. 2d 94 (D.D.C. 2002). On the latter case, see Rachel V. Stevens, Center for National Security Studies v. United States Department of Justice: *Keeping the USA PATRIOT Act in Check One Material Witness at a Time*, 81 N.C. L. Rev. 2157 (2003).

219. W. Mark Felt and Edward S. Miller, the only two officials convicted of COINTELPRO-related wrongdoing, were pardoned by President Reagan before they had exhausted their appeals or spent a day in jail. Churchill and Vander Wall, supra note 94 at il.

220. See, e.g., Handschu v. Special Servs. Div., 605 F. Supp. 1384 (S.D.N.Y. 1985), affirmed 787 F.2d 828 (2nd Cir. 1986) (consent decree limiting New York City Police Department). For a current case, see Am. Friends Serv. Comm. v. City and County of Denver, available at www.aclu-co.org/spyfiles/Documents/ClassActionComplaint.pdf (suit filed based on revelations that Denver police had "spy files" on over 3,400 individuals and organizations). The *Handschu* decree would be immediately terminated and a decree in the Denver case preempted by PATRIOT II. See PATRIOT II, Analysis at 18; Jerrold L. Steigman, *Reversing Reform: The Handschu Settlement in Post–September 11 New York City*, 11 J.L. & Pol'y 745 (2003). The only other curb on such activities has come from "guidelines" issued by the attorney general's office, which have been eviscerated by each successive administration. See Geoffrey R. Stone, *The Reagan Administration, the First Amendment, and FBI Domestic Security Investigations*, in Curry, supra note 113 at 272–88; Banks and Bowman, supra note 169 at 107–8.

221. Prison Litigation Reform Act, 18 U.S.C. § 3626; see PATRIOT II, Analysis at 18–19. On the steady increase in restrictions on prison reform litigation, see David M. Adlerstein, *In Need of Correction: The "Iron Triangle" of the Prison Litigation Reform Act*, 101 Col. L. Rev. 1681 (2001); *Developments in the Law II. The Prison Litigation Reform Act and the Antiterrorism and Effective Death Penalty Act: Implications for Federal Judges*, 115 Harv. L. Rev. 846 (2002); John Midgley, *Prison Litigation 1950–2000*, in Prison Nation, supra note 76 at 281–300; Matthew T. Clarke, *Barring the Federal Courthouses to Prisoners*, in Prison Nation, supra note 76 at 301–14. On the invalidation of consent decrees, see Anne K. Heidel, *Due Process Rights and the Termination of Consent Decrees under the Prison Litigation Reform Act*, 4 Univ. Penn. J. Const. L. 561 (2002).

222. PATRIOT II, § 312, Analysis at 18–19. Only decrees prohibiting racial discrimination and those "necessary to correct a current and ongoing violation of a Federal right," extending "no further than necessary to correct the violation of the Federal right," and

those "narrowly drawn and the least intrusive means to correct the violation" would be allowed to stand. *Id.*

223. PATRIOT II, § 405, proposing to amend 18 U.S.C. § 3142(e) to include crimes listed in 18 U.S.C. § 2332b(g)(5)(B), Analysis at 23.

224. USA PATRIOT Act, § 812, adding 18 U.S.C. § 3583(f).

225. PATRIOT II, § 408, Analysis at 24–26.

226. PATRIOT II, Analysis at 24.

227. PATRIOT II, § 410, Analysis at 26.

228. PATRIOT II, § 411, Analysis at 26–27.

229. PATRIOT II, § 424, Analysis at 29.

230. See text accompanying notes 171-172 supra.

231. PATRIOT II, § 504, Analysis at 32.

232. PATRIOT II, §§ 502, 505, Analysis at 31–33.

233. PATRIOT II, § 501, Analysis at 30–31.

234. Recognizing that in previous cases where the government has attempted expatriation, the Supreme Court has required a showing of intent to relinquish citizenship, the draft attempts to skirt this requirement by stating: "The voluntary commission or performance of [a qualifying act] shall be prima facie evidence that the act was done with the intention of relinquishing United States nationality." PATRIOT II, § 501, Analysis at 30–31.

235. See Harold Hongju Koh, *On American Exceptionalism*, 55 Stan. L. Rev. 1479 (2003); Natacha Fain, *Human Rights within the United States: The Erosion of Confidence*, 21 Berkeley J. Int'l L. 607 (2003); Mary Ellen O'Connell, *American Exceptionalism and the International Law of Self-Defense*, 31 Denv. J. Int'l L. & Pol. 43 (2002); Johan D. van der Vyver, *American Exceptionalism: Human Rights, International Criminal Justice, and National Self-Righteousness*, 71 Emory L.J. 775 (2001).

236. See text accompanying note 53 supra. For a summary of international law violations arising from the United States' post–September 11 detentions, see Saito, supra note 1 at 20–31.

237. On the convergence of the "war on terror" with general police powers to quell "civil disturbances" see Tom Burghardt, ed., Police State America: U.S. Military "Civil Disturbance" Planning (2002).

238. In addition to the complete erosion of privacy in everyday life, in the name of public health, safety, or "quality of life," we have seen a dramatic increase in the regulation and criminalization of everyday activity, as illustrated by ordinances prohibiting smoking, joking in airports, sleeping in public places, panhandling, or jaywalking. Thus a study of custodial arrests by the Atlanta police reports that of the 2,803 arrests made in July 2003, 1,039 were for "quality of life" violations. Metro Atlanta Task Force for the

Homeless, *Summary of Atlanta Detention Center Admissions Records for July 2003* (on file with author). See John J. Ammann, *Addressing Quality of Life Crimes in Our Cities: Criminalization, Community Courts and Community Compassion,* 44 St. Louis U. L.J. 811 (2000); Debra Livingston, *Police Discretion and the Quality of Life in Public Places: Courts, Communities, and the New Policing,* 97 Col. L. Rev. 551 (1997); Christine L. Bella and David L. Lopez, *Quality of Life—At What Price? Constitutional Challenges to Laws Adversely Impacting the Homeless,* 10 St. John's J. Leg. Comm. 89 (1994); Andrea McArdle and Tanya Erzen, eds., Zero Tolerance: Quality of Life and the New Police Brutality in New York City (2001); Parenti, supra note 70 at 69–110.

239. Senate Select Committee, Final Report, supra note 136 at 8.

240. *Id.* at 3.

241. See Jeffrey Reiman, The Rich Get Richer and the Poor Get Prison: Ideology, Class, and Criminal Justice (6th ed., 2001), 142–44 (noting that prior to their incarceration, prisoners were unemployed at three times the national average, and in 1994 about half of them had annual incomes one-third or less that of the U.S. median for males).

242. See Nunn, supra note 109 at 391–94; see also Mauer, supra note 104, Miller, supra note 107.

243. Edward N. Wolff, Top Heavy: A Study of the Increasing Inequality of Wealth in America (1997), 7 (also noting that disparities in both income and wealth have increased since the late 1970s).

2

The Pinkerton Detective Agency: Prefiguring the FBI

WARD CHURCHILL

By 1940 [FBI director J. Edgar] Hoover was the country's leading law enforcement officer. Much of what Hoover had done for the public and the police, however, had been done earlier by Allan Pinkerton and his two sons. Murray Kempton believed that Allan Pinkerton had invented most of the devices used by Hoover. The director of the Federal Bureau of Investigation "found the tablets already engraved; no further exercise was demanded of him except some tracing at the edges."

—Frank Morn, *The Eye That Never Sleeps*

On October 26, 2001, President George W. Bush signed the so-called USA PATRIOT Act—the title is actually an acronym standing for Uniting and Strengthening of America by Providing Appropriate Tools Required to Intercept and Obstruct Terrorism—thereby initiating what has been called "the most sweeping revocation of constitutional rights [and] civil liberties in the history of the United States."[1] Usually referred to simply as "the Patriot Act," the new law has been subjected to a range of substantive and often bitter critiques, most of them centering on the premise that, while it offers little by way of securing the country against the ravages of genuine terrorism, it provides a veritable carte blanche to domestic élites avid to preserve their own positions of power and privilege through the placement of arbitrary and generally severe constraints upon the range of activities/expression allowed dissident or "unruly" sectors of the body politic.[2]

Given that one of the better means of apprehending the implications inherent to a current phenomenon is to view it through the lens presented by analogous historical contexts, it is entirely appropriate that significant time and energy have been devoted to exploring the evolution of the Patriot Act out of what has come to be known as the "COINTELPRO era" of Federal Bureau of Investigation (FBI) political repression during the period 1954–71 (see, for example, Natsu Taylor Saito's contribution to this volume).[3] By the same token, of course, it is appropriate to peel the onion further, examining the antecedents of COINTELPRO, demonstrating its foundation in the post–World War II "Second Red Scare" period,[4] for instance, and, earlier still, the post–World War I Red Scare that gave rise to such little-remembered horrors as the Palmer Raids,[5] the Industrial Workers of the World (IWW) trials,[6] and the then-nascent FBI's campaign to destroy Marcus Garvey and his United Negro Improvement Association (UNIA), still the largest African American organization in U.S. history.[7]

A central conclusion drawn in every serious study that has sought to trace the trajectory at issue has been that the FBI, while by no means comprising the whole, has been at or very near the center of all that has proven most antidemocratic in American life during the past ninety years or more.[8] The purpose of this essay is to push the timeline back further still, to the beginning, sketching the template upon which the Bureau was itself constructed and thereby situating the origin of the repressive trend to which the Patriot Act presently serves as capstone, not in the fifth or even the second decade of the twentieth century, but rather in the mid-nineteenth.[9] The ramifications of taking this longer view are, to be sure, profound: given that the existence of an official/quasiofficial political police apparatus can be seen as defining the opposite of democratic order[10]—a proposition with which all but a handful of commentators would agree[11]—and insofar as such an apparatus has been demonstrably present in the United States for all but the most formative years of its existence, basic logic requires that the very term "American democracy" be understood as, at best, an oxymoron.

Democracy for Americans thereby becomes, in any but the most vulgarly rhetorical/propagandistic sense, not something that has been/is being "eroded" or "lost" by the passage of legislation like the Patriot Act and the concomitant functioning of agencies like the FBI. Instead, it must be viewed as something that, as a society—or, more accurately, as a multiplicity of societies—we've to all intents and purposes never experienced, but to which we might yet aspire. In no respect can the difference in perspectives thus described be considered of merely academic interest. To the contrary, it stands in very tangible ways not only to shape all that we might reasonably set out to achieve, socially and politically, but, perhaps more important, how it is we must ultimately go about achieving it.[12]

The Beginnings

The roots of what eventually became the FBI may be located in the post–Civil War setting. In 1871, Congress appropriated the sum of $50,000 to allow the newly created Department of Justice to form a component within the department devoted to "the detection and prosecution of those guilty of violating federal law."[13] Finding the amount insufficient to fashion an integral investigating unit of its own, the department opted to contract for such services in the private sector. Although there were several established concerns to select from—Cyrus Bradley's Chicago Detecting and Collecting Agency, for example—the government determined that the firm most suited to its purposes would be the Pinkerton National Detective Agency, founded by a Scottish immigrant, Allan Pinkerton.[14]

The choice is instructive. Although Pinkerton had come to America in 1842 largely to avoid the legal consequences of a youthful radicalism manifested in an engagement with the Chartist movement in his homeland, he had by the mid-1860s evolved into something of a reactionary.[15] Rather impoverished during his first years in the United States, he began to take jobs in law enforcement, first in Kane County, Illinois (1847–51), then in nearby Cook County (1853–54), meanwhile moonlighting as a private detective.[16] Two years later, Pinkerton's freelance activities translated themselves into the opening of a private agency, an enterprise that was, from its first moments, designed specifically to meet the needs of major business interests: "By the mid-1850s a few businessmen saw the need for greater control over their employees; their solution was to sponsor a private detective system. In February 1855, Allan Pinkerton, after consulting with six midwestern railroads, created such an agency in Chicago."[17]

Tellingly, at the same time that he began to form his cadre of "cinder dicks," as Pinkerton's railroad detectives came to be known, he was given his first federal appointment, as a special agent of the Chicago post office.[18] By January 1861, the agency's reputation for results had solidified within both the private and public sectors to the point that Pinkerton obtained his first contract outside the Midwest—with Samuel Morse Felton's Pennsylvania, Wilmington and Baltimore

Railroad—even as his personnel were employed in "protecting" president-elect Abraham Lincoln while he traveled to Washington, D.C., for his inauguration.[19] This last activity, conducted in an environment of flashpoint hostility between northern unionists and secessionist southerners, put Pinkerton in the national limelight for the first time.

> Pinkerton placed a number of key operatives in Baltimore. . . . He assumed the identity of John H. Hutchinson, a stockbroker, and went to Maryland also. Aware of the hostile feelings in that city, Pinkerton was not surprised when a letter came from William Stearns, master machinist of Felton's railroad, disclosing a plot to kill Lincoln in Baltimore. Operatives Timothy Webster and Joseph Howard infiltrated some secessionist societies and confirmed Stearn's [*sic*] fears that a Baltimore barber named Captain Fernandina was behind a conspiracy to cause a street riot when the president-elect arrived, commit the murder during the confusion, and then speed away to the South.[20]

Moving swiftly, Pinkerton convinced Lincoln to alter his schedule, "disguised the president as an old lady, placed special agents along the route, cut the telegraph wires, and allowed no other trains to travel the line until Lincoln's safe arrival."[21] The only problem with such heroics is that a congressional investigation, conducted shortly afterward, concluded that no conspiracy to assassinate the president had existed,[22] an opinion shared by John Wentworth of the *Chicago Democrat* and a number of other northern editors.[23] This viewpoint is reinforced by the fact that none of the alleged conspirators were ever arrested, much less tried and convicted.[24]

Whether or not there was a genuine threat to Lincoln, Pinkerton was able to parlay his "brilliant" response to it into a Secret Service commission for himself and a sequence of lucrative contracts for his agency during the Civil War, conducting espionage, counterespionage, and other security work for the military. Between September 1861 and November 1862 alone, such work garnered him profits of $38,567.[25] It also enabled him to acquire a long list of powerful connections, such as General George A. McClellan, commander of all Union forces during much of the period. By war's end, Pinkerton was very well positioned to capitalize upon his experiences.

> After the war, Pinkerton was a private businessman with two new offices in New York and Philadelphia. He had been a member of the government police system for about two years and had considerable exposure to the elite network

of business leaders who became military leaders, and military leaders who became postwar business leaders. In both cases, his fortunes moved along due to acquaintance with these interlocking elite systems.[26]

Indeed, by 1866, "in the United States and parts of Europe, the name Pinkerton was . . . synonymous with the protection of business and utilities by private police."[27] This was perhaps in some part due to Pinkerton's mounting proficiency in propagandizing himself through ghostwriters, mainly via publication of a dozen-and-a-half sensationalized accounts of his exploits, real or imagined, in "dime novel" format.[28] Much more important, the agency's prestige had to do with its creation of a "French-style" nationwide network of informants—augmented by the use of infiltrators when warranted—available to the highest bidder and without even the pretense of those safeguards supposedly associated with governmental oversight.

> Concern over government's role in the life of private citizens also touched the detective issue. Fears and expectations were colored by the obvious differences between French detectives (highly secret and effective [and] frequently used by the state to suppress civil liberties) and the English detectives, who were more visible and ineffective investigators in the 1870s and 1880s. In fact, many people in England, it was revealed in 1884, went to "private inquiry offices," the English equivalent to America's private detective agency, because London [police] detectives failed so often. William Pinkerton, looking for European models that best exemplified the main thrust of his father's business, declared a kinship with the French police. . . . To Pinkerton management, the public police detective in America resembled most nearly the English model, while the country's largest private police detective agency resembled and respected the French model.[29]

The dichotomy portrayed here is, of course, a bit too neat. Even as the Pinkertons were drawing such distinctions, key personnel like New York agency superintendent George H. Bangs were following the lead of Allan Pinkerton himself, securing positions in major police departments and other governmental investigative entities, thereby busily interlocking the ostensibly separate spheres of private and public detective work.[30] Most important of all, the agency's blossoming reputation was grounded in an increasing reputation among the emergent transatlantic corporate elite that it would go to virtually any length in satisfying the desires of its major business clientele. In this respect, two examples drawn from the 1860s and the 1870s—those focusing upon the Reno and James/Younger gangs—perhaps emblematize better than most others the kinds of techniques the Pinkertons were developing for such purposes. Insofar as the methods involved were often highly publicized, there can be little question but that the Justice Department, when it elected to retain Pinkerton as its primary investigative vehicle, was in effect not only condoning but rewarding their utilization.

The Reno Case

On October 6, 1866, an Indiana gang head by the brothers John, Frank, Simeon, and William Reno became the first in American history to rob a train.[31] Although the Renos appear to have possessed no political motivation—this holdup, along with the many that followed, seems to have been prompted by sheer pecuniary interest—there are indications that their action was received rather sympathetically by much of the local populace, discontented as it was with federal land impoundments and other policies designed to subsidize privately owned railroads at public expense.[32] In any event, local authorities proving unable or unwilling to pursue the matter, the Adams Express Company, which had lost $15,000 in the robbery, in collaboration with the Ohio & Mississippi Railroad, which had been hauling the safe containing the cash, retained the Pinkertons to "bring the gang to justice."[33]

Accepting the case, Pinkerton employed his favorite theory of "detection": that "a criminal enterprise could be successfully broken by infiltration."[34] Used for this task was an operative named Dick Winscott, who shortly opened a saloon in the Renos' hometown of Seymour, Indiana, hinting that he might be inclined to participate in activities a bit more profitable and exciting than selling drinks across the bar. Another operative, whose identity is not recorded, meanwhile set up shop as a gambler in the saloon and began dropping the same sorts of hints.[35] The gang was not long in taking the bait.

The outcome was that Winscott was able to provide photographs of gang members to the agency and, in late 1867, set up John Reno for arrest.[36] Tried and convicted, the bandit was sentenced to twenty-five years imprisonment. With their primary leader now on his way to prison, the rest of the gang became more canny, relocating their headquarters to Windsor, Canada. Still, acting on information provided by Winscott, the Pinkertons were able to nab three more gang members—Frank Sparks, Henry Jerrell, and John J. Moore—soon after a train robbery committed near Terre Haute, Indiana, on May 2, 1868. The prisoners were taken aboard an Ohio & Mississippi train under Pinkerton escort, supposedly for transportation to the jail in Seymore.[37]

They never made it, however. Having somehow "missed their connection" in Indianapolis, the Pinkerton men hired a wagon to complete the journey. En route, they were intercepted by a group of vigilantes who demanded that the shackled prisoners divulge the whereabouts of all remaining members of the gang. Once they'd complied, they were lynched, their Pinkerton guards having abandoned them to their fate. Afterward, the agency, acting upon information thus obtained, was able to arrest William and Simeon Reno on July 22, causing them eventually to be lodged in the jail at New Albany, Indiana. There they were joined in early October by Frank Reno and several other gang members, apprehended a month earlier in Windsor through the services of another Pinkerton infiltrator named Patrick O'Neil (their arrival in Indiana had been delayed by extradition proceedings, during which Allan Pinkerton had personally guaranteed their safety).[38]

On the night of December 12, 1868, another mob of vigilantes appeared at the door of the jail, where they were handed the keys. All three of the Renos, along with an associate named Charlie Anderson, were then taken from their cells and hanged in the corridor.[39] There was "a token investigation of the lynching [in which the Pinkertons did not participate], but nothing came of it. Secretly, state and county officials breathed a sigh of relief,"[40] while the agency, its "message" to those who would threaten the property interests of the rich and powerful loudly amplified, smugly closed its books on the matter. It was left to others, not U.S. officials and civic leaders, to be outraged over what had occurred. "England, through the Governor-General of Canada, demanded an apology for the 'shocking and indefensible lynching.' Diplomatic relations were strained, while legal experts predicted that England would eliminate the extradition clause [from its treaty of peace and friendship with the United States]."[41]

While federal diplomats scurried about containing the potential damages of the Reno murders, Pinkerton set himself to reaping the rewards accruing from his detectives' participation in orchestrating their summary executions: "After the Agency's 'war' with the Renos, the Pinkertons were retained to solve three major bank robberies: Those at the National Village Bank in Bowdoinham, Massachusetts; the Beneficial Savings Fund of America, Philadelphia; and the Walpole, New Hampshire, Savings Bank."[42] In 1874, the Pinkertons' performance against the Renos paid off even more handsomely when the agency was hired by the Rock Island, Union Pacific, and Kansas Pacific Railroads, as well as a consortium of banks, to conduct a similar war, this time against the James/Younger gang, operating in Missouri.[43]

That the Pinkertons orchestrated the vigilante actions against the Renos was tacitly confirmed by Allan Pinkerton himself. In an 1874 series of letters to his subordinate, George Bangs, he discussed the fact that a former employee was participating in a plan to blackmail him to the tune of $500,000 because of his role in the lynchings.[44] Although the blackmail plot appears to have been aborted by one or another means, the threat that his and his detectives' conduct in Indiana might be fully exposed was "obviously very disturbing" to Pinkerton, according to even his most sympathetic biographer.[45]

The James/Younger Case

In contrast to the Renos, the James/Younger gang exhibited discernible political characteristics. During the Civil War, its principal members had served in William Quantrill's Confederate guerrilla unit in the Kansas-Missouri region and, as even so harsh a chronicler as Paul Wellman was later to concede, they suffered postwar persecution as a result.[46]

> Some elements of the victorious Union party were vengeful and vindictive. Men who had served with or sympathized with the "Sesesh" were not infrequently called to their doors at night and shot down by masked gangs of men who called themselves "Regulators." Ex-guerrillas were particular targets of hatred. The general amnesty given Confederate soldiers after the war did not extend to Quantrill's men, who had been officially declared outlaws.[47]

The James brothers, Jesse and Frank, as well as their cousins, the Youngers—Cole, Jim, Bob, and John—responded to the situation by banding together in a sort of mutual defense group, rapidly incorporating as many as twenty other former Quantrill men. Almost as rapidly, their home territory of Clay County, Missouri, became relatively clear of Unionist terrorism, a matter that endeared them to much of the local populace. With their base secure, the gang shortly shifted from a defensive to an offensive posture, staging the nation's first bank robbery in the Clay County town of Liberty on February 14, 1866. Three bank jobs later, in May 1868, the Pinkertons were first called upon.[48]

The agency soon learned, to its dismay, that the James/Younger group was a far tougher opponent than the Renos. Extremely clannish and well entrenched in their community, the gang proved impossible to infiltrate, and the Pinkertons gave the matter up after about a year. In 1871, after it was retained by an Iowa bank that had been robbed in June, the agency returned briefly to the fray, but with equally poor results.[49] The bank robberies continued, and by 1873 the gang began to branch out, robbing a Rock Island line train on July 21, and a stagecoach on January 15, 1874. This was followed, on January 31, by the robbery of an Iron Mountain train, and the Pinkertons were hired again, this time on terms that caused them to remain involved for the duration.[50]

This was to be a long while, however, as Pinkerton's usual tactics fared no better during the second round than they had during the first. An attempt in March 1874 to insert three detectives into Clay County as "cattle buyers" left two of them—Louis J. Lull and James Wright—dead of gunshot wounds inflicted by Jim and John Younger (the latter also died as a result of the exchange, but this was unknown to the agency for some time).[51] On January 5, 1875, Pinkerton tried an outright assault on the James brothers' mother's home, where they were wrongly presumed to be visiting, sending a large group of armed men for the purpose. The attackers hurled an incendiary device through a window, supposedly intended only to "smoke out" the building's occupants. It exploded with sufficient force to kill eight-year-old Archie Samuel, the Jameses' half-brother, and to sever their mother's arm.[52]

> The blast in the Samuel home ended the usefulness of the Pinkertons. Public opinion swung violently against them. Newspapers, not only in Missouri but in other states, denounced the "night of blood" with furious editorial invective.... The Pinkerton Agency still remained on the railroad and bank association payrolls, and kept men going to every new point where a robbery was reported, but where before they had received public co-operation, they now found it difficult to get.[53]

Despite the gang's suffering a disaster—it attempted to rob a bank in Northfield, Minnesota, on September 7, 1876, but was ambushed and virtually shot to pieces by an alerted citizenry, with all the surviving Younger brothers being captured and eventually imprisoned for a quarter-century apiece—the Pinkertons were unable to run the Jameses to earth.[54] Five years later, in 1881, they were still operating with a certain abandon, robbing two trains, a bank, and a stagecoach between March and September. In some desperation, Pinkerton finally garnered success by advising Missouri governor Thomas Crittenden to pay the brothers Bob and Charley Ford, prospective gang members, the sum of

$10,000 to assassinate Jesse James. This was accomplished on April 3, 1882, after the Fords enjoyed dinner in their victim's home, when Bob Ford fired a bullet into the base of the outlaw leader's skull from less than five feet away. A few months later, Frank James surrendered under what amounted to a guarantee of no prison time, and the agency was able to mark another case closed.[55]

The War against Organized Labor

While the Pinkertons' campaigns against train robbers, especially the James/ Younger gang, brought it a certain fame—or notoriety, depending on one's point of view—the agency's bread-and-butter work became ever more centered in performing other, more critical tasks for big business. Primarily, this involved the undertaking of operations designed to thwart unionization of the labor force, allowing owners to maintain an artificially low wage structure in the face of rising prices, as well as institutions such as the twelve-hour workday and six-day workweek, and, in many cases, to avoid investing in even the most rudimentary measures to preserve worker health and on-the-job safety.[56]

The extent of company power over workers included outright ownership of the towns in which they lived, a matter enabling employers to garner additional profits by imposing exorbitant rates of rent, prices for subsistence commodities, tools, and such health care as was available. Conditions in these "company towns" were such that, by 1915, the Commission on Industrial Relations was led to observe that the towns displayed "every aspect of feudalism except the recognition of special duties on the part of the employer."[57] The job of the Pinkertons, first for the railroads, then more generally, was to prevent workers from organizing in a manner that might enable them to improve their own circumstances, thus reducing corporate profits.

> The agency remained largely a railroad police, but to the detectives' spying was added the watchmen's guarding of railroad property. A decade of contention and controversy occurred due to labor strife, and in the 1880s and early 1890s the Pinkertons became an industrial police force. Many railroads, taking cues from the monopolistic policies of notable industrial leaders like John D. Rockefeller, owned coalfields and ironworks. Appropriately enough, as industrial owners and managers increasingly equated crime and disorder with collective bargaining and work stoppages, Pinkerton's opportunities enlarged.[58]

In this, the agency was directly assisted by government. "The personnel," as has been observed elsewhere, "got their police power from the state legislature but were recruited, paid, and controlled by the company."[59]

> Beginning in 1865, the Pennsylvania legislature allowed state railroads to endow some employees with police power. Massachusetts provided for a railroad police in 1871, as did Maryland in 1880, and New York in 1890. Others followed, and by 1896, the Railway Association of Special Agents of the United States and Canada organized to encourage cooperation among the diverse railway police systems. These railway policemen were increasingly identified as enemies of labor.[60]

During this same span of time, "all of the various techniques used to repress labor were gradually developed and institutionalized by business and governmental elites . . . [notably] the use of private police, private arsenals and private detectives, the deputization of private police [and] the manipulation of governmental police agencies."[61] In this, the Pinkertons quickly assumed a status as an elite in their own right, coming to the fore by the early 1870s—that is, during the same period in which the Justice Department began, for its own purposes, to avail itself of the agency's unique talents—as the premier instrument of labor repression in the country. Here, one example, that of the Molly Maguires, speaks volumes to the nature of the expertise sought by the U.S. attorney general.

The Molly Maguire Case

The Molly Maguires were a secret society established in early-nineteenth-century Ireland to battle British landowners.[62] A number of them, forced to flee their homeland because of the midcentury famine, or because of charges brought against them by colonial authorities, found themselves in Pennsylvania's anthracite coal fields, living under conditions as bad as or worse than those they'd left behind.

> Miners . . . went underground to hack out coal under primitive conditions. There was no local or federal legislation to protect them. In 1871, 112 men were killed in the anthracite mines, and 332 permanently injured. In seven years, 556 men had been killed and 1,565 maimed or crippled for life. Out of 22,000 miners, more than 5,000 were sixteen years of age or under. . . . Take-home pay

was uncertain; deductions were often arbitrary or at the whim of the owners by means of what they called the "bobtail check." A typical week's wages for a miner at the time of the Molly Mcguires [*sic*] was $35; expenses, including rent, groceries, and a new drill, came to $35.03.[63]

Confronted by these circumstances, and finding no other avenue of redress available to them, the former Mollies reconstituted themselves to confront their new foe: the mine owners and their subordinates. After a wave of violent responses during the mid-1860s—arson, bombings, and the murder of several especially offensive mine officials—the group appears to have largely committed itself to achieving constructive change through the Workingman's Benevolent Association (WBA), a more conventional sort of union. After the so-called Long Strike of the early 1870s, during which the mine owners were able to destroy the WBA by "starving out" its membership, the Mollies returned to their earlier approach. Hence, in 1873 the Pinkertons were hired to destroy the group, and perhaps unionism in the coal fields more generally.[64]

The main contractor for the agency's services was Franklin Benjamin Gowen, a wealthy Philadelphia lawyer who had served briefly as a county pros-ecutor and as head of the legal department of the Reading Railroad before being named president of the line. Under his leadership, the railroad had acquired over 100,000 acres of coal land (more than double the acreage held by any other min-ing company) and a legally mandated monopoly on coal haulage from the entire Pennsylvania anthracite field.[65] In Gowen's behalf, Pinkerton launched his usual program of infiltration.

On October 27, 1873, [Pinkerton operative] James McParlan, posing as James McKenna, a fugitive from a murder charge in Buffalo, set out for the Pennsyl-vania coal fields. He hadn't shaved for ten days. A dirty reddish stubble covered his jaws and chin. He wore stained old clothes, carried a worn carpet bag, and smoked a clay cutty pipe. For two and a half years he would be engaged in an undertaking that, as J. Walter Coleman sums up in his history of the Molly Mcguires [*sic*], "was of such a nature that even the most calm recital of his deeds has all the aspects of the wildest fiction."[66]

At issue is the fact that McParlan was not only able to work his way into the Mollies, ultimately becoming rather close to the organization's nominal head, Jack "Black Jack" Kehoe, but seems to have functioned in the manner of a classic agent provocateur. At least he revealed a willingness to participate in, among other things, several murders while engaged in his stint of "undercover detection."[67] Ultimately, he was able to parlay his performance into a position as star witness during a series of trials that decimated the Mollies' leadership, but in the interim his employer became impatient, calling for a resumption of the technique that had liquidated the Renos a few years earlier. In a letter to George Bangs dated August 29, 1875, Allan Pinkerton offered the following instruction:

> The only way to pursue [the Molly Maguires] as I see it is to treat them as the Renos were treated in Seymour, Indiana. After they were done away with the people improved wonderfully and Seymore is a quiet town. Let [Pinkerton operative Robert] Linden get up a vigilante committee. It will not do to get many men, but let him get those who are prepared to take a fearful revenge on the M.M.'s. I think it would open the eyes of all the people and then the M.M.'s would meet with their just deserts. It is awful to see men doomed to death, it is horrible. Now, there is but one thing to be done, and that is, get up an organization if possible, and when ready for action pounce upon the M.M.'s when they are at full blast, take the fearful responsibility and disperse. . . . Place all confidence in Mr. Linden, he is a good man, and he understands what to do. . . . If you think it advisable, bring the matter before Mr. Gowen but none other than him. . . . In case of failure, bail may be required. Mr. Gowen will furnish it by his understanding it.[68]

Pinkerton's vigilance campaign seems to have commenced in the predawn of December 10, 1875, when a group of men burst into the home of Margaret O'Donnell, widow of a miner; her sons, James and Charles; and her daughter and son-in-law, Ellen and Charles McAllister. All three men were presumed to be active in the Mollies. Margaret O'Donnell was pistol-whipped, Charles McAllister badly wounded, and Charles O'Donnell shot "at least fifteen times" in the head. More of the same was perhaps averted only by a determination that an airtight case was now ready for presentation against key Molly leaders.[69]

During April 1876, a posse headed by Robert Linden effected wholesale arrests, and on May 6 McParlan made his first appearance on the witness stand, with Gowen himself rather than a state official serving as prosecutor. The outcome was a foregone conclusion: "In the winter of 1877, Jack Kehoe, 'King of the Mollies,' was found guilty. On April 16th, he was sentenced to be hanged. In June, 1877, nineteen of the Mollies went to the gallows; ten were hanged at one time."[70] Harold Aurand has summed up certain implications of the travesty as amounting to "one of the most astounding surrenders of sovereignty in

American history. A private corporation initiated the investigation through a private detective agency; a private police force arrested the offenders; the coal company attorneys prosecuted them. The state provided only the courtroom and the hangman."[71]

There is a distinct possibility that at least some of the convicted Mollies were innocent of the charges against them, and that the group as a whole might not have committed many of the acts of which it was accused. Certainly, the performance of infiltrator/provocateur McParlan in the Steunenberg case three decades later lends credence to the idea that he was not adverse to fabricating evidence to obtain convictions.[72] Similarly, the conclusion of a 1947 study—that Gowen and other "coal operators had instigated some of the attacks on the mines that were later attributed to the Mollies to provide an excuse for crushing both the Mollies and the WBA"—suggests the wrong parties went to the gallows.[73]

In any event, as noted labor historian Joseph Rayback has concluded, "Whoever was responsible for the Molly Maguire [violence], labor was their victim. . . . The trial temporarily destroyed the last vestiges of labor unionism in the anthracite area. More important, it gave the public impression that miners in general were inclined to riot, sabotage, arson, pillage, assault, robbery and murder. . . . The impression became the foundation of the anti-labor attitude held by a large portion of the nation to the present day."[74] Whatever else may be said, this was an outcome of which the government, big business, and their Pinkerton employees were self-evidently most desirous.

The Broader Antilabor Campaign

The dimension of labor strife in the United States during the last third of the nineteenth century is to some extent evident in the fact that business was disrupted, usually by strikes, on 22,793 occasions between 1875 and 1900.[75] In 47 of these instances, beginning with the Chicago "labor riots"—actually, the Chicago component of the national railroad strike—of August 1877, the National Guard was dispatched to protect the interests of business against those of unionized (or unionizing) workers.[76] On at least seventy occasions, beginning with the September 1866 coal strike in Braidwood, Illinois, the Pinkertons were called in to serve as a special corps of strikebreakers, while in hundreds of other instances they were utilized as a guard force to secure company property against "vandalism" by the workforce.[77] Most of all, the agency was retained by major corporations or corporate consortia to function as labor spies and provocateurs.[78]

So pervasive was the latter activity that by the early twentieth century an investigating committee headed by Wisconsin senator Robert La Follette was led to observe how the infiltration and disruption of labor unions was a "common, almost universal practice in American industry."[79] The purpose was to allow "private corporations [to] dominate their employees, deny them their constitutional rights, [and] promote disorder and disharmony."[80] So effective was this technique that in 1888, for example, two Pinkerton detectives were elected as voting delegates of the Reading, Pennsylvania, local of the Brotherhood of Locomotive Engineers and in that capacity attended the union's annual convention, providing "elaborate reports on the issues and discussions" immediately thereafter.[81] In another instance, reported by the La Follette committee, a "union organization" consisted of "five officers and no members, with the officers all Pinkerton detectives."[82] By 1929, it was officially estimated that as many as 200,000 labor spies of various sorts were employed by corporate America.[83] While most of these were undoubtedly amateurs of one type or another, during the mid-1930s General Motors alone was spending some $400,000 per year for the services of professionals.[84]

> Pinkerton's was [by far] the largest detective agency involved with union spying. . . . By 1935 Pinkerton's had twenty-seven offices and grossed over $2 million annually. There were 300 clients for whom Pinkerton did industrial work, the largest in the 1930s being General Motors. Between 1933 and 1935 the agency had 1,228 operatives, or "ops" as they were known in the business, in practically every union in the country. Five were in the United Mine Workers, nine in the United Rubber Workers, and seventeen in the United Textile Workers. Fifty-two members of the United Auto Workers were Pinkerton spies who reported on unionization in General Motors. . . . One spy was even the national vice president of one union. At least one hundred Pinkerton operatives held positions of importance in various unions. . . . One Pinkerton, Sam Brady, had been a spy for thirty years.[85]

This was during a period of time when, in the view of the committee, the "fear of incurring [additional] notoriety restricted Pinkerton's" in its antilabor activities.[86] Yet the committee also concluded that the agency's increasing revenues—from $1.4 million in 1933 to $2.3 million in 1935—derived primarily from labor spying, and that such activities were not designed to prevent "violence fostered by communists and other radicals in the union movement," as Pinkerton officials claimed (Pinkerton spymaster Joseph Littlejohn having been forced to admit that his personnel had never ferreted out a single individual meeting such specifications).[87] Rather, the committee concluded, labor "spying . . . was simply an excuse to wreck unions."[88]

The question of labor violence raises the issue of the "sharp end" of the Pinkertons' antilabor campaign. While there is no suggestion that agency personnel were killed by union members prior to 1892, the record shows the reverse to have been true in numerous places. At least as early as the autumn of 1866, a Pinkerton guard—one of 800 deployed in Chicago at the time—shot and killed an innocent bystander during the Chicago stockyard strike.[89] The number of such indiscriminate shootings increased steadily over the next twenty years. In January 1887, to give another example, a guard killed a young boy during a demonstration attending the Jersey City coal wharfs strike.[90] In 1890, during the massive Pennsylvania coal strike, "Pinkertons, hundreds of sheriff's deputies and the Pennsylvania militia occupied the strike area for two months, beating the strike, and in the words of the governor, 'had a very salutary effect on turbulent strikers,'" three of whom died at the hands of Pinkerton guards.[91] At about the same time, Pinkertons killed five people during a strike on the New York Central Railroad.[92]

"It was indicative of the general power relationship that existed in the United States during the late nineteenth century," one analyst has noted, "that during this period the Pinkerton Detective Agency, the most notorious private police force available for hire, had more men than did the U.S. Army."[93] The "Pinkerton guard was drilled and trained with military precision," and aside from whatever personal weaponry was owned by individual members—and by all indications it was considerable—the agency maintained arsenals in each of its branch offices: 250 rifles and 500 revolvers in Chicago alone.[94] Such firepower was, in turn, augmented by arsenals provided by the corporations contracting Pinkerton enforcers. By the 1930s, the four major American steel corporations each owned more tear gas equipment than any law enforcement agency in the country: Republic Steel maintained an inventory of 143 gas guns, more than 4,000 gas projectiles, and 2,700 gas grenades, as well as 500 revolvers, 64 rifles, and 245 shotguns.[95] There has never been a serious suggestion that any union in the United States was comparably equipped to dispense violence.

Strikebreaking, in the meantime, had become an increasingly prominent Pinkerton technique since the agency first experimented with the provision of substitutes ("scabs") for striking workers during the 1874 Braidwood lockout.[96] By 1888, the method had been perfected to the point that it was successfully employed to thwart a major strike of the Burlington Railroad, the agency using its guards to import thirty-five engineers and ninety-three switchmen to replace union personnel, and its detectives to arrest union members who responded by dynamiting railroad property in Aurora, Illinois.[97] Often, the Pinkertons' use of scabs to break strikes created the conditions for extreme violence, albeit of the sort perpetrated by parties other than themselves. A prime example occurred in Chicago on May 3, 1886, during the McCormick Harvester strike, when "police fired on a crowd of strikers who had attacked strikebreakers leaving the plant. Police gunfire killed one striker and seriously wounded five or six others."[98]

The events of May 3 led to what appears to have been one of the most sophisticated and lethal antilabor/antiradical actions of the nineteenth century. On May 4, the 7,000-member International Working People's Association (IWPA), a militant anarchist spin-off from Daniel DeLeon's Socialist Labor Party (SLP), scheduled a rally at Chicago's Haymarket Square to protest the police shootings of the McCormick strikers, as well as the killings of several others by Pinkerton guards.[99] Although the assembly was completely peaceful, a contingent of 180 police appeared just as things were wrapping up and ordered the few hundred people remaining in the square to disperse. A bomb was then tossed into the police ranks, and gunfire broke out. The toll came to seven police and as many as a dozen civilians dead, and about seventy police and an undetermined number of civilians wounded.[100]

> The aftermath of the bombing was a wave of hysteria directed against labor and radicals which convulsed the country. Without any evidence whatsoever, the press throughout the country identified the IWPA as the villains, and screamed for revenge. Police in Chicago opened up a reign of terror against radicals, making mass raids and arrests. . . . Meanwhile, a general roundup of anarchists and suspected anarchist followers was undertaken throughout the country. . . . Ultimately thirty-one persons [all IWPA leaders] were indicted in connection with the bombing, although only eight were tried, on charges of conspiracy to commit murder. . . . The trial was a judicial farce, with persons admittedly prejudiced against the defendants placed on the jury and the judge [Joseph E. Gary] displaying flagrant bias against the defendants throughout the case. No credible evidence was ever introduced linking the defendants to the bombing [but all of them] were found guilty and sentenced to hang, with the exception of one man [Oscar Neebe] who was given fifteen years.[101]

Four of those convicted—Albert Parsons, George Engel, August Spies, and Adolph Fischer—were executed on November 11, 1887. Another, Louis Lingg, had already committed suicide by exploding a dynamite cap in his mouth. Two others, Michael Schwab and Samuel Fielden, had appealed for executive clemency, and Illinois governor Richard Oglesby had commuted their sentences to life imprisonment.[102] Along with Neebe, the seven have come to be known as the "Haymarket Martyrs" in anarchist and labor histories, remembered by Spies's final words: "There will be a time when our silence will be more powerful than the voices you strangle today."[103]

In the prototypical "Red Scare" following hard on the heels of the Haymarket bombing, "the heavily immigrant composition of the IWPA . . . strengthened public identification with radicalism and violence" to the extent that it has been described as "the single most important incident in late nineteenth century nativism."[104] It also seemed to confirm the impression in "respectable" circles, fostered by the Molly Maguire episode a decade earlier, that unionists were "inherently criminal in character, inclined to riot, arson, pillage, assault and murder."[105] The only problems were that it turned out the Chicago police had fabricated such evidence as was introduced during the trial to suggest that any anarchists—much less the defendants—had been responsible for the carnage, and that it had most likely been a Pinkerton provocateur who had hurled the deadly device.[106]

Hence, in 1893 Governor John Altgeld finally pardoned the surviving defendants, observing in the process that he considered the "widespread and uncontrolled use of Pinkerton operatives by Chicago employers" and the city's failure "to bring the murderers to justice" to have been the causes underlying the bombing.[107] But by then the damage had long since been done, and the "net impact of the public reaction to Haymarket and . . . government repression [had] severely damaged the anarchist and radical labor movement in the U.S. and . . . set back the labor movement in general for about ten to fifteen years."[108] Perhaps ironically, it was not the anarchists and other radicals who suffered most heavily from the whole affair. Instead, the much more moderate (and more powerful) Knights of Labor experienced the sharpest decline in membership, from more than 729,000 members in 1886 to about 220,000 members three years later.[109]

According to analyst Daniel Bell, the Haymarket bombing "did more to induce the rank and file of trade unions to reject all associations with revolutionary ideas than perhaps all other things together."[110] In any event,

strike activity fell drastically in the last years of the 1880s, as did labor militancy. The Illinois Bureau of Labor Statistics reported that the bomb "abruptly ended" the eight-hour movement. . . . Similarly, the Wisconsin Bureau of Labor

observed in 1887 that "everywhere the life and spirit of 1886 have departed."
... It was not until 1889 that the [Illinois State Federation of Labor] deemed it
politic to publicly declare that the [Haymarket defendants] had not received a
fair trial.[111]

Under such conditions, the Knights, the first genuine mass membership
union in U.S. history—which for that reason had probably been the *real* target
of the corporations and, consequently, the Pinkertons—had by the turn of the
century declined to the point of ineffectuality.[112] In most respects, it had been
supplanted by an even more conservative rival, the American Federation of
Labor (AFL), and was soon to be confronted on the other flank by an altogether
more radical challenger, the IWW.[113] For its part, the Pinkerton Agency simply
continued in its well-subsidized and quasi-official drive to abolish organized
labor as a viable force in American society. Its very success was, however, to
cause the agency to indulge itself in an overconfidence that brought about an
interruption in its mode of operation in 1892.

Homestead and After

In the early 1890s, Homestead, Pennsylvania, was a small town of about 10,000
people, located seven miles east of Pittsburgh, which provided the labor force
for the local Carnegie, Phipps steel mill. In 1889, a strike for higher wages by
the AFL's Amalgamated Association of Iron, Steel and Tin Workers (AAISTW)
resulted in a battle between a mass of irate workers and around 100 sheriff's
deputies. The latter were routed, and the strikers got their raise. Hence, when a
new strike materialized in 1892, the plant manager, Henry Clay Frick, "bypassed
local police authority altogether and hired Pinkerton guards," 376 of whom were
assigned the job by the agency's Chicago, New York, and Philadelphia offices.[114]
The group assembled in Youngstown, Ohio, and from there debarked for Homestead on July 5. The following day, they were at last met with the sort of "authority" they were used to dispensing. "On July 6, strikers confronted three hundred
Pinkertons who tried to land from barges on the Monongahela River in order
to act as a strikebreaking force. During an ensuing gunfight . . . nine strikers
and seven [Pinkertons] were killed, scores were shot, and nearly all the [guards]
beaten . . . after they had surrendered to the strikers."[115]

The smoke had barely cleared from the debacle before, on July 18, warrants
were issued at the request of Carnegie, Phipps for the arrest of seven strike leaders

on charges of murdering the Pinkertons, who had supposedly been acting in the capacity of deputy sheriffs.[116] By September 22, the list had been extended to 167 union organizers on charges "ranging from murder to aggravated riot."[117] On September 30, a grand jury selected by the company added the charge of treason against thirty-five union members, including the entire strike committee. The jailing of virtually the entire AAISTW leadership pending trial had the effect not only of breaking the strike but the union itself, and "destroyed unionism in the steel industry for nearly fifty years."[118]

The combined cases collapsed, however, when it was disclosed that the Pinkertons had never been officially deputized by Pennsylvania authorities, and had therefore themselves been in violation of state law when they entered Pennsylvania bearing weapons.[119] When, predictably, there "were no indictments against the steel company or the Pinkertons" as a result of this and other illegalities that readily revealed themselves at trial, a certain negative public sentiment set in.[120] "The Pinkerton invasion of Pennsylvania looked," as the *New York Times* put it, "like the work of a mercenary army."[121] Before long, the agency found itself "denounced in a barrage of editorials" in most leading newspapers.[122]

> Fears of standing armies, an old standby in nineteenth century political rhetoric, were aired once more. References were made to Aaron Burr's military activities at the beginning of the century, as were remarks equating Pinkerton's to the Hessian mercenaries of the American Revolution. For those of an even more historical bent, Robert Pinkerton [nominal head of the agency, along with his brother, William, since the death of their father in 1884] resembled a medieval baron with an army for hire.[123]

Given such publicity, and the sheer clumsiness of what had happened, it was necessary for Congress to quell public outrage by convening an inquiry, not just into the disaster at Homestead, but with regard to the operations of private detective agencies more generally. In addition to Pinkerton's, smaller imitations like the Thiel Detective Agency, Illinois Detective Agency, U.S. Detective Agency, and Mooney and Boland's Detective Agency were taken under investigation by both the Senate and the House.[124] The result was a charade. "The House committee began its investigations in July, spending all its time in Pittsburgh. The Senate waited until November, and traveled to Pittsburgh, Chicago and New York. In both cases Congress seemed to be playing a political game. The hearings were filled with anti-Pinkerton rhetoric, but the final reports gave only conservative recommendations."[125]

When the committees' findings were released in February 1893, they merely passed the buck, acknowledging that "many problems" attended the activities of the Pinkertons and other such agencies, but concluding that "any attempts at mitigating the evils of the private detection system had to come from the states and not the federal government."[126] The latter then moved fairly swiftly to provide the appearance of having taken charge of the situation, following the lead established by Montana and Wyoming, each of which had "made constitutional provisions forbidding the importation of nonresidents for police work" in 1889.[127] Missouri had passed legislation to the same effect the same year, and Georgia had followed suit in 1890. In 1891, New Mexico, Washington, Minnesota, and Kentucky had joined in, while "New York and Massachusetts passed kindred laws in 1892, shortly before the Homestead violence."[128]

> In response to the congressional investigations, a flurry of anti-Pinkerton bills appeared and became law. On February 25 and 28, 1893, West Virginia and North Carolina passed laws forbidding armed [guards] from entering their states. On March 4, South Dakota passed a similar law, and the day before the District of Columbia stopped the federal government's policy of hiring private detectives. In April, both Nebraska and Wisconsin passed anti-Pinkerton legislation, as did Texas and Pennsylvania in May, and Illinois in June. By 1899, six more states followed, and a total of twenty-four states plus the District of Columbia forbade armed guards from entering their jurisdiction.[129]

Although much was made of the notion that such legislation put the Pinkertons "in their place," all that really happened was that state governments had rationalized an otherwise awkward situation, lending a veneer of legitimacy to the Pinkertons by ensuring that the agency would establish a permanent operational presence within their respective jurisdictions. The new structure, which "applied only to the guard," did little to "restrict the plain-clothed detective. Only Maine, Colorado, Pennsylvania, and Massachusetts attempted to regulate the detective by licensing laws by 1895."[130] Moreover, this structure facilitated coordination and cross-pollination with local police and entrenched the agency much more deeply than ever before in the very communities it was intended to repress.

Small wonder that, while the agency did de-emphasize its guard and scab-provision activities to some degree after Homestead—although by no means entirely, since the Pinkertons provided 176 scabs to break a strike against the Allis-Chalmers Corporation in 1902, for example, and it was the agency's importation of scabs during a United Mine Workers (UMW) strike in Ludlow,

Colorado, that provoked the confrontation resulting in the state militia's massacring sixteen people there on April 20, 1914—the Pinkertons continued to engage in antilabor activities with a very high degree of intensity, and "labor contracts were an important source of [the agency's] income" well into the twentieth century.[131] So much of this was done directly under the mantle of the states in which the agency operated that, ten years after Homestead, it "was not uncommon for the heads of foreign police systems to regard Pinkertons as America's official detective force."[132] In Pennsylvania, for example, at

> the request of business leaders the governor could issue special commissions conferring police power on persons employed by the various iron and coal companies. In 1901, the governor of Pennsylvania issued 570 such commissions. The following year he gave out 4,512 such commissions as strikes increased in the Pennsylvania coal fields. Railroad cars filled with company policemen [many of them provided by Pinkerton's] and mounted with Gatling guns visited mining towns to control worker discontent.[133]

If there are any particular distinctions to be noted between the pre- and post-Homestead periods, they are that the locus of antilabor operations shifted primarily to the western states, and reliance upon infiltrators was greatly accentuated. In both respects, the Pinkerton office in Denver, Colorado—headed by James McParlan, of Molly Maguire fame—figured prominently.

> The Denver office, under the leadership of McParlan . . . became [quite] active as labor problems grew in the early twentieth century. Secret operatives began to eclipse regular operatives as they infiltrated the Colorado, Montana, and Idaho mining areas. A. H. Crane was a member of a union in Colorado City in 1902. Operatives J. H. Cummins, Philander Bailey, and George Riddell, did much the same. The unexpressed expectations were that they might duplicate the exploits of their divisional leader, McParlan. The man who came closest to McParlan's Molly Maguire episode was A. W. Gratias. Gratias had joined the Western Federation of Miners [WFM] in 1902 and the following year was made chairman of the union relief committee. In 1904 Gratias was elected president of his local union and even went as a delegate to the annual convention.[134]

Actually, such activities had begun at least as early as 1892, shortly after McParlan was named superintendent in Denver, when an operative named Charles Siringo was assigned to infiltrate the WFM at about the same time it was

founded in northern Idaho.[135] The WFM, "the first strong, militant and realistic
. . . anticapitalist union in American history," was the major target of McParlan
and his men by 1894 at the latest, when Pinkertons comprised the core of "a large
force of deputies [used] to protect the re-opening of mines" closed by a strike in
Cripple Creek, Colorado.[136] Two years later, McParlan arranged for the importation of scabs to break a WFM strike at Leadville, Colorado, while he conspired
with the governor "to remove the local pro-union sheriff and replace him" with
a Pinkerton appointee.[137]

In 1899, the Denver office organized a company of guards behind which
the Bunker Hill and Sullivan mine in Coeur d'Alene, Idaho, enforced yellow dog
contracts—that is, refused to hire union labor—in defiance of state law. When
Idaho authorities did nothing to correct the situation, the WFM and/or Pinkerton provocateurs responded by dynamiting and burning Bunker Hill and Sullivan property. This, in turn, was used as the pretext upon which federal troops
were sent in to destroy the union and local radicalism more generally.[138]

> Martial law was proclaimed, and virtually any male remaining in the district be-
> came subject to arbitrary arrest and incarceration in boxcars or bullpens. [WFM
> president Edward] Boyce himself was arrested, along with a large number of
> Populist party leaders, including a local deputy sheriff. The Populist county
> sheriff and three Populist county commissioners were removed from office. No
> miner was allowed to return to work in the area unless he agreed to renounce
> allegiance to the WFM. While hundreds of miners were arrested, only fourteen
> were ever convicted of any crime. The repression of the strike broke the WFM
> in the area, and unionism remained insignificant in the area for years.[139]

The union leaders convicted included the WFM's Idaho head, George
Pettibone. Their imprisonment was obtained largely on the basis of testimony
provided by Pinkerton infiltrator Siringo, who was thereafter so disgusted with
McParlan's and his own performance that he declined a promotion to head up an
office of his own because "I know my conscience would not allow me to act as a
superintendent of the Agency . . . where so much dirty work would be expected
of me."[140] Eventually, he drifted away from the Pinkertons altogether and wrote a
rather contradictory volume of memoirs in which he sought to expose what he
thought was wrong with the agency's antilabor tactics while still justifying his
personal role in them.[141]

Contrary to McParlan's expectations, the WFM did not fold up after Coeur
d'Alene. Instead, it continued to grow in both numbers and militancy. From 1899

to 1903, the organization made rapid gains, reaching perhaps 50,000 members.[142] Hence, in 1901, when the Pinkertons again attempted to use scabs to break a WFM strike in Telluride, Colorado, miners were prepared to engage in pitched gun battles with both detectives and local police, seize the mine, and force the scabs to leave.[143] At that point, Colorado's reactionary governor, James Peabody, along with the state's mining interests and the Pinkertons, declared outright war on the WFM; over the next two years, among many other things, more than 400 key union organizers were forcibly deported from Colorado by the militia, while hundreds of others were beaten, shot, and confined to bull pens for weeks at a time.[144] Rather than causing it to disband, the onslaught led the WFM to seek allies, assuming a leading role in the establishment of the IWW in June 1905.[145]

War against the Wobblies

In many ways, the Industrial Workers of the World, or "Wobblies," was the most radical union of significant size ever formed in the United States (it is estimated that more than one million workers, a very high proportion of them non-Anglo immigrants, blacks, or members of other groups marginalized by conventional American unions, held IWW membership cards at some point between its founding and its demise as a viable entity in 1924).[146] The Wobblies' plan, in simplest terms, was to combine the American working class, and eventually workers all over the world, into one big trade union with an industrial basis, a syndicalist philosophy and a revolutionary aim. Its industrial departments were to act as syndicalist shadows of American capitalism, so that after the revolution they could quickly step in and help govern the workers' commonwealth. The revolution was to be achieved by a series of strikes, leading to a general strike that would force the capitalists to capitulate. Thus, "the IWW was to be both the embryo of the new society and the revolutionary instrument for achieving it."[147]

Although the union was always officially headquartered in Chicago, its initial energy center was Denver, operational base of its first president, WFM leader William "Big Bill" Haywood.[148] This geographical disposition, as well as Haywood's reputation for effectiveness and unrelenting militancy, caused "considerable fear [among governmental and business elites] that labor in Pacific Northwest and Rocky Mountain states would be radicalized."[149] Into the breach, to head off just such an eventuality, stepped the Denver office of the Pinkertons.

The IWW was hardly organized before it was dealt a crushing blow. On December 30, 1905, Frank Steunenberg, who had been governor of Idaho during the crushing of the Coeur d'Alene strike, was killed by a bomb explosion in Caldwell, Idaho. Subsequently, a man named Harry Orchard was arrested, and the state of Idaho hired Pinkerton detective James McPharland [*sic*] for the purpose of linking him to the WFM-IWW. After talking to Orchard at length, suggesting to him that the WFM was responsible for the crime and telling Orchard the story of how one person in the Maguire trials had gone free after turning state's evidence, [McParlan] obtained a statement from Orchard which implicated the WFM in virtually every major incident of labor violence in the West, including over twenty murders.[150]

In reality, McParlan had applied both the carrot and the stick to Orchard, a relative small fry who may have been an occasional Pinkerton operative as well, subjecting him to "third degree methods" for extended periods, even while promising to allow him to escape the noose.[151] This allowed McParlan to establish an "evidentiary basis" by which to arrest the three primary IWW leaders in Denver—Haywood, Pettibone, and WFM president Charles Moyer—for conspiracy to murder Steunenberg. He then arranged for their transport to Idaho without benefit of extradition—kidnapping—and assisted state prosecutor William E. Borah in assembling the case against them, in which Orchard's testimony was key.[152]

Although Orchard stuck to his story throughout the trials, and supplied many corroborating details about his confessed acts, his trial testimony also included confessions to acts of violence he could not have committed, and demonstrated that at least once in his long career of arson, theft, bigamy and murder he had worked as an agent provocateur of the Pinkerton Agency. In fact, the only incident of mysterious "labor" violence in Colorado which appears to have been solved [as a result of his testimony] was attributable to the mining companies.[153]

Haywood, Pettibone, and Moyer, ably defended by socialist attorney Clarence Darrow, were acquitted, but coming hard on the heels of Colorado's war on the WFM and right after the formation of the Wobblies, "the Steunenberg trial had a shattering effect on both the WFM and the IWW."[154] The former never recovered, while the latter found its growth potential permanently impaired.[155] Meanwhile, the manner in which McParlan and his operatives had contrived to trump up the Haywood-Pettibone-Moyer case had so appalled the stenographer in the Pinkerton Denver office, Morris Friedman, that he resigned in protest and wrote a scathing exposé, entitled *The Pinkerton Labor Spy*, in which he detailed the methods of the agency's antilabor operations.[156]

> Friedman's book, like so many muckraking books of the first decade of the century, described in detail the organization and operation of the Pinkerton business. Specifically he concentrated on the Denver office, but the general implication was aimed at the entire Pinkerton empire. . . . Numerous operatives' reports were reproduced, lending authority to his work. Pinkerton involvement in the Cripple Creek and Telluride strikes and the Haywood trial were recounted. . . . McParlan was accused of fabricating stories of union conspiracies to win new contracts. Never before had an employee so exposed the inner workings of Pinkerton operations. The agency was stunned into silence.[157]

The Pinkertons were more than usually quiet, perhaps, but hardly inactive. If anything, the agency's anti-IWW operations escalated after the publication of Friedman's book in 1907, pacing the union's efforts to expand to national proportions. And, after the death of his brother, Robert, in that year, William Pinkerton commenced a campaign of increasingly vituperative and ill-researched public denunciations of the Wobblies, including the contrivance of a number of catchy "meanings" for the union's acronym; over the next decade, the agency's owner was to make it fashionable in some circles to refer to the IWW as the "I Won't Work," the "I Want Whisky," the "International Wonder Workers," the "Irresponsible Wholesale Wreckers," and, during America's participation in World War I, "Imperial Wilhelm's Warriors."[158]

By 1910–11, the agency was up to many of its older tricks, organizing "vigilance" committees to visit summary punishment upon IWW organizers, providing large complements of guards and scabs to companies struck by the union, and infiltrating informers and provocateurs wherever possible. In most of this, as well as in antilabor activities of all types, it continued to enjoy much active complicity by state and local officials and police. Not the least indication of this was the enactment of state "criminal anarchy" or "criminal syndicalism" statutes banning the very philosophies espoused by the Wobblies and other radical organizations.[159]

> [Four] states passed legislation to outlaw the advocacy of anarchy in 1902 and 1903. The New York law, passed in April 1902, later became the model for

criminal syndicalism laws passed to outlaw the Industrial Workers of the World
. . . in 1917–20. The law defined criminal anarchy as the doctrine that organized
government should be "overthrown by force or violence or by assassination of
the executive head or of any of the executive officials of government, or by any
unlawful means." Persons who advocated such doctrines orally or in writing,
who helped disseminate such doctrines, or who organized, joined or "voluntarily" assembled with any group advocating such doctrines faced up to ten
years in jail and a fine of $5000. Also, any assemblage of two or more persons
for the purpose of advocating such doctrines was outlawed, and any person
knowingly allowing such meetings on their property, including janitors, also
faced arrest.[160]

The laws were ostensibly a response to the assassination of President William
McKinley by a self-described anarchist named Leon Czolgosz on September 6,
1901, but were always aimed in practice mainly against radical labor organizers.[161] In their implementation, the criminal anarchy statutes were coupled to
literally thousands of county and municipal ordinances, which began to prolifer-
ate around 1905, prohibiting agitation by radicals, especially IWW organizers,
within city or county limits.[162] It was in the enforcement of these local ordinances
that the Pinkertons, local authorities, and other reactionary social elements often
established tidy working arrangements. On November 27, 1911, for instance,
Pinkertons were among those deputized as "citizen police" by the mayor of
Aberdeen, Washington, and sent to put a stop to IWW organizing among area
lumberjacks; they then "blocked the entrance to a scheduled IWW meeting,
raided and ransacked the IWW hall, arrested forty men, including all the local
IWW leaders, and escorted the arrested Wobblies out of town."[163]

In San Diego, California, IWW activity was dispensed with on the night of
April 5, 1912, when the chief of police turned over nearly 200 union members
he'd jailed for making public speeches to a Pinkerton-organized vigilante mob
"who escorted the Wobblies to the county line, beat them with pickaxes and
sent them on their way."[164] Over 100 Pinkerton detectives were also sent to
break a 1912 lumber industry strike in Granbow, Louisiana, when the mostly
African American local of the Brotherhood of Timber Workers (BTW) voted
to affiliate with the IWW; the strike was broken after "company personnel"—
probably Pinkertons—fired on a workers' meeting, killing four and wounding
forty, and sixty-five BTW-IWW members were indicted. Although all were
eventually acquitted or released, "the trial paralyzed the organization for
months, drained its treasury and exhausted its resources."[165] A follow-up strike

by the BTW-IWW at Merryville, Louisiana, was broken in February 1913 when "a mob of townspeople and company gunmen [again including Pinkertons] raided and wrecked union buildings, and created such a reign of terror that most strikers were forced to flee for their lives. That was the end of the BTW and the southern lumber drive."[166]

During the much larger 1912 IWW strike of some 20,000 immigrant workers against the American Woolen Company, Atlantic Mill, and other textile manufacturers in Lawrence, Massachusetts, the Pinkertons deployed several hundred guards and detectives. All of their activities were closely coordinated with local police officials and, after dynamite bombs were discovered in three locations, militia commanders.[167] On January 29, a woman named Anna LoPezzi was shot to death by police during an attempt to halt a parade in support of the strikers. The following day, "a militiaman bayoneted to death a fifteen-year-old [Syrian immigrant named John Rami], and martial law was declared, making all public meetings illegal."[168] When the strikers then attempted to evacuate their children from Lawrence, this, too, was declared unlawful. A group of police, augmented by Pinkertons, stopped an attempt to load children aboard a train, "clubbed the children and their mothers, arrested over thirty persons for 'congregation,' and had fourteen children committed by the courts to the city farm."[169]

By the time the strike was successfully concluded in March—public outrage over the treatment of the women and children had been such that the companies were forced to capitulate—355 strikers had been arrested, 54 of whom were sentenced to jail terms. A "group of 34 strikers was given a year in jail each after five to ten minute trials. Although their sentences were later commuted to small fines on appeal, the IWW had to raise $27,000 for bail."[170] Much worse was the situation of IWW organizers Joseph Ettor and Arturo Giovannitti, who—although they had been three miles away at the time LoPezzi was killed—had been charged with complicity in her death by virtue of having called for the parade during which she was shot. They were held in jail without bail for ten months.[171]

> When the trial of Ettor and Giovannitti began in late September the two defendants were kept in metal cages in the courtroom; protesting strikers were brutally clubbed by police outside the [courthouse]. Massachusetts authorities indicted the entire defense committee on charges of conspiring to intimidate workers. Ettor and Giovannitti were acquitted in November.[172]

Before the trial ended, yet another telling illustration of the Pinkertons' operational methods had been revealed. It turned out that the dynamite bombs, which had been falsely attributed to "IWW radicals" by the police—and thus used as a pretext to bring in the National Guard, escalating the official violence that claimed the lives of both LoPezzi and Rami—were actually planted by John Breen, a member of the Lawrence school board. Breen admitted he'd acted on the instruction of William N. Wood, president of American Woolen, and in concert with two other men: Frederick H. Atteaux, a Boston businessman, and D. J. Collins, a sometime Pinkerton operative. Unlike Ettor and Giovannitti, Breen and Collins, who were eventually convicted of their offenses, were allowed low bail and were not caged in the courtroom. Each was fined $500 for his offense. The jury hung on Atteaux, and he was released. Wood was acquitted despite being implicated in the conspiracy by both Breen and Ernest Pittman, the man who provided the dynamite.[173]

Once again, public exposure of its covert techniques did little to slow the agency's anti-Wobbly campaign. During the 1913 textile strike in Patterson, New Jersey, in which the IWW once again displayed its ability to galvanize large numbers of immigrant workers, Pinkerton detectives engaged in all manner of provocation—including the killing of two strikers—in concert with the police and other authorities.[174] The U.S. Commission on Industrial Relations concluded, in a belated investigation, that "the police authority of the state was, in effect, turned over to the mill owners [who] trespassed every natural right and constitutional guarantee" of the strikers.[175]

At the same time, during an IWW strike of rubber workers in Akron, Ohio, police and Pinkerton-organized "vigilante groups broke the strike by attacking, beating and arresting scores of strikers. The strike defeat ended attempts to organize the Akron rubber workers until the 1930s."[176] Similarly, an "IWW loggers' strike in Coos Bay, Oregon, in May, 1913, was defeated by vigilante raids, beatings, arrests and deportations."[177] Elsewhere, "local police and sheriff's deputies killed two strikers and wounded many others by firing into picket lines at Ipswich, Massachusetts, and Rankin, Pennsylvania, while private [Pinkerton] guards killed five and wounded many by firing into a group of strikers at Metuchen, New Jersey."[178] In 1914, in Stockton, California, Pinkerton "strikebreakers armed with guns and blackjacks were deputized during labor strife, while Stockton employers tried to plant dynamite to implicate [IWW] members."[179] And the hammer blows kept falling.

During June, 1915, 6 strikers at the Standard Oil plant at Bayonne, New Jersey, were shot and killed by private [Pinkerton] guards. . . . A year later at the same plant, police and "deputies" swept through workers' residential areas after six

police and strikebreakers were wounded by gunfire during a strike, killing four
persons as they clubbed and shot at strikers and wrecked strikers' saloons. . . .
Riots broke out at East Youngstown, Ohio, and at Braddock, Pennsylvania, during 1916 when private guards fired at strikers, killing four and wounding many.
In both cases state troops had to be called in to restore order. During the same
year, Pennsylvania state troops [acting on information provided by a Pinkerton
detective] broke up a strike of IWW coal miners by the simple technique of
raiding a union meeting and arresting all 250 miners present.[180]

During the massive strike of immigrant mine laborers in Minnesota's Mesabi
iron range during 1916, the IWW demonstrated for a third time its capacity to
organize large numbers of strikers under extremely adverse conditions. This was
met with another ferocious response by the agency and its employers.

Four hundred mine guards [many of them Pinkertons] were deputized even
after they had shot and killed one striker and wounded two others. The deputized guards dispersed parading strikers, arrested IWW organizers without
cause, and generally established a reign of terror in the area. The climax of the
Mesabi violence came when several of the deputized guards forced themselves
without warrant into the home of a miner, allegedly to make an arrest on a li-
quor violation; in the subsequent melee a deputy was killed along with a nearby
soft drink peddler. All the miners present were jailed on charges of first degree
murder, along with IWW leaders who had not even been in the area. Eventually,
a settlement was reached in which the IWW leaders were released, while three
miners pled guilty to manslaughter. . . . [Governmental] investigating agencies
placed the major share of blame on the mining companies and the police [in-
cluding the Pinkerton deputies]. A report of the U.S. Commission on Industrial
Relations found that the miners endured the "abuse and violence of beating up,
shooting and terrorizing." The Mesabi strike eventually collapsed due to the
miners' exhaustion.[181]

Then there was the Everett Massacre of November 4, 1916, in some ways a
mirror image of the battle at Homestead twenty-four years earlier. Beginning in
July, efforts by the IWW to organize workers at a sawmill in Everett, Washington,
were met by "repeated arrests, brutal beatings and deportations" by the local
sheriff and a growing number of "deputized members of the business community," including numerous Pinkertons.[182]

During October, 1916, alone about five hundred Wobblies trying to enter the city were deported by local police. On October 30, forty-one Wobblies trying to enter Everett were beaten by deputies with saps, clubs, rifles and fists. . . . The climax of the Everett affair came on November 4 when two hundred fifty Wobblies trying to land by boat were met at the dock by armed, and, in many cases, drunken deputies who tried to prevent their disembarkation. During a subsequent gun battle five Wobblies and two deputies were killed and scores wounded. Although the source of the first shot was never determined, seventy-four Wobblies were arrested. No action was ever taken against the deputies, although it seems likely that most of the deputies' casualties resulted from gunfire from other deputies. The arrested Wobblies were all released after the first man was acquitted.[183]

After 1916, the Pinkertons' reliance upon vigilantism, already pronounced against the Wobblies, appears to have increased substantially. During the summer of 1917, the Anaconda Mining Company retained the agency to break an IWW strike at its facility in Butte, Montana. In response, the union sent Frank Little, one of its best, most dynamic, and militant organizers. What happened next harkened back to the Reno and Molly Maguire cases of the 1860s and 1870s.

Following a speech at the ball park in Butte on July 31, 1917, Little went to his room at the Finn Hotel. That night, six masked and armed men broke into his room, beat him, and dragged him by a rope behind their automobile to a Milwaukee Railroad trestle on the outskirts of Butte. There he was hung. On his coat was pinned a card: "First and last warning! 3–7–77. D-D-C-S-S-W." It was said that the numbers referred to the measurements for a grave and the initials corresponded to the first letters of the names of other strike leaders in Butte, thereby warning them of similar treatment if their strike activities were not stopped.[184]

It is generally conceded that the "vigilantes" who lynched Little were in fact "agents of the copper corporation," a description that strongly implies Pinkerton personnel.[185] Indeed, Pinkerton operative Dashiell Hammett (later to win fame as a writer of detective fiction) is believed to have served as lookout for those who did the actual killing.[186] Be that as it may, local authorities plainly shielded the perpetrators from incurring any penalties as a result of their deed: the "police kept up a pretense of looking for the man they called their prime suspect, a mentally deranged drug addict from the Western underworld, but no serious attempt was made to bring Little's killers to justice."[187]

After 1917, the federal government assumed overall responsibility for destroying the Wobblies,[188] although the Pinkertons and the vigilante organizations they facilitated continued to figure prominently in violence directed against the union. A prime example concerns the case of Wesley Everest, an IWW organizer and much-decorated First World War hero who was murdered while wearing his uniform by a mob of self-proclaimed "patriots" in November 1919.

> On November 11, the so-called "Centralia Massacre" occurred. The IWW had been driven out of Centralia, Washington, by a mob attack in March, 1918, but had re-established a hall there in September, 1919. During [an] armistice parade, a group of American Legion members attacked the hall, and were fired upon by Wobblies who had armed themselves as a result of widespread rumors of impending assault. Three legionnaires were killed in the battle; an IWW named Wesley Everest who was arrested was turned over to a mob by jail guards that night and lynched. The Centralia incident set off a true reign of terror in Washington; hysterical mobs assaulted Wobblies, and ransacked IWW headquarters, while police arrested at least one thousand alleged IWWs. The "white terror" decimated what was left of the IWW in the state. When the Seattle *Union Record* asked that judgment be suspended until the facts about Centralia became known, federal agents seized the press plant, banned the issue from the mails and arrested several of the editors [for "sedition"].[189]

Describing what happened to Everest as a "lynching" is actually a bit too sanguine. The fate visited upon him by the American Legion—that squalid equivalent to the protofascist *Freikorps* movement, which was simultaneously rampaging in Germany—was to smash his teeth with a rifle butt, castrate him, hang him three times in three separate locations, and then riddle his corpse with bullets before disposing of the remains in an unmarked grave. The official coroner's report listed the victim's cause of death as "suicide."[190] Afterward, "eleven Wobblies were tried for the incident in a courtroom packed with legionnaires and with federal troops stationed on the courthouse lawn. Two defense witnesses were arrested for perjury during the trial, and the judge ruled out arguments for self-defense. Seven defendants were sentenced to twenty-five to forty years in prison, with the last not released until 1939. No effort was made to find the lynchers of Everest."[191]

THE MODERN AGENCY

After the death of William Pinkerton in December 1923, the agency's chief executive slot was taken by Robert's son, Allan Pinkerton II. When he died in 1930, his son, Robert Pinkerton II, took over the job.[192] Despite these changes in leadership, and the ever-increasing role assumed by federal agents in repressing labor radicalism, the Pinkertons remained consistent for some time in peddling their wares as a business instrument against labor: "In the 1920s and early 1930s the Agency provided operatives for use in large industrial plants to report on union activities. . . . By 1936, 30 percent of the firm's business was made up of its industrial services, aside from providing uniformed guards and criminal investigation."[193]

To be fair, the agency was hardly alone in this. A number of other private firms, following the Pinkertons' pioneering record of profitability, were also specializing in antilabor activities by the early twentieth century. In fact, the William Burns International Detective Agency, the Pinkertons' main competitor, "made a concerted effort to specialize in guard services" as well as industrial espionage, taking up most of the slack the agency left in these fields.[194] Other "industrial contractors" included the Archer, Baldwin-Felts, Waddell-Mahon, John Sherman, and Gus Thiel agencies.[195] In addition, there were enterprises that excelled exclusively in strikebreaking.[196]

Jack Whitehead was the first to specialize in this activity in the early 1890s when he maintained an army of forty men solely to break strikes. The practice, however, was formalized by Jim Farley, "King of the Strikebreakers," at the turn of the century. As a New York detective, Farley saw the chaos resulting when several different detective agencies provided scabs for the same strike. A centralized force of workers that could be mobilized and moved quickly by a strikebreaker general was needed, he believed. In 1895 Farley gave up any pretense of detective work and specialized in strike services. It was rumored he earned nearly a million dollars from one strike in San Francisco. After ten years of specializing, Farley retired, noting that he had not lost any of his thirty-five strike jobs. Others, like Pearl L. Bergoff, followed Farley's example. Between 1910 and 1922 Bergoff was idle only a few months a year as strikebreaking became a profitable business. He charged the Erie Railroad two million dollars to smash the switchmen's walkout in the 1920s. The government did nothing to restrict these activities, and the number of agencies offering extensive strikebreaking services grew to sixty by the 1930s, when [the Wagner Act] was passed forbidding the mass transportation of scabs.[197]

Initially, the Pinkertons' antilabor operations survived passage of the Wagner Act in 1935 relatively unscathed. On April 8, 1937, however, in the wake of an extremely negative finding by the La Follette committee after its investigation of private sector industrial espionage activities, Pinkertons finally acknowledged the handwriting on the wall. In their own words, the firm's board of directors "recognized the change in recent years in the field of employer and employee relations and that the public sentiment generally was condemning of such practices which had been in effect for a long time."[198] The board then resolved "that management be authorized and instructed to take such steps as the management may feel necessary that this Agency in the future not furnish information to anyone concerning the lawful attempts of labor unions or employees to organize and bargain collectively."[199] As Robert Pinkerton II later put it in the *New York Times*, "That is a phase of our business that we are not particularly proud of and we're delighted we're out of it. However, there was nothing illegal about it at the time."[200]

The change was partly real, partly subterfuge. In 1938, a year after the resolution was taken, the agency's income dipped to $1,244,661, its lowest ebb since 1921.[201] It was, nonetheless, simply attempting to repackage itself for operation in the post–Wagner Act world, in which thoroughly co-opted unions such as the AFL had been federally legitimated.[202] Rather than strikebreaking and industrial espionage, the agency sought, with considerable success, to trade in industrial "security" services. In this it was greatly assisted both by the Second World War and by the subsequent period of sweeping repression usually—and rather misleadingly—referred to as the "McCarthy Era."[203]

> The Agency's business and profits increased sharply during the war years when the Pinkertons supplied protection for war plants. The top year, 1944, saw the gross income from war-plant operations come to $1,748,584 of the Agency's total of $4,089,969. As national business became more security conscious in the postwar years, the Agency's income continued to rise. In 1946, it was $5,309,772, and in the following year slightly under that figure.[204]

Another lucrative area of endeavor, police consulting, dovetailed handily with the agency's new profile. This had begun at least as early as 1893, when both Robert and William Pinkerton, taking the lead set by their father's and assistant director George Bangs' holding of official federal and local police detective positions earlier in the century, accepted appointments as honorary members of the newly formed National Association of Chiefs of Police (NACP).[205] In this capacity, William took a leading role in establishing a committee—on which he served until 1923—to lobby for congressional funding to establish a "Central Bureau of Identification."[206] He also arranged a publisher for the NACP's official periodical, *Detective*, in 1896.[207]

With respect to identification, what William Pinkerton originally had in mind was the adoption by police departments nationally of the French system of Bertillonage (recording a complex series of physical measurements theoretically unique to each individual). The National Bertillon Identification Center was actually established near Pinkerton's Chicago office in 1897; it employed a French expert named George Porteous as director and had thirty-nine subscribing police departments by 1900. The initiative was undone in 1903, however, when it was discovered that two prisoners in the federal facility at Leavenworth, both named William West, exhibited precisely the same bodily measurements.[208] Pinkerton thereupon abandoned the notion of Bertillonage and formed a new three-person subcommittee—including himself and W. G. Baldwin of the Baldwin Railroad Detective Agency—to explore fingerprinting methods, which were more-or-less universally adopted after they were accepted by a court as conclusive evidence in the 1911 *Caesar Calla* case.[209]

Despite his obviously self-serving and somewhat bumbling approach, Pinkerton's efforts at creating a centralized criminal identification center, in combination with a series of keynote addresses he delivered each year at the annual NACP conventions—the organization was renamed the International Association of Chiefs of Police (IACP) in 1902—established him and his agency as the preeminent examples of scientifically efficient crime fighting.[210] By 1900, "the Pinkerton agency was [also] widely applauded for its sophisticated managerial style," and served as a model for reorganizing a number of police departments around the country.[211] The payoff in terms of interlock between the agency and the police was readily apparent.

Robert Linden, superintendent of the Philadelphia Pinkerton office in the 1880s, became the head of the Philadelphia police department in the late 1890s. Linden, personally or through his protégés, continued to influence that police department well into the twentieth century. After twenty-three years with Pinkertons, George Dougherty became the deputy commissioner and chief of detectives for the New York City police department in 1911. Dougherty later joined the faculty of the New York School for Detectives and led several crusades for the adoption of a comprehensive fingerprinting system in America. Allan Pinkerton II . . . turned down an invitation to be the police commissioner of New York City in 1913. Other members of Pinkerton management [also] split off and . . . became police officials . . . creating a network of proselytizers for Pinkerton's brand of private policing.[212]

Such de facto integration of private and public police detective capacities allowed Pinkerton's to position itself favorably against potential competitors, and thus to become the sole agency retained by the Jewelers Protective Alliance from its founding in 1883, and the American Bankers Association, beginning in 1894.[213] When added to police consulting and industrial security, commercial security and investigation activities added up to a tidy package. Following the trajectory thus defined enabled the agency to expand its personnel roster to 13,000 full-time and more than 9,000 part-time employees by 1945, and its gross revenues rose to more than $71,000,000 by the mid-1960s.[214] Under the leadership of Edward J. Bednarz, who replaced Robert Pinkerton II as CEO in 1967, Pinkerton's, Inc. (as the agency began to call itself in 1956) also moved full tilt into the design, manufacture, installation, and maintenance of electronic security, monitoring, and surveillance systems, and into the formal training of governmental security personnel.[215]

Bednarz has played a key part in creating a more sophisticated image for the Agency. He established a research department to study new techniques in industrial security and a school for the study of sophisticated electronic devices. The school was selected by the State Department as the only private agency included in the training program of State's Agency for International Development [AID] for Security Officials sent to the United States by other world governments. In 1962, Bednarz arranged for the purchase of a New England company, manufacturing space alarms along radar principles. This subsidiary of the Agency, Pinkerton-Elector Security Company, is now marketing an anti-intrusion device for industry and homes known as Radar-Eye. . . . It was also Bednarz who gained for the Agency membership in the Ligue Internationale des Sociétiés de Surveillance, with headquarters in London. This international group extends membership to only one security agency in each country. Pinkerton's represents both the United States and Canada.[216]

While Pinkerton's, which by the 1980s remained the largest firm of its type in North America,[217] has long claimed to have gotten completely out of the kind of politically repressive work that so indelibly marked its earlier history, the AID's training program for foreign security personnel was a primary mechanism by which the death squad apparatus, which has been used so extensively against leftists and labor organizers in Latin America and other third world localities, was assembled and perfected.[218] Moreover, the Ligue Internationale des Sociétiés de Surveillance has always evidenced a decidedly antiradical, antilabor cant. In addition, the facts that the agency has at this point reversed the flow of personnel from itself to various police agencies and finds one of its own major recruitment pools to be composed of former FBI agents, and that by 1980 it was known to have compiled more than four million dossiers on the activities of "suspect" individuals tend to speak for themselves.[219]

There is also the matter of clones. The Florida-based Wackenhut Corporation, for example, employs upward of 3,500 personnel—many of them ex-FBI men—making it the third largest private detection/security firm in the United States, right behind Pinkerton's and Burns. The corporation was established in the late 1950s by George R. Wackenhut, a John Birch Society member and former FBI agent, and, until their deaths in the late 1970s and mid-1980s, respectively, included on its board Orange County Birchite attorney Lloyd Wright and former FBI assistant director Stanley J. Tracy.[220] Even more straightforward is Fidelifacts, a twenty-two-office operation that promotes itself as being "The National Organization of Ex-FBI Agents" and includes on its staff over 200 former Bureau men.[221] Still another Pinkerton-style detection and security outfit is Dale Simpson & Associates, of Dallas, also run by men who learned their trade in the FBI.[222]

All of these "private" concerns feed information on the political activities of American citizens directly into the FBI data banks—and receive classified information in return—if the murky operation once run by retired Military Intelligence chief Ralph H. Van Deman is any indication. In early 1971, it was accidentally discovered that the former major general had, for a quarter-century after he left service, been compiling tens of thousands of dossiers on the people and groups he considered "subversive" (Nobel Prize winner Linus Pauling, for instance, and the actress Joan Crawford, as well as political figures such as Franklin Roosevelt, Harry Truman, and Wayne Morse).[223] He was at least partially funded in this enterprise by the U.S. Army, and his files included thousands of pages of supposedly confidential material provided by the FBI.[224]

It was established during a preliminary investigation by the Senate that Van Deman had, over the years, freely provided the results of this "entrepreneurial intelligence gathering" not only to the military and the FBI but also to the House Un-American Activities Committee, Senator Joseph McCarthy, and the

Tenny Committee in California.[225] Further revelations were avoided by the army, which—when it appeared that the files would be subpoenaed by Senator Sam Ervin's Subcommittee on Constitutional Rights—quickly turned them over instead to the Senate Subcommittee on Internal Security, headed by archreactionary James O. Eastland, who promptly clamped a permanent "National Security" classification over the entire lot. Consequently, at present, more than a quarter-century later, the full dimension of Van Deman's operation and the disposition of much of the information he collected remain unknown.[226]

PINKERTON INFLUENCES ON THE FBI

It is important that the impact of the Pinkerton mode of repressing labor radicalism upon the U.S. polity be understood from the vantage point of its having no counterpart anywhere in the industrialized world. As Val R. Lorwin has observed,

> American workers had to fight bloodier industrial battles than the French for the right of unions to exist and to function. . . . [The] rail strikes of 1877, the pitched battle of Homestead, the Ludlow massacre were far bloodier than Fourmies and Draveil and Villeneuve-Sainte-Georges. The 1919 steel strike was more brutally suppressed than the French general strike of 1920. "Bloody Harlan" had no rival in the coal country of France. France had nothing like the private armies, factory arsenals and industrial espionage services exposed by the La Follette Committee.[227]

Or, as Stuart Jamieson has remarked with respect to the evolution of unionism in Canada, "The use of professional strike-breakers, labor spies, 'goon squads,' 'vigilante' groups, armed militia and other spectacular features of industrial warfare in the United States . . . have been absent from the Canadian scene."[228] The same can be said of Great Britain, Italy, Scandinavia, the Low Countries, even Germany. Indeed, in no other ostensibly democratic country "have employers been so much aided in their opposition to unions by the civil authorities, the armed forces of government and their courts."[229] The level and forms of repression manifested during the period of "Pinkertonism" are all the more remarkable when it is considered that—with the exceptions of the IWW, WFM, and a few fringe groups like the IWPA—the American labor movement has been the least ideologically developed of any on the planet.

The rate of industrial violence in America is striking in light of the fact that no major American organization [including the IWW] has ever advocated violence as a policy, that extremely militant class conflict philosophies have not prevailed here, and that the percentage of the American labor force organized in unions has always been (and is now) lower than in most advanced industrial countries. With a minimum of ideologically motivated class conflict, the United States has somehow had a maximum of industrial violence.[230]

In addressing the question of industrial violence in the United States, it is thus inappropriate to ask, as orthodox analysts insist upon doing, whether and to what extent labor precipitated or "provoked" it. Rather, the sole relevant question is why American government at all levels not only acquiesced in but often vigorously supported big business usage of the Pinkertons and their counterparts to visit such unparalleled barbarity upon persons, citizens and noncitizens alike, who, for the most part, never asked more than a living wage, decent working conditions, and perhaps a brighter future for their children. To this, Robert Justin Goldstein provides the only reasonable response.

> The fundamental explanation for the government-business alliance against labor ... lies in the fact of business' tremendous power [and consequent utility to government]. . . . Just as the amalgamation of church and state in colonial America made religious dissent in effect a political challenge to state authority, calling for state repression, so during most of the 1837–1937 period did the challenge posed to American capitalism by labor become transformed by the state-business amalgamation into a challenge to the ruling orthodoxy of the state.[231]

It was to preserve this status quo that the Pinkertons were unleashed with such sustained ferocity. In this sense, it is rather academic to ask whether the creation of an official entity to assume those functions performed by the Pinkerton Agency for the U.S. Department of Justice from 1871 to 1892 might not tend to reflect or even replicate the Pinkertons' tactics and priorities in the process.[232] This is all the more true when it is considered that many of the personnel staffing the Justice Department's "detection unit" in its early days had learned their trade while working as Pinkerton detectives. The only questions, then, go not to whether the agency left an imprint upon its federal successor, but to which methods and to what degree.

Some things, identification methodologies for example, are fairly straightforward. At its inception, the Justice Department's investigative bureau utilized the Bertillon System favored by William Pinkerton, and then shifted to a reliance upon fingerprinting when the Pinkerton chief switched preferences.[233] Pinkerton reciprocated by seeing to it that the IACP provided the new bureau with duplicates of both its Bertillon and fingerprint records, and in 1924 the Bureau's recently appointed acting director, J. Edgar Hoover, was finally able to convince Congress to allocate funds for purposes of establishing the national identification center Pinkerton had long sought: "The importance of William Pinkerton's plan in the 1890s to centralize Bertillon and photographic records within a national bureau of criminal identification—later the basis for the present FBI's enormous files—is obvious."[234]

Actually, it appears that Hoover may have gone well beyond anything Pinkerton had in mind, creating "a Division of Identification and Information [DII] within the Bureau that would include the fingerprints of law abiding citizens as well as criminals."[235] By 1993, the DII database would include cards on some 196 million people—a total estimated to have since grown at a rate of 9 million per year—only 107 million of them classified as "criminals" by some definition or another (the FBI's National Crime Information Center [NCIC] also maintains an estimated 23 million additional "items of interest to law enforcement").[236] In any event, the division, by now the largest in the Bureau, functions very much as Pinkerton originally envisioned, with state and local police "subscribers"—a term now encompassing virtually every police agency in the country—continuously feeding in data, and the identification center continuously disseminating it.[237]

Hoover plainly followed Pinkertonian tradition in developing other interlocks with the police, from offloading personnel to serve as chiefs, commissioners, and heads of detective divisions in major city departments, as well as county sheriffs and even district attorneys. Agent Joseph I. Woods, for example, left the FBI in 1961 to become sheriff in Cook County, Illinois, while Peter J. Pitchess, Los Angeles County sheriff during the 1960s, was also an FBI alumnus, as was Los Angeles district attorney Evelle J. Younger.[238] Similarly, Dade County (Florida) sheriff E. Wilson Purdy was a former FBI man, while the "late Arthur Cornelius, Jr., once [head agent] in Albany, was named superintendent of the New York state police in 1959 and brought with him a large contingent of Bureau alumni, including former Assistant Director John J. McGuire."[239] The list of such situations could be extended for pages.

In 1960, former FBI assistant director Quinn Tamm became executive director of the IACP; among the more important IACP members during his tenure were Kansas City police chief Clarence Kelley, still another former agent (and future FBI director).[240] As to the IACP itself, Hoover and his Bureau picked up exactly where William Pinkerton left off.

> The Washington-based International Association of Chiefs of Police claimed more than sixty-two hundred members as of 1970. Police officials from the rank of captain up were eligible, as were industrial security men, many of whom were former FBI agents. . . . For years the IACP-FBI relationship was incestuous. On Hoover and Associate Director Clyde Tolson was bestowed the honorific title of life member. Year after year, in ritual symbolism, special resolutions—usually written by FBI personnel and approved by the Director—lavishly praised the FBI chief and were unanimously passed. Hoover's nod or frown could make or break proposals under consideration. At the conventions, FBI officials were invited as keynote speakers. . . . [In 1969, Santa Ana, California, police chief Edward J.] Allen "flatly asserted that the FBI . . . controls the IACP."[241]

Aside from infusion of FBI personnel into the higher ranks of public and private police forces, one means to the desired end has been the Bureau's production and distribution of "professional" publications such as the *Law Enforcement Bulletin*, "a monthly slick mailed to some fifty-seven thousand police officers, sheriffs and prosecuting attorneys."[242] Another has been the provision, free of charge, of some 5,000 training sessions each year for local police departments around the country on such topics as arrest techniques, firearms, and defensive tactics.[243] In 1935, the FBI once again surpassed the Pinkertons' record in cultivating such handy cross-pollination, this time by establishing a by-invitation-only "National Police Academy" through which to inculcate not merely the Bureau's investigative techniques but its "perspective" among state and local police personnel.[244]

> Once an officer has been through the academy, he is automatically thought, by the FBI and usually by himself and others, to be a member of the select (although larger all the time) fraternity of Bureau men among the nation's estimated four hundred thousand law enforcement personnel. If he is in a big city, he is invited to special events by the local FBI office. In a small town, he is the first person consulted by a Bureau agent who is a stranger and has come looking for information. . . . He is invited to regional "retraining" sessions where Bureau agents dispatched from Washington lecture on a current problem in law enforcement and present the FBI's ideas for a solution. And he is almost sure to be a member of the FBI National Academy Association complete with blazer

patches, coasters, and festive reunions and conventions. . . . Because of the status and honor attached to the National Academy, local police departments and the officers within them often compete to be chosen.[245]

Small wonder that, by 1948, FBI assistant director Hugh N. Clegg, while delivering a keynote address at the annual IACP convention, could assert—to considerable applause from those assembled—that the "ideal" police chief was one "who cooperates with the FBI in such a generous manner that he has earned our undying gratitude," consistently sending in fingerprints and "laboratory problems," and having his men trained to Bureau specifications.[246] As this intimate relationship between the FBI and the police was being forged, the same was being done with the security forces maintained by private corporations. In 1923, for example, H. C. Ruch, a close friend and assistant to Hoover, left the Bureau to head up a labor espionage operation for the H. C. Frick Coal Company.[247] By the 1980s, the "security chiefs of Texas Instruments of Dallas, Lockheed at Sunnyvale, California, the giant Wynn-Dixie [sic] supermarket chain, and Reynolds Metals, to name only a few, were former Hoover minions."[248] During the 1990s, Richard Wallace Held, a ranking specialist in COINTELPRO-style operations and head of the FBI's San Francisco field office, took early retirement from the Bureau to become chief of security for the Visa corporation.[249] Again, the list could be extended to great length.

Such carefully calculated placements of its personnel allowed the FBI to avoid the appearance of direct involvement in certain of the more unsavory aspects of antilabor activity, even while exerting a steadily increasing degree of indirect control over them. Nor did Hoover neglect the cultivation of personal relationships with the rich and powerful. Following the pattern set forth by Allan Pinkerton's "friendship" with McClellan, the FBI director ingratiated himself with a cast of characters, including politicos like Wisconsin's Red-baiting senator Joseph McCarthy, California's Richard Nixon, and Texas liberal Lyndon Johnson, as well as right-wing billionaires such as Clint Murchison and Sid Richardson.[250]

There are also more than a few Pinkertonesque elements embodied in Hoover's propensity to popularize himself and his Bureau by writing—or causing to be written under his byline—a lengthy stream of material glamorizing and mythologizing his version of the "craft of detection." Unmistakably, this activity on the part of the Bureau and its director, complete with the 1935 creation of an internal propaganda mill euphemistically dubbed the Crime Records Division (CRD), found its roots in the literary efforts of Allan Pinkerton and his prose hacks in the 1800s.[251]

Allan Pinkerton, the most famous real-life detective of the nineteenth century, probably was more famous for the eighteen volumes of casebooks his ghost writers turned out from 1873 until 1886 than anything he did as a detective. When Hoover began issuing his own ghost-written casebooks (*Persons in Hiding* in 1938, *Masters of Deceit* in 1958, along with scores of magazine articles and several movies), these literary performances seemed incongruous to many, but only because his critics did not know the popular tradition of the "great detective" who has always been a storyteller as well as a hero.[252]

In the same vein, the FBI, like the Pinkerton Agency before it, was packaged as the nation's premier crime-fighting force when in fact the preponderance of its resources and attention were always devoted to antiradicalism, pure and simple. While the Pinkertons made much of their campaigns against the Reno and James/Younger gangs—and, later, the apprehension (twice) of Willie Sutton, a notorious bank robber of the 1920s—there is no indication that the agency made any effort at all to confront such precursors of twentieth-century organized crime as the Whyos and other New York gangs.[253] Meanwhile, as was shown above, the agency specialized in deploying literally thousands of employees to break strikes, infiltrate labor unions, and disrupt anarchist and other radical political activities, regardless of their legality.

By the same token, the FBI hyped itself as being composed of "gang busters" after a series of easy successes during the mid-1930s against such small-time rural hoodlums as John Dillinger, Baby Face Nelson, Pretty Boy Floyd, Machine Gun Kelly, Alvin Karpis, and the Barker family.[254] At the same time, it did absolutely nothing to interfere with the rise of syndicated crime in the United States, with Director Hoover even going so far as to state publicly—repeatedly and officially—that so far as his Bureau knew, organized crime, as such, "did not exist."[255] Yet while allegedly being too shorthanded to discover the operations of urban crime bosses like Al Capone, Lucky Luciano, Meyer Lansky, Bugsy Siegel, Albert Anastasia, Tony Acardo, and Vito Genovese,[256] the FBI always had sufficient resources to blanket labor radicals like Harry Bridges, maintain a fifty-year vendetta against the American Communist Party, and so on.[257]

In other words, the Bureau unquestionably inherited its predecessor's tendency to veil its true identity and priorities, masquerading as society's main defense against rampant crime while largely ignoring major criminal enterprises in favor of a steadily increasing concentration on the repression of radical political activity.[258] Even when he was willing to come out of the closet with regard to his Bureau's real priorities, the stilted concepts and rhetoric used by Hoover in such books as *Masters of Deceit* and *A Study of Communism* to describe the "subversive menace" he assigned his agents to combat bear more than passing resemblance to those used early on by Allan Pinkerton in his *The Molly Maguires and the Detectives* and *Strikers, Communists, Tramps and the Detectives*, as well as Robert Pinkerton's 1901 essay, "Detective Surveillance of Anarchists."[259] As Hoover biographer Richard Gid Powers has observed:

> Hoover's performance [from 1919 onward] might be interpreted as a variation on a technique developed by the Pinkerton Agency in the nineteenth century: "Every group was assumed to be led by a tight inner circle of conspirators whose program and tactics were closely held secrets. These insiders were, in theory, surrounded by an outer ring of followers, many of them unaware of the criminal purposes of the leaders."[260]

Administrative, propagandistic, and ideological similitude aside, however, a genuine question might still be posed as to the extent to which the FBI assimilated the Pinkertons' vernacular of utterly illegal tactics in waging its own, more official campaigns against radicalism. Here, we again encounter a veritable point-by-point correspondence, beginning with the use of "Big Lie" techniques—such as those evident in Allan Pinkerton's 1861 "Lincoln Assassination Plot" fable—in order to garner from those in power an extra measure of support at critical moments. There have been a number of instances in which the FBI has clearly resorted to such stratagems, perhaps most notably when Hoover testified before a congressional subcommittee in 1970, while seeking increased funding, that his agents had uncovered a plot by a group of pacifist Roman Catholic clergy nominally headed by the priests Daniel Berrigan and Philip Berrigan to sabotage Washington, D.C., and assassinate presidential assistant Henry Kissinger. It took months before the sheer falsity of the director's assertions became apparent, and by then his purpose(s) had been long since accomplished.[261]

As concerns the orchestration and/or organization of vigilante groups to neutralize targets, à la the Pinkertons' performances against the Renos, Molly Maguires, and IWW, the FBI's record is also imbued with many counterparts, especially during the First World War, and again in the 1960s and early-to-mid-1970s.[262] One example drawn from the latter period, that of the so-called Secret Army Organization (SAO) in southern California, should be sufficient to illustrate the point. Among other things, the SAO was responsible for the attempted murder, in San Diego, of radical economist Peter G. Bohmer on January 9, 1972, and the firebombing of the Guild Theater, also in San Diego, on June 19 of the same year.[263]

An ex-FBI informer, Nanda Zocchino, recounted in the January 26, 1976, editorial of the *Los Angeles Times* how the Bureau had created and financed this "crypto-fascist" group in San Diego during 1969–70. During the early-1970s the SAO engaged in a range of activities including burglary, mail thefts, bombings, kidnappings, assassination plots and attempted murder. . . . A second informant to the San Diego FBI office, Howard Berry Godfrey, has substantially corroborated Zocchino's story. . . . According to the Citizens Research and Investigation Committee (CRIC), the SAO was established specifically to "use violence against radicals" and, at its peak, had cadres in eleven western states.[264]

The record is also replete with examples of the FBI utilizing agents provocateurs in essentially the same role as was played by the Pinkertons' James McParlan against the Molly Maguires. Notable in this regard was the Bureau's insertion of at least thirty operatives into the Black Panther Party during the late 1960s,[265] but this hardly exhausts the list of possible illustrations. Consider the following, taken from the chronicle of FBI provocation within Students for a Democratic Society (SDS) during the same period.

Probably the most well-known *agent provocateur* was Thomas Tongyai, known as Tommy the Traveler. Tongyai, who was paid by both the FBI and local police, spent over two years traveling among the colleges in western New York State, urging students to kill police, make bombs and blow up buildings. . . . Tongyai constantly talked of violence, carried a grenade in his car, showed students how to use an M-1 rifle and offered advice on how to carry out bombings. After some students at Hobart College apparently took his advice and bombed the Hobart ROTC building, and Tongyai's cover was exposed, the local sheriff commented, "There's a lot of difference between showing how to build a bomb and building one." As a result of disturbances connected with Tongyai's activities on the Hobart campus, nine students and faculty faced criminal charges.[266]

Another FBI-sponsored provocateur, Charles Grimm, maintaining that he acted on instructions of the Bureau, openly admitted to the burning of Dressler Hall on the campus of the University of Alabama at Tuscaloosa on May 7, 1970.[267] Still another, Horace L. Packer, who became the government's star witness during the "Seattle Eight" conspiracy trial, conceded to having supplied all manner of illegal weapons, explosives, and drugs to the defendants and their associates.[268]

Probably the most incredible provocation incident involved an FBI and Seattle police informer, Alfred Burnett, who lured Larry Eugene Ward into planting a bomb at a Seattle real estate office on the morning of May 15, 1970, by paying Ward $75, providing him with the bomb and giving him transportation to the bombing scene. Ward, a twenty-two year old veteran who had been twice wounded and decorated three times for service in Vietnam, was shot and killed by waiting Seattle police as he allegedly fled after the bombing attempt, although he was unarmed, on foot, and boxed in by police cars. . . . Burnett, the FBI informer, was a twice-convicted felon who had been released from jail as a result of FBI statements to the Seattle police.[269]

By and large, the FBI seems not to have manifested the Pinkertons' proclivity to engage directly in the murder of targeted individuals, preferring instead to manipulate vigilantes, rival political organizations, or local police into such lethal pursuits. An example of the Bureau's deliberate provocation of interorganizational violence for purposes of physically neutralizing members of one or both groups concerns the 1969 "war" precipitated at least in part by the FBI's dissemination of forged cartoons attributed to the Black Panther Party and defaming US, a black cultural nationalist organization. By the FBI's own tally, six members of the party died at the hands of US gunmen as a result.[270] The assassination of Illinois Black Panther leaders Fred Hampton and Mark Clark on December 4, 1969, is probably the best-known instance of police being used by the Bureau in much the same manner.[271]

There have, of course, been exceptions to such indirect approaches to mayhem, as when agents cold-bloodedly gunned down bank robber John Dillinger in a Chicago alley on the night of July 22, 1934, and their execution, in what amounted to firing squad fashion, of another minor desperado, Pretty Boy Floyd, on October 21 of the same year.[272] In other instances, the Bureau appears to have utilized "nonagent personnel" to infiltrate targeted organizations with express instructions to assassinate selected political leaders. Such is the case with provocateur Louis Tackwood, who insists—and passed a polygraph to punctuate his point—that he was assigned by his FBI handlers to murder Black Panther field marshal George Jackson inside San Quentin, the California maximum security prison, in 1970.[273] Where one should look to find a clearer repetition of the Pinkertons' endgame move against Jesse James is difficult to imagine.

As concerns usurpation of the judicial system for purposes of staging the sort of "trial" inflicted by the Pinkertons and their cohorts upon the Molly Maguires and the Haymarket defendants, no shortage of counterparts can also be drawn from the FBI's subsequent performance. Probably the most spectacular have been the mass trials of IWW leaders/organizers in 1918 and the so-called Chicago Eight conspiracy trial of 1969–70.[274] Another is the abovementioned trial of the Seattle Eight, growing out of a February 1970 demonstration in that city.

> Although the demonstration—called to protest contempt sentences handed down in the Chicago case—had been planned only ten days before it occurred, four of the defendants were charged with crossing state lines the previous December with intent to incite riot; another defendant (a visiting photography professor at the University of Washington) was charged with using interstate telephone lines with intent to incite riot as a result of a long distance call placed a week before the demonstration. . . . The judge, George H. Boldt, declared a mistrial when the defendants protested his refusal to give any kind of shelter in the entire courtroom building to spectators who were waiting outside in the rain to gain entrance to the trial. He then sentenced five defendants to a year in jail for contempt and two to six months for contempt (one defendant had gone underground and never shown up), based on the "totality" of their behavior during the trial.[275]

Boldt then denied bail on the contempt convictions, even after an appeals court instructed him to grant it. In March 1973, the government finally dismissed the original charges, but by then the defendants had all served jail time as a result of their malicious prosecution. Moreover, "the once thriving radical movement in Seattle," of which they were key organizers, "had been made a shambles."[276]

Much the same pattern prevailed in the so-called Wounded Knee Trials pursued against the American Indian Movement (AIM) during the same period. Although the FBI caused a total of 562 felony charges to be filed against AIM members and supporters following a protracted 1973 confrontation on the Pine Ridge Reservation in South Dakota, a total of only fifteen convictions resulted, all for minor offenses.[277] The purpose of the prosecutorial onslaught had been far from the obtaining of guilty verdicts, however. During the more than two years in which the trials occurred, almost the entire roster of AIM's key leaders and organizers were continuously tied up in the struggle to defend themselves in court against a seemingly unending stream of baseless allegations, their out-of-court activities constrained by conditions attached to the posting of their usually excessive bails, and their organization ultimately bankrupted by its ever-mounting legal expenses.[278]

Worst of all have been the cases in which extralegal manipulation of the judicial process by "law enforcement officials" has resulted in imprisonment of those falsely accused. Among the more striking examples is that of Dhoruba bin Wahad (Richard Moore), a New York Black Panther leader who served nineteen years in a maximum security prison before being released in 1990 after it was conclusively established that the FBI had not only fabricated evidence leading to his conviction on charges of attempting to murder police but also to have withheld evidence that would have exonerated him.[279] Another is that of Geronimo ji Jaga (Elmer Gerard Pratt), a one-time leader of the Los Angeles Panther chapter, released from prison in 1996 after serving twenty-seven years on a murder conviction engineered in much the same fashion as bin Wahad's.[280] Still another is that of AIM member Leonard Peltier, now in his thirty-first year of maximum security incarceration, despite formal acknowledgment by the U.S. Eighth Circuit Court of Appeals as long ago as 1986 that the evidence used to obtain his conviction was utterly invalid.[281]

These and myriad other examples demonstrate conclusively that the essence of nineteenth- and early-twentieth-century Pinkertonism has infected the FBI from the moment of its birth through the present day.[282] Moreover, insofar as the Bureau has continued to evolve and refine the criminal techniques of political repression pioneered by the Pinkertons, to have expanded their application to include a span of targets vastly broader than the labor radicalism that preoccupied its "private" predecessor, and to have fully institutionalized the result, the FBI must be seen as having accomplished things far worse than anything even the most malignantly visionary of the Pinkertons might ever have conceived. Far from diminishing as the country has matured, the unique terms of American class warfare remarked upon above by Lorwin, Jamieson, and others must therefore be understood as having become ever more pronounced over the past nine decades. We must calculate the nature of our own actions accordingly.

NOTES

1. David Cole, excerpt from a presentation made at Princeton University, aired on radio station KGNU, Boulder, Colo., March 2003.

2. See, as examples, David Cole and James X. Dempsey, *Terrorism and the Constitution: Sacrificing Civil Liberties in the Name of National Security* (New York: New Press, 2002); Cynthia Brown, ed., *Lost Liberties: Ashcroft and the Assault on Personal Freedom* (New

York: New Press, 2003); James Bovard, *Terrorism and Tyranny: Trampling Freedom, Justice, and Peace to Rid the World of Evil* (New York: Palgrave, 2003).

3. Also see, e.g., David Cole, "The Course of Least Resistance: Repeating History in the War on Terrorism," in Brown, *Lost Liberties*, 13–32; Natsu Taylor Saito, "Whose Liberty? Whose Security? The USA PATRIOT Act in the Context of COINTELPRO and the Unlawful Repression of Political Dissent," *Oregon Law Review* 81, no. 4 (Winter 2002). The term COINTELPRO was derived from the FBI's designation of such operations as "counterintelligence programs."

4. Probably the best overview remains David Caute's *The Great Fear: The Anti-Communist Purge Under Truman and Eisenhower* (New York: Simon and Schuster, 1978). Also see Athan Theoharis, *Seeds of Repression: Harry S. Truman and the Origins of McCarthyism* (Chicago: Quadrangle Books, 1971).

5. An excellent examination is provided in Robert W. Dunn, ed., *The Palmer Raids* (New York: International, 1948). For further backdrop, see Robert K. Murray, *Red Scare: A Study in National Hysteria, 1919–1920* (New York: McGraw-Hill, 1964).

6. The centerpiece of this juridical offensive was the mass trial—by far the largest in U.S. history (bleachers had to be installed in the courtroom to seat the defendants)—of 113 IWW leaders on an average of 100 charges each, all devolving upon the notion of "sedition" and "seditious conspiracy." Beginning on April 1, 1918, the trial lasted until August 31, when, their having been convicted en masse, Judge Kenesaw Mountain Landis sentenced fifteen of the accused to twenty years imprisonment, thirty-three to ten years, and thirty-five to five years. More or less simultaneously, mass trials of IWW organizers also occurred in Wichita, Kansas, and Sacramento, California. In Wichita, thirty-four persons were tried, twenty-seven convicted and sentenced to serve from one to nine years imprisonment; in Sacramento, where there were forty-six defendants, all were convicted and received sentences of up to ten years. For one of the best treatments of these proceedings, see Philip A. Taft, "The Federal Trials of the IWW," *Labor History*, No. 3 (Winter 1962).

7. On Garvey and the UNIA, see Robert A. Hill Jr., "The Foremost Radical of His Race: Marcus Garvey and the Black Scare, 1918–1920," *Prologue*, No. 16 (Winter 1984). More broadly, see Theodore Kornweibel Jr., *"Seeing Red": Federal Campaigns against Black Militancy, 1919–1925* (Bloomington: Indiana University Press, 1998).

8. This is a point I've made elsewhere and repeatedly. See, e.g., my "'To Disrupt, Discredit and Destroy': The FBI's Secret War Against the Black Panther Party," in Kathleen Cleaver and George Katsiaficas, eds., *Liberation, Imagination, and the Black Panther Party: A New Look at the Panthers and Their Legacy* (New York: Routledge, 2001), 78–79; "The FBI's Secret War Against the Black Panther Party: A Case Study in

Repression," in Curtis Stokes, Theresa Meléndez, and Genice Rhodes-Reed, eds., *Race in the 21st Century* (East Lansing: Michigan State University Press, 2001), 268.

9. In terms of legislation, there are of course much earlier examples, notably the Alien and Sedition Acts of 1798–1800. Nonetheless, I locate the point of departure in the juncture at which the apparatus of enforcement of such ideologically repressive statutes is formally established, if not as a component integral to the central government itself, then through the regularized employment of surrogate entities retained for this specific purpose. On the early legislation, see John C. Miller, *Crisis in Freedom: The Alien and Sedition Acts* (Boston: Atlantic-Little, Brown, 1951).

10. Again, this is a theme I've elsewhere developed more fully. See, e.g., my preface to the recent Classics Edition of my and Jim Vander Wall's *The COINTELPRO Papers: Documents from the FBI's Secret Wars Against Dissent in the United States* (Cambridge, Mass.: South End Press, 2002), xxv–lxxxviii.

11. For a penetrating analysis of the broader reality within which this seeming consensus is embedded, see Noam Chomsky, *Necessary Illusions: Thought Control in Democratic Societies* (Boston: South End Press, 1989).

12. For explication, see the essay titled "Acts of Rebellion: Notes on the Interaction of History and Justice," which serves as the introduction to my *Acts of Rebellion: The Ward Churchill Reader* (New York: Routledge, 2003), esp. xi–xvii.

13. U.S. Congress, *Appropriations to the Budget of the United States of America, 1872, Section VII: United States Department of Justice* (Washington, D.C.: Government Printing Office, 1872).

14. Max Lowenthal, *The Federal Bureau of Investigation* (New York: William Sloan, 1950), 6–10.

15. Frank Morn, *The Eye That Never Sleeps: A History of the Pinkerton National Detective Agency* (Bloomington: Indiana University Press, 1982), 19–20, 52; Sigmund A. Lavine, *Allan Pinkerton: America's First Private Eye* (New York: Dodd, Mead, 1963), 18–22. More generally, see Ray Boston, *The British Chartist Movement in America, 1839–1900* (Manchester: Manchester University Press, 1971).

16. Morn, *Eye*, 21–23.

17. Ibid., 18.

18. Ibid., 23, 93.

19. Ibid., 39.

20. Ibid., 39–40. For Pinkerton's own account of this episode, see his *The Spy of the Rebellion, Being a True History of the Spy System of the United States Army during the Late Rebellion* (New York: G. W. Dillingham, 1888), 46, 54–56, 62, 68. Also see his self-published *History and Evidence of the Passage of Abraham Lincoln from Harrisburg, Pa.*

to *Washington, D.C. on 22d and 23d of February, 1861* (Chicago: Pinkerton National Detective Agency, 1861).

21. Morn, *Eye*, 40.

22. U.S. House of Representatives, *Reports of the Committees of the House of Representatives, No. 79, Vol. 2: Alleged Hostile Organization Against the Government Within the District of Columbia* (Washington, D.C.: 36th Cong., 2d Sess., 1861), 2.

23. "There was no conspiracy at all, save in the brain of the Chicago detective [Pinkerton]." *Chicago Democrat*, March 5, 1861.

24. Morn, *Eye*, 41.

25. Ibid., 45.

26. Ibid., 46.

27. James D. Horan, *The Pinkertons: The Detective Dynasty That Made History* (New York: Crown, 1967), 238. Also see Richard Wilmer Rowan, *The Pinkertons: A Detective Dynasty* (Boston: Little, Brown, 1931).

28. Pinkerton's bibliography of potboilers is extensive. Aside from *Spy of the Rebellion* and *History and Evidence*, he also authored, among many other tomes, *General Principles of Pinkerton's Police Agency* (Chicago: Church, Goodman and Donnelley, 1869); *The Expressman and the Detectives* (Chicago: W. B. Keen, Cooke, 1875); *The Model Town and the Detectives* (New York: G. W. Dillingham, 1876); *The Molly Maguires and the Detectives* (New York: G. W. Dillingham, 1877); *The Spiritualists and the Detectives* (New York: G. W. Carleton, 1877); *Strikers, Communists, Tramps and Detectives* (New York: G. W. Carleton, 1878); *Mississippi Outlaws and the Detectives* (New York: G. W. Carleton, 1879); *The Gypsies and the Detectives* (New York: G. W. Dillingham, 1879); *Professional Thieves and the Detectives* (New York: G. W. Carleton, 1880); *The Railroad Forger and the Detectives* (New York: G. W. Dillingham, 1881); *Bank Robbers and Detectives* (New York: G. W. Dillingham, 1882); and *Thirty Years a Detective* (New York: G. W. Dillingham, 1884).

29. Morn, *Eye*, 68–69.

30. Ibid., 50.

31. Wilgus Wade Hogg, *The First Train Robbery* (Medford, N.J.: Plexus, 1978).

32. For a succinct explanation, see Howard Zinn, *A People's History of the United States* (New York: Harper and Row, 1980), 213–15.

33. Cleveland Moffett, *True Detective Tales of the Pinkertons* (New York: Sharp, 1897), 164.

34. Horan, *Pinkertons*, 162.

35. Ibid.

36. John Reno, *John Reno: Life and Career* (New York: self-published, 1887).

37. Frederick Volland, "The Reno Boys of Seymore" (master's thesis, University of Indiana, 1959; on file in the Pinkerton Archives, Chicago).

38. Ibid.; Horan, *Pinkertons*, 168–73.

39. Ibid., 176–78.

40. Ibid., 178.

41. Ibid., 179.

42. Ibid.

43. Ibid., 191–96.

44. See, e.g., Allan Pinkerton to George Bangs, November 1, 1874, Pinkerton Archives.

45. Horan, *Pinkertons*, 234.

46. Perhaps the best book on Quantrill remains William Elsey Connelly's *Quantrill and the Border Wars* (Cedar Rapids, Iowa: Torch Books, 1910; reprint, New York: Pageant Books, 1956). Also see Charles W. Breihan, *Quantrill and His Civil War Guerrillas* (Denver: Sage Books, 1959).

47. Paul I. Wellman, *A Dynasty of Western Outlaws* (Lincoln: University of Nebraska Press, 1961), 65.

48. Ibid., 68–79.

49. Ibid., 69; Horan, *Pinkertons*, 191–92.

50. The James/Younger group was falsely accused of many things, including the commission of two bank robberies 400 miles apart on the same day. The robberies and dating used here are taken from a "clarifying list" provided by gang member Dick Liddil after he turned state's evidence in exchange for clemency in 1881; it is included in full in Wellman, *Dynasty of Outlaws*, 120–21.

51. Ibid., 87–94. Also see William A. Settle, *Jesse James Was His Name* (Columbia: University of Missouri Press, 1966).

52. The attackers were operating on the basis of erroneous information provided by an operative named Jack Ladd. The remains of the "smoker" thrown by the Pinkertons into the Samuel residence are consistent with being a Civil War vintage iron hand grenade. Wellman, *Dynasty of Outlaws*, 96–97.

53. Ibid., 97–98.

54. Augustus C. Appler, *The Younger Brothers* (New York: Alfred A. Knopf, 1955); Carl W. Breihan, *The Outlaw Brothers: The True Story of Missouri's Younger Brothers* (San Antonio, Tex.: Naylor, 1961).

55. Frank James underwent a pro forma trial for his role in a single train robbery, but was quickly acquitted after Governor Crittenden took the stand to testify in his behalf. All state charges were then dropped, and Missouri authorities refused to honor extradition requests from Minnesota in connection with the Northfield raid. T. J. Styles, *Jesse James: Last Rebel of the Civil War* (New York: Alfred A. Knopf, 2002), 379–81.

56. Analyses of these dynamics are legion. Two of the best are Paul M. Sweezy and Paul Baran, *Monopoly Capital* (New York: Monthly Review Press, 1966); and Harry Braverman, *Labor and Monopoly Capital: The Degradation of Work in the Twentieth Century* (New York: Monthly Review Press, 1974).

57. Quoted in Jerold S. Auerbach, *Labor and Liberty: The La Follette Committee and the New Deal* (Indianapolis: Bobbs-Merrill, 1966), 15.

58. Morn, *Eye*, 93.

59. Ibid.

60. Ibid., 94.

61. Robert Justin Goldstein, *Political Repression in Modern America, 1870 to the Present* (Cambridge/New York: Schenkman/Two Continents, 1978), 23.

62. Wayne G. Broehl Jr., *The Molly Mcguires* (Cambridge, Mass.: Harvard University Press, 1964), 93.

63. Horan, *Pinkertons*, 206.

64. Goldstein, *Political Repression*, 29. Also see Arthur H. Lewis, *Lament for the Molly Maguires* (New York: Harcourt, Brace and World, 1964).

65. Horan, *Pinkertons*, 207–8.

66. Ibid., 209. The book referred to is J. Walter Coleman, *The Molly Maguire Riots* (Richmond, Va.: Garrett and Massie, 1936).

67. Broehl, *Molly Maguires*, 230–1.

68. Quoted in Horan, *Pinkertons*, 224.

69. Ibid., 225–26.

70. Ibid., 236.

71. Harold W. Aurand, *From the Molly Maguires to the United Mine Workers* (Philadelphia: Temple University Press, 1971), 25.

72. Vernon H. Jensen, *Heritage of Conflict* (Ithaca, N.Y.: Cornell University Press, 1950), 192–218.

73. Joseph Rayback, *A History of American Labor* (New York: Free Press, 1966), 133; Goldstein, *Political Repression*, 28.

74. Rayback, *History of Labor*, 133.

75. U.S. Department of Labor, *Sixteenth Annual Report of the Commissioner of Labor, 1901* (Washington, D.C.: Government Printing Office, 1901), 803–6.

76. Morn, *Eye*, 97; *National Guard Association Annual Convention Proceedings, 1881*, 13–14.

77. U.S. Senate, *Report on an Investigation of Labor Troubles at Homestead, Pennsylvania* (Washington, D.C.: S. Rep. 1280, 52d Cong., 2d Sess., 1893), 242; Herbert G. Gutman, "The Braidwood Lockout of 1874," *Journal of the Illinois State Historical Society*, No. 53 (1960).

78. See Leo Huberman, *The Labor Spy Racket* (New York: Modern Age Books, 1937).

79. Quoted in Auerbach, *Labor and Liberty*, 101.

80. Ibid., 99.

81. Morn, *Eye*, 98; *Pinkerton Reports of the Annual Convention of the Brotherhood of Locomotive Engineers,* Burlington Papers, Newberry Library, Chicago.

82. Auerbach, *Labor and Liberty*, 97–99.

83. Irving Bernstein, *The Lean Years: Workers in an Unbalanced Society* (Boston: Houghton-Mifflin, 1960), 149.

84. Auerbach, *Labor and Liberty*, 99.

85. Morn, *Eye*, 187–88.

86. U.S. Senate, Committee on Education and Labor, *Violations of Free Speech and the Rights of Labor: Strikebreaking Services* (Washington, D.C.: S. Rep. 6, Pt. 1, 76th Cong., 1st Sess., 1939), 23.

87. U.S. Senate, Committee on Education and Labor, *Violations of Free Speech and the Rights of Labor: Industrial Espionage* (Washington, D.C.: S. Rep. 46, No. 3, 75th Cong., 2d Sess., 1938), 9–10, 12–15, 17, 21, 24, 26, 28, 53, 58–59, 63.

88. Ibid., 53.

89. Harry J. Carman, Henry David, and Paul N. Guthrie, eds., *The Path I Trod: The Autobiography of Terrence V. Powderly* (New York: Columbia University Press, 1940), 149, 154.

90. Morn, *Eye*, 100.

91. Leon Wolff, *Lockout! The Story of the Homestead Strike of 1892* (New York: Harper and Row, 1965), 70; also see William Serrin, *Homestead: The Glory and Tragedy of an American Steel Town* (New York: Vintage Books, 1993).

92. John Higham, *Strangers in the Land* (New York: Atheneum, 1970), 89.

93. Goldstein, *Political Repression*, 12.

94. Morn, *Eye*, 104; U.S. House of Representatives, *Employment of Pinkerton Detectives during the Homestead Mining Strike, Pennsylvania* (Washington, D.C.: 52d Cong., 2d Sess., 1893), 213.

95. Auerbach, *Labor and Liberty*, 101.

96. Morn, *Eye*, 101; also see Gutman, "Braidwood Lockout."

97. Donald L. McMurry, *The Great Burlington Strike of 1888: A Case History in Labor-Relations* (Cambridge, Mass.: Harvard University Press, 1956), 192–204, 287.

98. Goldstein, *Political Repression*, 38.

99. On the IWPA, SLP, and related matters, see Henry David, *The History of the Haymarket Affair* (New York: Collier, 1963); on the Pinkerton shootings, see John Altgeld, *Live Questions* (Chicago: George S. Bowen, 1899), 385–87, 391; on Daniel DeLeon, a major figure in American socialist history, see his autobiographical *The American Anarchist:*

Reflections on Indigenous Radicalism (Baltimore: Johns Hopkins University Press, 1978).

100. Sidney Lens, *The Labor Wars: From the Molly Maguires to the Sitdowns* (Garden City, N.Y.: Doubleday, 1974), 63–75; Samuel Yellin, *American Labor Struggles* (New York: Monad Press, 1974), 39–71.

101. Goldstein, *Political Repression*, 39–40.

102. Lens, *Labor Wars*, 75.

103. See, e.g., Lucy E. Parsons, *Life of Albert Parsons with a Brief History of the Labor Movement in America* (Chicago: Charles Kerr, 1889).

104. Maldwyn Jones, *American Immigration* (Chicago: University of Chicago Press, 1960), 252–53; Higham, *Strangers in the Land*, 54.

105. Rayback, *History of Labor*, 168.

106. On the police, see David, *History of the Haymarket Affair*, 191; on the Pinkerton provocateur, see Morn, *Eye*, 99.

107. Quoted in Norman J. Ware, *The Labor Movement in the United States, 1860–1895: A Study in Democracy* (New York: D. Appleton, 1929), 359.

108. Goldstein, *Political Repression*, 41.

109. Harold Dick, *Labor and Socialism in America: The Gompers Era* (Port Washington, N.Y.: Kennikat, 1972), 16; Goldstein, *Political Repression*, 43.

110. Daniel Bell, *Marxian Socialism in the United States* (Princeton, N.J.: Princeton University Press, 1967), 39–40.

111. Goldstein, *Political Repression*, 43.

112. Dick, *Labor and Socialism*, 16; Ware, *Labor Movement*, 316.

113. On the accommodationist posture of the AFL, even during the earliest phases of its development, see David, *Labor and Socialism*, 343; Ware, *Labor Movement*, 182.

114. Morn, *Eye*, 103. Also see Wolff, *Lockout!*

115. Goldstein, *Political Repression*, 46; Lens, *Labor Wars*, 76–88; also see Jeremy Brecher, *Strike!* (San Francisco: Straight Arrow Press, 1972), 53–63.

116. Wolff, *Lockout!* 164: Yellin, *American Labor Struggles*, 72–100.

117. Goldstein, *Political Repression*, 46.

118. Horan, *Pinkertons*, 358; Henry David, "Upheaval at Homestead," in Daniel Aaron, ed., *America in Crisis* (1952; reprint, New York: Shoe String Press, 1971), 133–70.

119. Wolff, *Lockout!* 164–65.

120. Goldstein, *Political Repression*, 46.

121. *New York Times*, November 19, 1892.

122. Horan, *Pinkertons*, 350.

123. Morn, *Eye*, 104; Horan, *Pinkertons*, 35.

124. Ibid., 103; *Labor Troubles at Homestead*, 121–25.

125. Morn, *Eye*, 103; Horan, *Pinkertons*, 350–58.

126. Morn, *Eye*, 107; U.S. Senate, *Investigation of Labor Troubles at Homestead*; and U.S. House of Representatives, *Employment of Pinkerton Detectives*. Also see William Oates, "The Homestead Strike: A Congressional View," *North American Review*, No. 155 (September 1892).

127. Morn, *Eye*, 107.

128. Ibid.

129. Ibid. For further analysis, see J. Bernard Hogg, "Public Reaction to Pinkertonism and the Labor Question," *Pennsylvania History*, No. 2 (July 1944).

130. Morn, *Eye*, 107; Henry Warrum, *Peace Officers and Detectives: The Law of Sheriffs, Constables, Marshals, Municipal Police and Detectives* (Greenfield, Ind.: William Mitchell, 1895), 106, 108–9, 112–13.

131. Morn, *Eye*, 165–66; on the Ludlow Massacre, see Goldstein, *Political Repression*, 92.

132. Morn, *Eye*, 164; Jürgen Thorwald, *The Twentieth Century Detective* (New York: Harcourt, Brace and World, 1964), 91.

133. Morn, *Eye*, 168. Also see Jeremiah Patrick Swallow, *Private Police: With Special Reference to Pennsylvania* (Philadelphia: American Academy of Political and Social Science, 1933).

134. Morn, *Eye*, 158; Morris Friedman, *The Pinkerton Labor Spy* (New York: Wilshire Books, 1907), 30–40, 51–64.

135. Morn, *Eye*, 156, 160.

136. Goldstein, *Political Repression*, 51; Jensen, *Heritage of Conflict*, 38–53.

137. Melvin Dubofsky, "The Leadville Strike of 1896–1897," *Mid-America*, No. 48 (April 1966).

138. William J. Gaboury, "From State House to Bull Pen: Idaho Populism and the Coeur d'Alene Troubles of the 1890s," *Pacific Northwest Quarterly*, No. 58 (January 1967): 18–22; Jensen, *Heritage of Conflict*, 72–87.

139. Goldstein, *Political Repression*, 71.

140. Charles A. Siringo, *Two Evil Isms: Pinkertonism and Anarchism* (Chicago: self-published, 1915), 93.

141. Ibid.

142. Melvyn Dubofsky, "Origins of Western Working Class Radicalism," *Labor History*, No. 7 (Spring 1966): 152.

143. George C. Suggs, *Colorado's War on Militant Unionism: James H. Peabody and the Western Federation of Miners* (Detroit: Wayne State University Press, 1972), 20–22.

144. Ibid.; Jensen, *Heritage of Conflict*, 130–31; Lens, *Labor Wars*, 148.

145. Perhaps the best account of the role of the WFM in founding the IWW—especially with regards to the preliminary "secret meeting" conducted in Chicago in January

1905—remains Paul Brissenden, *The I.W.W.: A Study of American Syndicalism* (New York: Columbia University Press, 1920).

146. John S. Gambs, *The Decline of the IWW* (New York: Columbia University Press, 1932), 164–69.

147. Patrick Renshaw, *The Wobblies: The Story of Syndicalism in the United States* (Garden City, N.Y.: Doubleday, 1967), 22.

148. The first office was at 146 West Madison St. in Chicago; ibid., 92.

149. Morn, *Eye*, 167.

150. Goldstein, *Political Repression*, 73; Jensen, *Heritage of Conflict*, 192–218; David H. Grover, *Debaters and Dynamiters: The Story of the Haywood Trial* (Corvallis: Oregon State University Press, 1964); Stewart H. Holbrook, *The Rocky Mountain Revolution* (New York: Holt, 1956).

151. Morn, *Eye*, 158.

152. Grover, *Debaters and Dynamiters*, 53, 98–105.

153. Goldstein, *Political Repression*, 73; Jensen, *Heritage of Conflict*, 134–35. The conclusion is entirely in line with that drawn by Suggs (*Colorado's War on Militant Unionism*, 191–92) in his definitive study of the 1903–4 Colorado Labor War, that "at no time did the WFM engage in armed resistance against constituted authorities even when their extreme harassment and provocation might have justified it."

154. Goldstein, *Political Repression*, 73.

155. Finally intimidated by the concerted repression directed against it, the WFM adopted the formulation of Moyer, its president, that "if to be conservative meant to stay out of prison, he was going to be conservative," withdrew from the IWW in 1908, and rejoined the AFL. This, of course, severely reduced the IWW's early membership, especially with regard to experienced organizers. Jensen, *Heritage of Conflict*, 236–44; Melvin Dubofsky, *We Shall Be All: A History of the IWW* (Chicago: Quadrangle, 1969), 105.

156. Morn, *Eye*, 158; also see Friedman, *Pinkerton Labor Spy*.

157. Morn, *Eye*, 158–59; for contextualization, see Louis Filler, *Crusades for American Liberalism: The Story of the Muckrakers* (New York: Collier Books, 1961), 214, 216–17.

158. Renshaw, *Wobblies*, 22.

159. A good assessment is found in Leonard Whipple, *The Story of Civil Liberty in the United States* (New York: Vanguard, 1927), 304.

160. Goldstein, *Political Repression*, 68.

161. Sidney Fine, "Anarchism and the Assassination of McKinley," *American Historical Review*, No. 9 (July 1955).

162. This precipitated what the Wobblies called the "Free Speech Fight," resulting in about thirty major confrontations, mostly along the West Coast, from 1907 to 1916. Renshaw, *Wobblies*, 120.

163. Goldstein, *Political Repression*, 86–87; on this and other confrontations in Washington and Oregon, see Robert L. Tyler, *Rebels of the Woods: The I.W.W. in the Pacific Northwest* (Eugene: University of Oregon Press, 1967).

164. Goldstein, *Political Repression*, 87.

165. Ibid.; Ronald Radosh, *American Labor and Foreign Policy* (New York: Vintage, 1970), 17.

166. Goldstein, *Political Repression*, 88.

167. Lens, *Labor Wars*, 203.

168. Goldstein, *Political Repression*, 88–89; Renshaw, *Wobblies*, 139–40.

169. Goldstein, *Political Repression*, 89.

170. Ibid.; U.S. House of Representatives, *Report on the Strike of Textile Workers in Lawrence, Mass.* (Washington, D.C.: 62d Cong., 2d Sess., 1913), 19.

171. Goldstein, *Political Repression*, 89.

172. Ibid.

173. Renshaw, *Wobblies*, 140–41.

174. Morris Schonbach, *Radicals and Visionaries: A History of Dissent in New Jersey* (Princeton, N.J.: Von Nostram, 1964), 62–65; Joyce L. Kornbluh, *Rebel Voices: An I.W.W. Anthology* (Ann Arbor: University of Michigan Press, 1972), 197–226.

175. Quoted in Philip S. Foner, *The History of the Labor Movement in the United States* (New York: International, 1965), 4:370–71.

176. Goldstein, *Political Repression*, 90; Foner, *History of the Labor Movement*, 4:373–90.

177. Goldstein, *Political Repression*, 90; Foner, *History of the Labor Movement*, 4:224–25.

178. Goldstein, *Political Repression*, 95; Philip Taft and Philip Ross, "American Labor Violence: Its Causes, Character and Outcome," in Hugh D. Graham and Ted R. Gurr, eds., *Violence in America* (New York: Bantam Books, 1969), 326–27.

179. Goldstein, *Political Repression*, 95; Richard H. Frost, *The Mooney Case* (Stanford, Calif.: Stanford University Press, 1968), 56–61.

180. Goldstein, *Political Repression*, 95; Taft and Ross, "American Labor Violence," 326–27; Kornbluh, *Rebel Voices*, 292.

181. Goldstein, *Political Repression*, 96; Dubofsky, *We Shall Be All*, 321–22; Neil Betten, "Riot, Revolution and Repression in the Iron Range Strike of 1916," *Minnesota History*, No. 41 (Summer 1968).

182. Goldstein, *Political Repression*, 97; Norman H. Clark, "Everett 1916, and After," *Pacific Northwest Quarterly*, No. 57 (April 1966).

183. Goldstein, *Political Repression*, 97–98; Kornbluh, *Rebel Voices*, 98; Dubofsky, *We Shall Be All*, 337–42.

184. Kornbluh, *Rebel Voices*, 306.

185. John Steuben, *The Truth About Butte* (1940, attributed to Mike Byrnes; reprint, Butte, Mont.: Old Butte, 2003).

186. Correspondence from independent researcher Bobby Greene, May 13, 1986.

187. Renshaw, *Wobblies*, 208.

188. See note 10.

189. Goldstein, *Political Repression*, 155–56; Robert L. Tyler, "Violence at Centralia," *Pacific Northwest Quarterly*, No. 45 (October 1954).

190. Jules Archer, *Bullets, Strikes and Bombs: Big Bill Haywood and the IWW* (New York: Julian Messner, 1972), 169. On the *Freikorps*, see Robert G. L. Waite, *Vanguard of Nazism: The Free Corps Movement in Postwar Germany, 1918–1923* (Cambridge, Mass.: Harvard University Press, 1952).

191. Goldstein, *Political Repression*, 601; Dubofsky, *We Shall Be All*, 455–56.

192. Horan, *Pinkertons*, 502, 507.

193. Ibid., 507.

194. Morn, *Eye*, 184.

195. Ibid., 166.

196. See F. B. McQuiston, "The Strike Breakers," *Independent*, No. 53 (October 17, 1901); John H. Craige, "The Professional Strike-Breaker," *Colliers Weekly*, No. 46 (December 3, 1910).

197. Morn, *Eye*, 166; Leroy Scott, "Strikebreaking as a New Occupation," *World's Work*, No. 10 (May 1905); William Brown Melony, "Strikebreaking as a Profession," *Public Opinion*, No. 38 (March 25, 1905); Edward Levinson, *I Break Strikes! The Technique of Pearl L. Bergoff* (New York: Robert McBride, 1935); Auerbach, *Labor and Liberty*, 97–107.

198. Quoted in Horan, *Pinkertons*, 509.

199. Quoted in ibid.

200. Quoted in ibid.

201. Ibid., 510.

202. On the Wagner Act and its implications, see Broadus Mitchell, *Depression Decade: From New Era through New Deal* (New York: Harper and Row, 1969), 277–83; Foster Rhea Dulles, *Labor in America* (New York: Crowell, 1966), 264–76.

203. See Caute, *Great Fear*. Also see Walter Goodman, *The Committee: The Extraordinary Career of the House Committee on Un-American Activities* (New York: Farrar, Straus and Giroux, 1968).

204. Horan, *Pinkertons*, 511.

205. Brian S. Boyd, "The Founding of the I.A.C.P., 1893," *Police Chief*, No. 38 (May 1971). They were nominated by Milwaukee police chief J. T. Janssen, a one-time Pinkerton and private policeman for the Chicago, Milwaukee & St Paul Railroad. Actually, such consulting, sometimes pro bono, probably began much earlier. In 1871, for example, Allan Pinkerton delivered a paper entitled "The Character and Duties of a Detective Police Force" to a national police convention organized by St. Louis police chief James MacDonough. Morn, *Eye*, 123.

206. Morn, *Eye*, 124.

207. On Pinkerton's role in originating the publication, see *Detective*, No. 20 (January 1905): 2.

208. John L. Thompson, "National Identification Bureau's I.C.A.P. Pioneer's Legacy," *Police Chief* (January 1968): 15, 17.

209. Berthold Laufer, "History of the Finger-Print System," *Annual Report of the Smithsonian Institution, 1912* (Washington, D.C.: Smithsonian Institution, 1912); Jürgen Thorwald, *The Century of the Detective* (New York: Harcourt, Brace and World, 1965), 94, 98, 100–101.

210. Samples of Pinkerton's NACP lectures include "The Yeggman" (1904), "Forgery" (1905), "The Professional Sneak Thief" (1906), and "The Porch Climbers" (1907). Morn, *Eye*, 127.

211. Morn, *Eye*, 151; Friedman, *Pinkerton Labor Spy*, 4.

212. Morn, *Eye*, 165–66; on Linden, see George Barton, *The True Stories of Celebrated Crimes: Adventures of the World's Greatest Detectives* (New York: McKinlay Stone and Mackenzie, 1909), 159; on George S. Dougherty, see his *The Criminal as Human Being* (New York: D. Appleton, 1924), 3, 8–9, 14–15; on the offer to Pinkerton, see the *New York Times*, December 14, 1913.

213. Tom Duggan, *The History of the Jewelers Security Alliance of the United States, 1883–1950* (New York: Alliance, 1958), 5, 20–22, 35; W. Espey Albig, "The Origin of the American Bankers' Association," *Banking*, No. 35 (September 1942).

214. Horan, *Pinkertons*, 512–13.

215. Ibid., 513–14.

216. Ibid., 514.

217. Jim Hougan, *Spooks: The Haunting of America—The Private Use of Secret Agents* (New York: William Morrow, 1978), 17n.

218. See, e.g., A. J. Langguth, *Hidden Terrors: The Truth About U.S. Police Operations in Latin America* (New York: Pantheon, 1978).

219. Horan, *Pinkertons*, 514; Hougan, *Spooks*, 71.

220. William W. Turner, *Hoover's F.B.I.*, 2nd ed. (New York: Thunder's Mouth Press, 1993), 305–6. Among many other things, the corporation was hired by Florida governor

Claude Kirk to serve as a "private gestapo" in that state. It also publishes the *Wackenhut Security Review*, which purports to expose "the threat of communism" in areas as diverse as civil rights and environmental protection legislation, opposition to Latin American oligarchies, and domestic educational reform.

221. Ibid., 207. A hint of the agency's operational emphasis is offered in the fact that one of its detectives, former FBI agent Vincent W. Gillen, admitted to a congressional committee in 1966 that he had been retained by General Motors to spy on consumer advocate Ralph Nader.

222. Ibid. Simpson & Associates performs "specialized security and detection work" for several major oil companies known to underwrite extreme right-wing causes.

223. Curt Gentry, *J. Edgar Hoover: The Man and His Secrets* (New York: W. W. Norton, 1992), 706.

224. See the series of articles on the Van Deman files written by Richard Halloran and published in the *New York Times* in September 1971.

225. Gentry, *Hoover*, 706–7.

226. See note 224.

227. Val R. Lorwin, "Reflections on the History of the French and American Labor Movements," *Journal of Economic History*, No. 17 (March 1957): 37.

228. Quoted in Arthur M. Ross and Paul T. Hartman, *Changing Patterns of Industrial Conflict* (New York: John Wiley, 1960), 165.

229. Lewis Lorwin, *The American Federation of Labor* (Washington, D.C.: Brookings Institution, 1933), 355.

230. Richard Hofstadter and Michael Wallace, "Perspectives," in Richard Hofstadter and Michael Wallace, eds., *American Violence: A Documentary History* (New York: Vintage, 1971), 19.

231. Goldstein, *Political Repression*, 5.

232. From the point in 1892 when Congress banned employment of Pinkerton operatives by the government until its own Bureau of investigation was formed, the Justice Department's "investigative services were usually performed by federal bank examiners and agents discretely borrowed from the Customs Bureau, the Interior Department, and the Treasury Department's Secret Service." Sanford J. Ungar, *FBI: An Uncensored Look Behind the Walls* (Boston: Atlantic–Little, Brown, 1976), 39.

233. Ibid., 55.

234. Horan, *Pinkertons*, 515.

235. Ungar, *FBI*, 55.

236. Ronald Kessler, *The FBI* (New York: Pocket Books, 1993), 216; on the NCIC specifically, see Turner, *Hoover's F.B.I.*, 315.

237. Thompson, "National Identification Bureau," 16–17; Kessler, *FBI*, 216–17.

238. Turner, *Hoover's F.B.I.*, xii, xiii.

239. Ibid., 304.

240. Ibid., 222; Ungar, *FBI*, 578–80.

241. Turner, *Hoover's F.B.I.*, 220, 222.

242. Ibid., 210.

243. For a range of views on these relationships, see Ovid DeMaris, *The Director: An Oral Biography of J. Edgar Hoover* (New York: Harpers, 1975).

244. See Ungar, *FBI*, 20–22, 31–34, 428–34, 437–41.

245. Ibid., 329–30.

246. Quoted in Turner, *Hoover's F.B.I.*, 220.

247. Gentry, *Hoover*, 81.

248. Turner, *Hoover's F.B.I.*, 306.

249. Richard Wallace Held is the son of COINTELPRO architect Richard G. Held. Among other things, the father, while serving simultaneously as head of the FBI's Internal Security Section and as special agent in charge of the Chicago field office, presided over the cover-up of the Bureau's role in the 1969 Hampton-Clark assassinations (see note 271), before being appointed FBI assistant director. The younger Held got his start working on the "Panther Squad" of the Los Angeles field office, where he was instrumental in concocting a "shooting war" between the Panthers and the US organization (see note 270), as well as framing Los Angeles Panther leader Geronimo ji Jaga (see note 281). After a stint on the Pine Ridge Reservation working under his father's command against AIM (see note 277), he was assigned to head up the San Juan field office, where he coordinated repression of the Puerto Rican independence movement. Posted next to San Francisco, he retired shortly after it was revealed that agents working under his supervision had been involved in the attempted assassination of Earth First! activists Judi Bari and Darryl Cherney on May 24, 1990. For further details, see my "COINTELPRO as a Family Business: The Strange Case of the FBI's Two Richard Helds," *Z Magazine*, March 1989; "The FBI Targets Judi Bari: A Case Study in Domestic Counterinsurgency," *Covert Action Quarterly*, No. 47 (Winter 1993–94).

250. On Hoover's personal relationships, see Richard Gid Powers, *Secrecy and Power: The Life of J. Edgar Hoover* (New York: Free Press, 1987): 315, 440 [Nixon]; 315 [Murchison and Richardson]; 320 [McCarthy]; 393–94 [Johnson].

251. As Ungar puts it in *FBI* (383), the CRD functions as not merely "a typical public relations office but rather [as] a part of the bureaucracy responsible for calculating and acting aggressively upon the Bureau's best interest at any given moment." Concerning Pinkerton's impact on the genre, see Frank Smyth and Miles Ludwig, *The Detectives: Crime and Detection in Fact and Fiction* (Philadelphia: Lippincott, 1978); also see Thorwald, *Century of the Detective*.

252. Richard Gid Powers, *G-Men: Hoover's FBI in Popular Culture* (Carbondale: Southern Illinois University Press, 1983), 91–92.

253. See Herbert Asbury, *The Gangs of New York: An Informal History of the Underworld* (New York: Alfred A. Knopf, 1927); there is not so much as an index reference to the Pinkertons.

254. On the FBI's PR effort attending its 1930s "War on Crime," see Gid Powers, *G-Men*, 33–50. For good surveys of the reality involved, see John Toland, *The Dillinger Days* (New York: Random House, 1967); Steven J. Nickel and William J. Helmer, *Baby Face Nelson: Portrait of a Public Enemy* (Nashville, Tn.: Cumberland House, 2002); Michael Wallis, *Pretty Boy: The Life and Times of Charles Arthur Floyd* (New York: St. Martin's Press, 1992); Alvin Karpis with Bill Trent, *The Alvin Karpis Story* (New York: Coward, McCann and Geoghegan, 1971).

255. Quoted in Ungar, *FBI*, 392.

256. Contrary to FBI-fostered mythology, the Bureau had nothing to do with the imprisonment of Chicago mob kingpin Al Capone in 1932. That, instead, was the work of a team of IRS auditors. See John Kobler, *Capone: The Life and World of Al Capone* (New York: G. P. Putnam's Sons, 1971), 323–54; also see Robert J. Schoenberg, *Mr. Capone: The Real—and Complete—Story of Al Capone* (New York: William Morrow, 1992), 287–325. More broadly, there are a number of good histories of organized crime in America, several of them written well before the FBI formally acknowledged the existence of such an enterprise. See, e.g., Fred A. Pasley, *Al Capone: Biography of a Self-Made Man* (Garden City, N.Y.: Garden City, 1930); Burton B. Turkus and Sid Feder, *Murder, Inc.: The Story of the Syndicate* (1951; reprint, New York: De Capo Press, 1992); Ed Reid, *Mafia: The History of the Ruthless Gang That Runs the Nationwide Crime Syndicate* (New York: Random House, 1952); Frederick Sondern Jr., *Brotherhood of Evil: The Mafia* (New York: Farrar, Strauss and Cudahy, 1959). For a reasonably accurate recent effort, see William Balsamo and George Carpozi Jr., *Crime Incorporated: The Inside Story of the Mafia's First Hundred Years* (Far Hills, N.J.: New Horizon Press, 1991).

257. See, e.g., Charles Larrowe, *Harry Bridges: The Rise and Fall of Radical Labor* (Westport, Conn.: Lawrence Hill, 1972).

258. This is a standard ploy; see Jacques Ellul, *Propaganda: The Formation of Men's Attitudes* (New York: Alfred A. Knopf, 1965). Also see Chomsky, *Necessary Illusions*; Edward S. Herman and Noam Chomsky, *Manufacturing Consent: The Political Economy of the Mass Media* (New York: Pantheon, 1988).

259. J. Edgar Hoover, *Masters of Deceit* (New York: Holt, 1958); J. Edgar Hoover, *A Study of Communism* (New York: Holt, 1962); Pinkerton, *Molly Maguires and the Detectives*; Pinkerton, *Strikers, Communists, Tramps and the Detectives*; Robert A. Pinkerton,

"Detective Surveillance of Anarchists," *North American Review*, No. 173 (November 1901). Also see J. Edgar Hoover, *J. Edgar Hoover on Communism* (New York: Random House, 1967).

260. Gid Powers, *Secrecy and Power*, 91.

261. Jack Nelson and Ronald J. Ostrow, *The FBI and the Berrigans: The Making of a Conspiracy* (New York: Coward, McCann and Geoghegan, 1972).

262. Aside from the American Legion, the classic example is that of the American Protective League (APL), a quarter-million-member vigilante group founded in 1916 by Chicago advertising executive A. M. Briggs and financed by a range of corporations. In 1917, the APL was endorsed as a "patriotic organization" by U.S. Attorney General Thomas W. Gregory and A. Bruce Bielaski, director of the department's budding investigative bureau (then known as the BoI). Thereafter, every APL thug was provided with a police-style badge bearing the inscription, "American Protective League, Auxiliary to the U.S. Department of Justice." Ungar, *FBI*, 42. Thus "deputized," APL goon squads were employed by the BoI to execute a range of tasks, not least the conducting of raids on IWW headquarters in twenty-four cities on September 17, 1917—at that point the most spectacular single antiradical action in U.S. history—seizing the union's books, minutes, financial records, correspondence, and membership lists in preparation for the mass trials discussed in note 10. Gentry, *Hoover*, 71.

263. Everett R. Holles, "A.C.L.U. Says F.B.I. Funded 'Army' to Terrorize Antiwar Protestors," *New York Times*, June 27, 1975; Nanda Zoccino, "Ex-FBI Informer Describes Terrorist Role," *Los Angeles Times*, January 26, 1976.

264. See my and Jim Vander Wall's *Agents of Repression: The FBI's Secret Wars Against the Black Panther Party and the American Indian Movement*, Classics ed. (Cambridge, Mass.: South End Press, 2002), 182. Also see Michael Parenti, *Democracy for the Few* (New York: St. Martin's Press, 1980), 24.

265. For details, see Citizens Research and Investigation Committee and Louis E. Tackwood, *The Glass House Tapes: The Story of an Agent Provocateur and the New Police-Intelligence Complex* (New York: Avon Books, 1981).

266. Goldstein, *Political Repression*, 474–75. Also see Frank J. Donner, "Hoover's Legacy," *Nation*, June 1, 1974.

267. Paul Chevigny, *Cops and Rebels* (New York: Pantheon, 1972), 251–52.

268. *Seattle Times*, December 7, 1970; *New York Times*, December 8, 1970.

269. Goldstein, *Political Repression*, 473; Chevigny, *Cops and Rebels*, 258–59.

270. Churchill and Vander Wall, *COINTELPRO Papers*, 133–35. Also see Kenneth O'Reilly, *"Racial Matters": The FBI's Secret File on Black America, 1960–1972* (New York: Free Press, 1989), 305–9.

271. See Roy Wilkins and Ramsey Clark, *Search and Destroy: A Report by the Commission of Inquiry into the Black Panthers and the Police* (New York: Metropolitan Applied Research Center, 1973). Also see Churchill and Vander Wall, *Agents of Repression*, 64–77.

272. Although by the early 1930s the entry requirement for FBI hopefuls was ostensibly a "degree in law, accounting or some comparable field," Hoover recruited and maintained a "Special Squad" of hired guns whose only qualification for agent status was the demonstrated willingness to "exterminate" those named "public enemies" by the director. Headed by Melvin Purvis, this hit team—no other description is really adequate—included ex-Texas Ranger Gus T. Jones, as well as former policemen like John Keith, Charles Winstead, C. G. Campbell, and Clarence Hurt. Gentry, *Hoover*, 169. For details on two of the Special Squad's more sensational summary executions, see Toland, *Dillinger Days*, 320–25; Wallis, *Pretty Boy*, 340–45. As concerns Charley Arthur "Pretty Boy" Floyd, moreover, it is a virtual certainty that he had no involvement at all in the crime used as a pretext in Hoover's declaring him Public Enemy Number 1; see Robert Unger, *The Union Station Massacre: The Original Sin of J. Edgar Hoover's FBI* (Kansas City, Mo.: Andrews McMeel, 1997).

273. Louis E. Tackwood, "My Assignment Was to Kill George Jackson," *Black Panther*, April 21, 1980. On Tackwood's polygraph examination, see Jo Durden-Smith, *Who Killed George Jackson? Fantasies, Paranoia and the Revolution* (New York: Alfred A. Knopf, 1976), 131–32. In this case, the plot failed. Jackson was therefore murdered by San Quentin guards on August 21, 1971. For further context, see Gregory Armstrong, *The Dragon Has Come: The Last Fourteen Months in the Life of George Jackson* (New York: Harper and Row, 1974).

274. On the IWW trials, see note 10. On the Chicago Eight, see Jason Epstein, *The Great Conspiracy Trial: An Essay on Law, Liberty and the Constitution* (New York: Random House, 1970).

275. Goldstein, *Political Repression*, 492; Bernard Weiner, "What, Another Conspiracy Trial?" *Nation*, November 2, 1970; Bernard Weiner, "The Orderly Perversion of Justice," *Nation*, February 1, 1971.

276. Goldstein, *Political Repression*, 492.

277. On the trials, see John William Sayer, *Ghost Dancing the Law: The Wounded Knee Trials* (Cambridge, Mass.: Harvard University Press, 1997). On AIM more generally, see Paul Chaat Smith and Robert Allen Warrior, *Like a Hurricane: The American Indian Movement from Alcatraz to Wounded Knee* (New York: New Press, 1996).

278. That such was the result desired by the federal officials involved was made clear at the outset by Colonel Volney S. Warner, a military adviser to the FBI personnel deployed on Pine Ridge, when he publicly observed that "AIM's most militant leaders are under

indictment, in jail or warrants are out for their arrest. [So] the government can win, even if no one goes to [prison]"; quoted in Martin Garbus, "General Haig of Wounded Knee," *Nation*, November 9, 1974.

279. Winston A. Grady-Willis, "The Black Panther Party: State Repression and Political Prisoners," in Charles E. Jones, ed., *The Black Panther Party Reconsidered* (Baltimore: Black Classic Press, 1998), 380–82.

280. On the mechanics of ji Jaga's framing, see Churchill and Vander Wall, *Agents of Repression*, 77–94. On his release, and for information on the man himself, see Jack Olsen, *Last Man Standing: The Triumph and Tragedy of Geronimo Pratt* (New York: Doubleday, 2000).

281. For the most detailed analysis of the case itself, see Jim Messerschmidt, *The Trial of Leonard Peltier* (Boston: South End Press, 1984). For the best contextualization, see Peter Matthiessen, *In the Spirit of Crazy Horse: The Story of Leonard Peltier*, 2nd ed. (New York: Viking Press, 1991).

282. Readers desiring additional illustrations of the Bureau's fabrication of evidence to obtain convictions will find more than enough material in John F. Kelly and Phillip K. Wearne, *Tainting Evidence: Inside the Scandals at the FBI Crime Lab* (New York: Free Press, 1998). Those seeking amplification on the theme of FBI lethality will find plenty in David T. Hardy and Rex Kimball, *This Is Not an Assault: Penetrating the Web of Official Lies Regarding the Waco Incident* (San Antonio, Tex.: Xlibris, 2001).

3

Between Hegemony and Empire: Africa and the U.S. Global War against Terrorism

Darryl C. Thomas

In recent years there has been a proliferation of studies revolving around globalization, benevolent imperialism, empire, and U.S. hegemony. First, there is the ongoing debate over whether Pax Americana during the current wave of globalization constitutes hegemony or empire. Most of these studies compare and contrast the British and American experience with empire.[1] Patrick Karl O'Brien and Armand Clesse, for example, expend most of their efforts in trying to clarify the relationship between empire, imperialism old and new, and globalization. These studies are concerned with the uniqueness of Pax Americana in comparison with the trajectory of the British efforts at constructing an empire. The British were not reluctant empire builders once they embarked on this enterprise and did not register any reluctance until the Anglo-Boer War of 1904, when the cost of imperialism began to climb. Similarly, the Soviet Union also was not hesitant to expand its Eurasian empire until its military fiasco and devastation in Afghanistan in the 1980s. In the black Atlantic world, the Haitian revolutionaries' defeat of the Napoleon and other Western armies resulted in French imperial retreat from much of this vast zone in the world system.

Naill Ferguson seeks to glean lessons from the British imperial legacy for future Great Powers contemplating empires, including the United States.

Ferguson's work traverses an expansive arena, including the rise of consumerism, the largest mass migration in history—20 million emigrants between the early 1600s to the 1950s—the impact of missionaries, the triumph of capitalism, the spread of the English language, and globalization. Ferguson revisits the enduring unwillingness of Americans to make sacrifices in the name of empire. He also notes that the British acknowledge their imperial project as an effort to construct an empire, while Americans, except for a small cadre of intellectuals and policy makers, cast their "grand majestic" projects under the umbrella of bringing democracy, civilization, and freedom.[2] Nevertheless, both of these projects fail to address the human cost in terms of number of lost lives in indigenous populations, particularly with reference to the Opium War in China and the lack of liberty during the British colonial rule of India—examples of contradictions to Britain's civilizing mission.

Others have drawn attention to the providential destiny, realities, and consequences of America's power as well as its imperial projects toward the rest of the world. These scholars are concerned with the continuity and discontinuity in U.S. foreign policy as well as the similarities and differences between U.S. and British hegemony or empire.[3] Robert Kagan's work draws attention to the tensions and growing adversarial relations that are developing between American and European leaders over the conduct of world affairs in the age of globalization and a lone superpower.[4]

There are a growing number of studies that question whether the United States can sustain its global hegemony indefinitely.[5] Charles Kupchan offers a critical resistance to the notion that the United States can continue its dominance of the international system for an indefinite period into the future. Similarly, Joseph S. Nye advises American policy makers to support multilateral approaches to world order in this era of one superpower (at least in the military arena) and avoid the temptations of unilateralism for sustaining America's hegemony in the age of globalization. While most of these studies emphasize the expansion of American power in terms of military capability reinforced by economic and financial preponderance during this era of globalization, Immanuel Wallerstein and Giovanni Arrighi, along with Giovanni Arrighi, Beverly Silver, and Iftikhar Ahmad, may be the exceptions, arguing that American power may be waning since the end of the Cold War and that the contemporary wars in Afghanistan and Iraq after September 11, 2001, will probably accelerate the deterioration of American power. The studies by Wallerstein and Arrighi provide a lucid analysis on how this hegemonic decline is tied to the American model of capital accumulation.[6] They employ the world system analysis as a methodology for understanding the interrelationship and linkages between American capitalism, hegemony, and empire. Arrighi, Silver, and Ahmad[7] introduce the notion of chaos and crisis that accompany the crisis of accumulation that eventually leads to world leadership crisis and decline and the emergence of a new hegemony. David Harvey locates the driving force behind contemporary economic globalization in the structure of capitalism. For Harvey, globalization is the latest phase of capitalist accumulation and a new form of postcolonial imperialism aided by the exercise of imperial power. He defines the exploitative tendencies of this new form of imperialism through the dual processes of accumulation by dispossession or accumulation by appropriation. For Harvey, it is the accumulation by dispossession or appropriation that is generating resistance and contestation to globalization.[8] The burst of the U.S. housing bubble in 2008 and the fall of several Wall Street denizens, from Merrill Lynch and Citigroup to Bear Stearns, may reinforce the analysis of the United States as a declining hegemon. Most of these accounts fail to adequately address the violence that accompanies these systemic changes. Martin Luther King Jr. captured the racial dimension of American and the Western attitudes toward the non-Western world and how race has been critical in understanding these relations. King observed: "Men of the white West have grown up in a racist culture, and their thinking is colored by that fact. . . . They don't respect anyone who is not white."[9]

The focal point of this chapter is an analysis of the role of African states in the U.S. war against terrorism and the extent that the American and African military partnership exacerbates human rights violations on the African continent and continues the marginalization of people of African descent. In order to elucidate these relationships, it is important to examine how the American empire emerged and to what extent the intensification in the use of military power signals a return to imperialism and empire under the guise of the war against terrorism. How does this new American and African military partnership in the war against terrorism also reduce the sovereignty of African states? The U.S. war against Saddam Hussein and Iraq and the U.S. occupation that followed represent the attempt to dispossess the Iraqis and later Iran and others of their oil and petroleum resources, and also represent the return to empire. The new bellicose attitude toward preemptive nuclear strikes and nuclear utilization theories targeted toward the so-called axis of evil—that is, Iraq, Iran, and North Korea—enumerating regime change and democracy through the barrel of a gun, marks a stark transition toward empire. Historically, racism and ethnocentrism have remained key components of American foreign policy. The spread of democracy in the nineteenth century was integrally linked to racism. During this era, racism penetrated U.S. policy-making processes in both the domestic and international arena side by side with the development of science. Hence, such concepts as manifest destiny, the "white man's burden," eugenics, and racial hierarchy are essential to the development of the "national interest" of the elites that controlled and managed U.S. foreign policy.[10]

SITTING ON TOP OF THE WORLD

The traditional American belief in possessive individualism, manifest destiny, anti-Communism and, more recently, antiterrorism became the driving force behind the emergence of not only the Pax Americana but also additional strategies aimed at revitalizing and sustaining American hegemony and structural dominance of the world economy through economic globalization since the end of the Cold War era. This way of thinking, which accompanied the American rise to globalism, has had two ramifications for the global community. It has helped to provide a cultural context for the postwar era in the West, and its mainly liberal economic principles serve as organizing concepts for the debates between, and practices of, important decision makers from a range of countries. Thus, elements of legitimization and ideology interact at a deeper epistemological level to create a global synergy of ideas beneficial to the outward extension or maintenance of American power. American policy makers have been successful in building a broad-base consensus of beliefs, values, and ideology to support America's position as a hegemon. Consequently, most of the strategies, agendas, questions, and prescriptions to combat antisystemic alliance systems and states, ranging from the Russians and the Warsaw Pact nations to would-be rogue state and terror networks from North Korea, Syria, Iran, Iraq, and Al-Qaeda, have been American-centered since the end of the Second World War. The global economy still operates primarily from a neoliberal (American) framework. At the same time, the discourses around U.S. hegemony have also become code words that obscure American imperialism and its informal empire.

The Road to the U.S. Informal Empire

Sidney Lens has noted that the terms "colony" and "protectorate" have never been part of American official discourse, for the understandable reason that they clash with the tradition of anticolonialism.[11] The roots of American empire can be traced back to the early nineteenth century, when the United States declared all of Latin America its sphere of influence and busily enlarged its territory at the expense of the indigenous people in North America, as well as at the expense of French, British, and Spanish colonialists and neighboring Mexico. In a similar vein to their contemporaries in Australia, Algeria, and tsarist Russia, Americans devoted much energy to displacing the indigenous populations and dispossessing them of their land and transforming ownership to the new settlers.[12]

Since the end of the Cold War, the United States has been the lone superpower and arguably has the greatest ability to shape the future of world politics. America enjoys a preponderance of overwhelming power through military, economic, technological, and cultural means. America's military has unquestioned superiority with regard to all potential adversaries. The power and influence of the dollar, along with the size of the U.S. economy, provide Washington with enormous influence in the trade and financial arenas. Economic globalization has provided American transnational corporations the means to penetrate virtually every market. The information technologies that were was developed and spawned in Silicon Valley, along with the other high-tech centers, provide U.S. firms, media, and culture with unprecedented global reach. Whether they like it or not, in every corner of the world, governments and ordinary people are affected by decisions emanating from Washington.[13]

Between 1901 and 1917, the United States began its new phase of empire building or developing its informal empire by transforming the small countries in the Caribbean and Central America into protectorates, compromising their sovereignty in the interest of Washington. The Platt Amendment, giving Washington the unilateral right to occupy Cuba at will, and the leases granted the United States in perpetuity in Panama, as well as the guarantee of maintaining independence, reduced both to protectorates without mentioning the word. In a short period of time, the United States, through treaties and threats of intervention, converted the whole region into an American lake, no more independent than Long Island or the state of New York.

Once the purely strategic linchpins of the new U.S. empire—Guantanamo Bay, Cuba, Puerto Rico, and the Panama Canal—were in place, successive American governments were motivated to maintain U.S. hegemony in the region, as well as promote political, economic, and social stability within the empire's sphere of influence. With the ascendancy of the U.S. Navy to second place, in a three-way tie with Germany and France, who together with the United Kingdom, the world's naval leader, held substantial economic interests in the region, the Monroe Doctrine ceased to be an international joke. "The Monroe Doctrine," proclaimed Theodore Roosevelt, "is as strong as the United States Navy, and no stronger." [14]

At this juncture, European colonization in the hemisphere was no longer an issue; however, European military intervention, to safeguard investments and nationals, was. The Caribbean and Central American states—notably Haiti, the Dominican Republic, Honduras, and, starting in 1909, Nicaragua—were riddled with endemic internal conflicts. By the time Theodore Roosevelt assumed the presidency of the United States, the presence of expeditionary European naval forces in America's front yard could no longer be tolerated.

To strengthen America's newfound role as Western hemispheric policeman, Roosevelt devised his controversial corollary to the Monroe Doctrine, whereby the United States could militarily and unilaterally intervene in any regional state where the political, economic, or social conditions invited European protective response in force. It was Woodrow Wilson's invocation of the corollary that provided for the intervention and nineteen-year occupation of Haiti by the Marine Corps and the establishment of an ill-conceived American military government under the navy and the Marine Corps in the Dominican Republic (1916–1924). [15] A political stalemate between the Dominican Republic president, parliament, and the military precipitated the crisis and the United States military intervention and occupation.

In the course of resolving the crisis in San Domingo (the Dominican Republic), the Monroe Doctrine was modified by adding what became known as the Roosevelt Corollary. The Monroe Doctrine was designed to deter European intervention into the Americas; the corollary undermined the sovereignty of the nations throughout this zone of the world system. It reaffirmed that the United States would not tolerate direct European intervention in the Americas, but, since intervention was sometimes necessary, added a new feature that accorded only the United States the right to intervene in the internal affairs of other countries. It was in the wake of the Dominican Crisis that Theodore Roosevelt, in his inaugural message to Congress delivered on December 6, 1904, restated the corollary already enunciated in May 1904, but in more unambiguous language: "Chronic wrongdoing, or an impotence which results in a loosening of the ties of civilized society, may in America as elsewhere, ultimately require intervention by some civilized nation, and in the Western Hemisphere, the adherence to the Monroe Doctrine may force the United States, however reluctantly, in flagrant cases of such wrongdoing or impotence, to the exercise of an international police power." [16]

The enunciation and implementation of the Roosevelt Corollary by the United States went beyond the Monroe Doctrine, which was largely defensive in nature, and the United States began to assume the responsibility of bringing political and financial order to the hemisphere through unilateral action. The United States emerged as the major architect of "global apartheid" in the Americas through the enunciation and implementation of this doctrine. The notion that the United States had the right to wield power against "uncivilized" or "impotent" people had been of course articulated throughout the nineteenth century with respect to Native Americans, Spaniards, and Mexicans. This ultimatum clearly defined, for Europe and Latin America, U.S. hegemony in this important zone of the world system. It was an assertion that the United States was both a patron and a policeman. These words were reinforced with a show of force via naval power off the coast of the Dominican Republic, and in 1905 American officials stepped in to take charge of this island nation's custom collections in order to guarantee the repayment of debts to American and European banks.[17]

The Roosevelt Corollary provided the United States with a justification for intervention into its neighbors' domestic affairs. The United States intervened in Mexico in 1848 and 1916 and Columbia in 1903, ending with the creation of the Panama Canal. Panama was dealt with in 1915, 1918, 1921, 1963, and in 1989; Nicaragua on a number of occasions, including 1909–10, 1912–25, 1926–33, and, more recently, through counterinsurgency efforts of the Contras in the 1980s; Haiti in 1915; the Dominican Republic in 1912, 1916–24, and 1960; and Cuba in 1898–1902, 1906–9, 1912, 1917–33, and in the Bay of Pigs fiasco in 1961, when the United States suffered a defeat. The Arbenz government in Guatemala was overthrown in 1954, and through covert means the Allende government in Chile was overthrown in September 11, 1973. American intervention into Grenada in 1982 and Panama in 1989 has led to major changes in both societies.

After the Second World War, the United States emerged as the richest and most powerful nation on earth and the self-designated successor to the British Empire. Most American leaders were very enthusiastic about embracing the global leadership mantle, while most U.S. citizens were less reticent and demanded that the country demobilize its military and turn to the task of full employment and domestic development. The fragile peace did not last long, as the Cold War began and the growing conviction that the United States' vital interests and even national survival demanded the containment of the Soviet Union. Before long, the U.S. informal empire turned into hundreds of military installations around the world, as well as the largest military ever maintained in peacetime.[18]

During the military and diplomatic impasse that lasted for the fifty years that constituted the Cold War, American policy makers denied that many of their activities were a variation on the imperialism theme. They cloaked their policies and actions as merely reactions to the menace of the "evil empire" of the Soviet Union and its satellites. It took the Vietnam War and the Watergate scandal to uncover the "imperial presidency" and the power and influence of the military-industrial complex, where both the Central Intelligence Agency (CIA) and the Pentagon wielded unchecked power.

The Soviet Union collapse in 1991 initially caught American leaders, policy makers, and ordinary citizens by surprise. With the end of the Cold War came the loss of the rationale for the continuation of U.S. containment policies, as well as for U.S. military installations around the world. Chalmers Johnson observed that many Americans simply concluded that they had "won" the Cold War and so deserved the imperial fruits of victory. Several ideologues began to argue that the United States was indeed a "good empire" and should act accordingly in a world with one superpower. To demobilize the military and turn these resources to peaceful uses would mark a return to isolationism.[19]

The Pentagon announced in the early 1990s that it would brook no challenge to American supremacy, pledging to "prevent the emergence of a new rival."[20] Although the Cold War was over, the United States would remain the global policeman. During the post–Cold War era, the United States mounted many actions to perpetuate and extend its global power, including wars and "humanitarian" interventions in Panama, the Persian Gulf, Somalia, Haiti, Bosnia, Columbia, and Serbia, while maintaining its Cold War–related deployments in East Asia and the Pacific. Increasingly, American people developed the perception that America had an informal empire, even though it had no formal colonies. Its massive military forces were deployed around the world to either maintain stability, guarantee mutual security, or promote a liberal order, free elections, and open markets.[21]

9/11 Terrorist Attacks on the United States and Back to Empire

For many Americans, the world changed after the terrorist attacks on the World Trade Center and the Pentagon. The Hart-Rudman Commission had warned in a report released in 1999, "America will become increasingly vulnerable to hostile attack on our homeland, and our military superiority will not entirely protect us."[22] The report went on to predict that during the early twenty-first century, Americans would likely die on U.S. soil, possibly in large numbers. Nevertheless, despite similar reports and warnings from other agencies, American leaders failed to enact policies that would improve coordination among a dozen agencies responsible for domestic security. Likewise, they failed to shut down terrorist networks working abroad.

The 9/11 attacks produced a profound change in thinking of some American leaders, who began to envision the United States as a genuine empire, the new Rome, the greatest colossal in history, no longer bound by international law, the concerns of allies, or any constraints from deploying military force. The George W. Bush administration declared war on terrorism, Al-Qaeda networks in Afghanistan and worldwide, Iraq for its alleged weapons of mass destruction, and the remaining states associated with the "axis of evil" for their pursuit of nuclear weaponry. The Bush foreign policy team also enunciated a new doctrine of preemptive war against new global enemies, sanitizing human rights violations through such euphemisms as "collateral damages," "regime change," "illegal combatants," and "preventive wars"—as if these explain away the growing gross violations of human rights and civilian deaths that emanated from the war on terrorism.

In June 2003, President Bush made a trip to Baghdad as part of a seven-day, six-nation trip and celebration of the American victory in the Iraq War. During his trip, Bush encountered many of the world leaders who opposed the war in Iraq. The Bush foreign policy team had set in motion the American unilateral approach to foreign policy. Bush emphasized the proactive doctrine of preemption and de-emphasized the reactive strategy of deterrence and containment. He promoted forceful interdiction, preemptive strikes, and missile defenses as a means to counter proliferation of weapons of mass destruction. The Bush team downplayed the U.S. traditional support for treaty-based nonproliferation regimes. They also had a preference for regime change rather than negotiation with regimes and leaders they loathed. Under Bush's leadership, the United States developed ad hoc alliances or "coalitions of the willing" rather than permanent alliances and coalitions. At this juncture, the Bush team retreated from support of the European integration and exploited Europe's internal divisions. President Bush also sought to create a united effort on the part of the Great Powers against terrorism.[23]

By 2004, American troops in Iraq found themselves engaged in guerrilla warfare and a brewing civil war between various religious factions, including the Shiites, Kurds, and Sunnis, as well as ethnic factionalism. The Bush administration's initial celebration had been premature, as the military and political situation worsened. Anger also swelled overseas at what was perceived as the arrogance of American power. American troops are fighting in both Afghanistan and Iraq, which is sapping their energies in a war with no apparent end. This state of affairs has led the military and policy makers to seek new partners in the war against terrorism. Therefore, African states have emerged as important new actors in the war against terrorism.

AFRICA AND U.S. FOREIGN POLICY BEFORE 9/11

The historical period focused on earlier was followed by decades of race war on a global scale. Indeed, two of the most intensive sites of the war were the United States and South Africa.[24] As Cedric Robinson notes, the Cold War, as the official world contestation, was believed to have subsumed all other conflicts; it is now possible to cast the competition between the two imperial hegemons, the United States and the Soviet Union, as a historical sidebar to the struggle to either obtain or vanquish racial domination. Contrary to the colossal cultural, political, technological, military, and propaganda industries contrived on behalf of the Cold War obsession for the past fifty years, the awe-inspiring and more lasting dualism has been what Franz Fanon recognized as the racial order of a Manichaean colonial domination: "The cause is the consequence: you are rich because you are white, you are white because you are rich." From there he calculated, "It was not the *organization of production* but the *persistence and organization of oppression* which formed the primary social basis for revolutionary activities."[25] Furthermore, the West's political leaders gave secondary significance to the impulses of racial domination so central to imperial wars of the nineteenth century and the global wars of the twentieth century, masked as they were beneath the discursive veil of internation (international) conflict. Corporate and political elite/leaders ratcheted up the clash with the Soviet Union and China, providing them with an ideological apparatus with which to preserve imperial and colonial "adventures" among darker peoples and to suppress democratic movements at home.[26]

The African continent has not been historically identified with U.S. strategic interests or priorities, particularly for the U.S. military, and the American military engagement on the continent has been at best sporadic. During the height of the Cold War, delegates from third world nations gathered in Bandung, Indonesia, setting the stage to launch the nonaligned movement. African Americans were represented at this gathering by Congressman Adam Clayton Powell Jr. and Richard Wright. Nevertheless, the independence of Ghana in 1957 marked the beginning of the end of colonialism in Africa. During the 1950s and the 1960s, the international community witnessed the growth and proliferation of independence throughout the continent. Charles Henry observed that a younger generation of African Americans began to interact with and were influenced by African leaders and intellectuals, including Kwame Nkrumah, Sekou Toure, Jomo Kenyatta, Julius Nyerere, and Amilcar Cabral.[27] The civil rights and Black Power movements challenged both the American-style apartheid known as "Jim Crow" and the remaining pillars of global apartheid in the international system.

King's 1967 rupture with U.S. foreign policy on Vietnam marks a defining moment in African American perspectives on such policies as the Vietnam War itself and laid the groundwork for the historic breakup of the bipartisan Cold War consensus on anti-Communism. Nevertheless, King was not the first African American leader to register opposition to the war in Vietnam. Malcolm X, Stokely Carmichael (who later changed his name to Kwame Ture), and Muhammad Ali had preceded King in public opposition to the war. However, no leader of King's stature and reputation had taken the position outlined in King's sermon at Riverside Church in New York on April 4, 1967. Charles Henry summarizes seven points made in King's speech opposing U.S. policy in Vietnam:

1. Spending on the war was draining funds for domestic programs;
2. Young black men were being killed at an extraordinarily high rate in integrated army units yet still faced segregated schools at home;
3. It was morally inconsistent for him to urge nonviolence at home while America applied violence abroad;
4. Winning the Nobel Peace Prize gave him the responsibility to work for peace everywhere;
5. He opposed all forms of imperialism;
6. America needed a radical revolution in values that would lead it to place human rights above profits;
7. He opposed the war because he loved America and wanted to see it become a "divine Messianic force," not a world policeman.[28]

These views of King are not celebrated on the annual American commeration of his birthday. King's speech was condemned by prominent African American leaders, key members of the Johnson administration, and the U.S. foreign policy elites. By the time of the Tet Offensive in 1969, a larger sector of the establishment elites had joined King in opposition to the war. Powerful elites from Reinhold Niebuhr, Arthur Schlesinger, and Hans Morganthau to John Kenneth Galbraith were now proclaiming that the Communist world was polycentric and that Vietnam was not crucial to U.S. national security.[29] At this critical stage, the containment policy that had influenced American foreign policy since 1948 was torn asunder. Hence, the debate over the Vietnam War set in motion the events that eventually led to the fall of the Berlin Wall in 1989 and the elimination of anti-Communism as the raison d'être of postwar U.S. foreign policy.

During the Cold War, U.S. foreign policy toward Africa had very little to do with Africa. Africa, like most third world zones, was conceptualized as a pawn on the chessboard of the East-West conflict between the United States and the Soviet Union. Even the U.S. support for the apartheid regime in South Africa and for white rulers in what was Rhodesia, Southwest Africa, and Portuguese colonies in southern Africa was structured by the East-West conflict.

After the fall of the Soviet Union, most U.S. policy makers considered the U.S. military role and responsibilities in Africa to be minimal. At this juncture, U.S. military involvement revolved around the deployment of U.S. forces to Somalia to secure humanitarian operations, first in 1992 under the U.S.-led Unified Task Force (UNITAF), also known as Operation Hope, and later under the United Nations Operation in Somalia. In April 1992, the United Nations Security Council established the United Nations Operations in Somalia (UNISOM) in an effort to mediate an end to the country's civil war and to permit the delivery of much-needed food relief.[30] American military efforts in Somalia were unique on the continent. Accompanied by military forces from twenty-four other countries, approximately 25,000 U.S. troops were deployed by President George H. W. Bush under UNI-TAF. When Bill Clinton assumed the presidency, the number of U.S. troops was significantly reduced as operational responsibility from UNITAF shifted to UNI-SOM. In October 1993, U.S. Special Operations forces in the U.S.-led Task Force Ranger engaged Somali militia forces in the battle of Mogadishu, which ultimately resulted in the death of eighteen American soldiers and hundreds of Somalis. President Clinton ultimately ordered the withdrawal of U.S. forces from Somalia in March 1994, the same month that a limited U.S. deployment of 3,600 soldiers was dispatched to central Africa to assist in humanitarian efforts for Rwandan refugees and provide protection for humanitarian supplies in Rwanda. The killing of U.S. soldiers in Mogadishu dampened American policy makers' enthusiasm for humanitarian intervention to Rwanda to stop the genocide in comparison of the American-led North Atlantic Treaty Organization (NATO) campaign in Bosnia.[31] In February 1995, UNISOM withdrew from Somalia, having failed in its goal of fostering political stability there, although the operation was credited with having provided significant humanitarian assistance.[32]

In 1995, the Department of Defense articulated its perspective of Africa in its U.S. Security Strategy for Sub-Saharan Africa, "asserting that ultimately we see very little traditional strategic interest in Africa." The department's document did, however, note significant U.S. political and humanitarian interest in the region. Nevertheless, following terrorist attacks on two U.S. embassies in East Africa, the United States conducted retaliatory strikes against a pharmaceutical factory in Khartoum, Sudan, that Clinton administration officials initially contended was producing precursors that might lead to chemical weapons for Al-Qaeda.[33] Many analysts consider the embassy bombings and the retaliatory strikes against Sudan to be a turning point in U.S. strategic policy toward the African continent.

In 2002, the Bush administration's report *The National Security Strategy* reflected a need for a more targeted strategic approach toward the African continent. "In Africa, promise and opportunity sit side by side with disease, war, and desperate poverty. This threatens both a core value of the United States— preserving human dignity—and our strategic priority—combating global terror." The report went on to assert that U.S. security strategy must focus on building indigenous security and intelligence capabilities through bilateral engagement and "coalitions of the willing."[34] The Bush administration elaborated further on the growing economic and strategic importance of the African continent in its 2006 National Security Strategy, identifying Africa as a "high priority of this administration," and "recognizing that our security depends upon partnering with Africans to strengthen fragile and failing states and bring ungoverned areas under the control of effective democracies."[35] Increasingly, the African continent emerged as a new epicenter of U.S. national security in the global war against terrorism. The African continent was conceptualized in a manner reminiscent of Latin America and the Caribbean during the era of the Roosevelt Corollary, making apparent an American imperial intent to gain control over the natural resources of the African continent.

AFRICA AND THE U.S. WAR AGAINST TERRORISM

In 1998, terrorist networks associated with Al-Qaeda launched twin bombings of U.S. embassies in Nairobi, Kenya's capital, and Dar es Salaam, Tanzania's largest city. The Nairobi attack killed 201 Kenyans and 12 Americans; approximately 4,000 people were injured. In Tanzania, the bombers never reached their intended target but still killed twelve people and wounded eighty-five. Then, two years following the terrorist attack on the World Trade Center on September 11, 2001, terrorists fired two shoulder-launched missiles at an Israeli airliner taking off from Mombasa, Kenya.[36] Despite the 1998 attacks, Kenya, Uganda, and Tanzania were reluctant to introduce legislation to deal with terrorism. Their reluctance was premised on the view that Americans and other foreigners were the targets of these attacks. Nevertheless, African states in East Africa and elsewhere have come under increasing pressures since September 11, 2001, to join the "coalition of the willing" against terrorism. Kenya has not passed an antiterrorism law. Opponents have stated that most of the draft legislations contain unconstitutional elements, while others see such laws encouraged by another state as a threat to Kenya's sovereignty. In 2002, the Tanzanian government enacted an antiterrorism law similar to the one stalled in Kenya. Uganda's 2002 Anti-Terrorism Act criminalizes aiding and abetting terrorism, establishing terrorist organizations, and supporting, financing, or carrying out acts of terrorism. It also grants government-wide latitude in eavesdropping on suspects. In Uganda, terrorist suspects face double jeopardy as they are increasingly tried before military and civilian courts.[37]

The United States has expanded its military relations throughout East Africa and the Horn of Africa with special relations with Djibouti since the September 11 attacks. Before the September 11 attacks, Djibouti was off the U.S. military and diplomatic radar, but Djibouti has emerged as an important site in the global war against terrorism. Djibouti offers the United States and the West a very strategic geographical location with reference to the global war against terrorism. It is located on the mouth of the Red Sea, directly across a narrow strait near Yemen, the ancestral home of Osama bin Laden's father and a site with a legacy of Islamic extremism. To the south lies the failed state of Somalia, simmering with warlords and Islamists, which the United States claims is the sanctuary of Al-Qaeda training camps.[38] The Pentagon negotiated usage of a former French Legion outpost in Djibouti for its war against terrorism.

In 2002, the U.S. military conducted a number of operations against terrorism in this region, including a predator drone attack that killed six men in Yemen, and one of the casualties was an Al-Qaeda operative. In January 2007, a U.S. AC-130 gunship reportedly took off for a mission to attack what the United States had identified as an Al-Qaeda outpost in southern Somalia. It is the only military base in sub-Saharan Africa that employs special operation teams as well as troops to carry out humanitarian missions, which seems to indicate a decisive return toward empire building. According to the 2006 Amnesty International report, CIA jets known to have participated in "extraordinary renditions"—kidnapping of terror suspects who are transported for questioning outside of any legal process to friendly countries that may permit torture—had landed in Djibouti en route to Afghanistan and possibly Pakistan.[39]

Djibouti is the site of Camp Lemonier, which houses the U.S. Combined Joint Task Force–Horn of Africa (CJTF-HOA), created in 2002. The primary mission of the approximately 1,500 civilian and military troops is detecting, disrupting, and ultimately defeating transnational terrorist networks operating in the region, and denying safe havens, external support, and material assistance for terrorist activity. The CJTF-HOA covers the land and airspace in Kenya, Somalia, Sudan, Seychelles, Ethiopia, Eritrea, Djibouti, and Yemen, as well as the coastal waters of the Red Sea, the Gulf of Aden, and the Indian Ocean.[40] Prior to September 11, 2001, Djibouti received money from the U.S. State Department for removal of land mines and antiterrorism training. During the first three years after 2001, Djibouti received funds through the Economic Support Fund, a program encompassing a range of activities used to funnel money to allies; also, foreign aid from the United States to Djibouti went from zero to approximately $25 million. At the same time, foreign military financing increased from $100,000 total in the three years before the attacks to more than $21 million after. Djibouti also was the recipient of more than $5 million from the Pentagon's new post–September 11 Coalition Support Funds.

Starting in 2002, the State Department launched the Pan Sahelian Initiative (PSI) program to increase border security and counterterrorism capacities of four West African nations: Mali, Chad, Niger, and Mauritania. The Bush administration expanded the PSI program in 2005 under the rubric, "Enduring Freedom–Trans Sahara"; implemented by the United States European Command (EUROCOM), U.S. forces work with their African counterparts from Algeria, Chad, Mali, Mauritania, Morocco, Niger, Nigeria, Senegal, and Tunisia to improve intelligence, command, control, logistics, and border control, and to execute joint operations against terrorist groups.[41] All military and security issues related to the African continent operated under (EUROCOM) before the creation of the AFRICOM in February 2006.

The Launching of the U.S. Military African Command

In February 2006, President Bush announced the formation of a unified military command for the African continent. For the first time, this puts the continent on par with the Pacific Rim (Pacific Command), Europe (European Command), Latin America (Southern Command), and North America (Northern Command). The growing strategic importance of the African continent has played a critical role in establishing the African Command. Bush went on to assert

that the unified command in Africa will enhance efforts to bring peace and security to the people of Africa. A transition team has begun to establish Africa
Command (AFRICOM), which is expected to have initial operating capability
as a sub-unified command under European Command (EUCOM) by October
2007 and full operating capability as a stand-alone command by October 2008.
President Bush has nominated General William E. "Kip" Ward, currently deputy
commander of EUCOM, to serve as commander of the new command.[42]

In his 2006 State of the Union Address, President Bush called for the United
States to "replace more than 75 percent of our oil imports from the Middle East
by 2025." According to the Department of Energy Information Administration,
the United States has already advanced significantly in its efforts to lessen its
dependency on hydrocarbons originating in the volatile Persian Gulf, thanks in
large part to the abundant energy resources of Africa. According to the report,
in March 2007 Nigeria edged past Saudi Arabia to become America's fifth largest
supplier, delivering 41,717,000 barrels of oil that month compared to the desert
kingdom's 38,557,000. When Angola's 22,542,000 barrels are included with Nigeria's, the two African states alone account for more of America's energy needs
than Saudi Arabia, Iraq, Kuwait, and the United Arab Emirates combined.[43]

The Pentagon and other analysts point to the growing strategic importance
of the African continent that necessitates a dedicated regional command. Nevertheless, some experts have suggested that the growing Chinese presence in this
critical zone of the world system and oil have been major motivating factors. The
natural resources of the African continent have emerged as an inviting target for
the People's Republic of China, whose dynamic economy, averaging 9 percent
growth per year over the last couple of decades, has an insatiable thirst for oil and
other commodities. China imports approximately 2.6 million barrels of crude
oil per day, about half of its consumption. More than 760,000 barrels—roughly
a third of its imports—come from African sources, that is, Sudan, Angola, and
Congo (Brazzaville). In addition, Chinese president Hu Jintao announced a
three-year, $3 billion program in preferential loans and expanded aid to Africa
as part of his twelve-day and eight-nation tour of Africa. These funds came on
top of the $3 billion in loans and $2 billion in export credits that Hu announced
in October 2006 at the opening of the historic Beijing Summit of the Forum on
China-Africa Cooperation (FOCAC), which attracted nearly fifty heads of state
and ministers to the Chinese capital.[44]

The quest for energy security is also transforming China's relations with Africa and other regions of the developing world, including Central Asia. Beijing's
demand for oil is projected to rise from the present requirements of 60 million

tons to 250 million tons by 2020, and, like the United States, China wants to reduce its dependency on West Asian (Middle Eastern) oil. If a conflict should erupt over Taiwan, current oil supply lines would be seriously affected. Therefore, participation in energy development projects in Africa and other Third World regions is vital to the Chinese energy strategy.[45]

The Bush administration has sought to make it very clear that the new AFRICOM does not represent a "new scramble for Africa." At the same time, it has also emphasized that the United States is not at war with Africa, and that AFRICOM is concerned with enhancing security in the region and combating global terrorism. Most African leaders have been lukewarm to this initiative. Zambia president Levy Mwanawasa has made it clear that none of the member states of the Southern African Development Community (a network of fourteen nations) is interested in hosting the command. Similarly, South Africa defense minister Mosiuoa Lekota has refused to meet with General Ward, who will command AFRICOM. Recently, Lekota stated that "Africa must avoid the presence of foreign forces on her soil."[46] Several African states—Senegal, Mali, Ghana, Gabon, and Namibia—have agreed to participate in AFRICOM. Liberia, historically a close ally to the United States, has aggressively promoted AFRICOM. President Ellen Johnson has lobbied hard to secure AFRICOM headquarters in Liberia. The United States is also pursuing Sao Tome, Principe, Equatorial Guinea, Kenya, Djibouti, and Ethiopia as a possible host. Currently, AFRICOM operates out of Stuttgart, Germany, and it is anticipated to be based on the African continent by October 2008.

It's the Oil Stupid!

During the current wave of globalization, the United States has sought to increase its trade with Africa. Foreign trade between the United States and Africa tripled between 1990 and 2005.[47] In 2000, the Clinton administration introduced a comprehensive U.S. trade and investment policy for the continent in the African Growth and Opportunity Act (AGOA). Congress has amended AGOA on several occasions, including most recently in 2006. Most of the trade between the United States and Africa under AGOA has been primarily concerned with natural resources, and especially energy-related resources.

Currently, Nigeria is the African continent's largest supplier of oil, and is the fifth largest global supplier of oil to the United States. The Niger Delta region is a highly unstable area of Nigeria where output has been reduced periodically by much as 25 percent. Global oil prices rose above $60 a barrel in April 2007 after Nigeria's disputed national elections and above $70 per barrel in May 2007 after attacks on pipelines in the delta.

The American/international financial institutions and transnational corporations were content to continue business as usual, notwithstanding the increase in human rights violations and corruption—including the hanging of writer and political activist Ken Saro-Wiwa in 1995 along with eight other Oguni activists—that accompanied the General Sani Abacha era. As long as the oil continued to flow, the nature of the regime was less important than the interests of the West. U.S. policy makers even sought to persuade a reluctant Chief Abiola to renounce any desire to assume the presidency in Nigeria in exchange for release from prison. Chief Abiola paid a high price for the democratic forces in Nigeria, suffering a deadly heart attack in 1997. Subsequently, a heart attack also took the life of General Abacha in the summer of 1998. Afterward, Nigeria made critical steps toward a democratic transition.

In the latter part of 1998, people throughout the Niger Delta region staged protests against continuing corruption and collusion between the recently elected civilian democratic government and the oil multinationals. Citizens in this area are alarmed at the environmental degradation that is taking place in the oil region. Oil companies have not demonstrated any concern for the environment in their exploitation of the petroleum resources in Nigeria. Their behavior in Nigeria mirrors the action of other transnational corporations in other areas of the developing world where environmental racism is rampant. The same scenario as in Nigeria is taking place in minority communities in the United States, where environmental racism is also problematic.

The threat to disrupt oil supplies from Nigeria followed the arrest of a factional leader of the Movement for the Emancipation of the Niger Delta, Henry Okah, in Angola on arms trafficking charges on September 3, 2007. The group bombed facilities and kidnapped foreign workers in the southern delta from late 2005 to May 2007, when President Umaru Yar'Adua took office promising to solve the problem. Threats to resume attacks have accused the government of trying to divide and rule the inhabitants of the delta and attempting to bribe militants and leaders from the region. The group stated: "We will not sit back and allow our birthright to be exchanged for a bowl of porridge." The group also declared that effective midnight September 23, 2007, it would commence attacks on installations and abduction of expatriates.[48]

In February 2008, President George W. Bush made a tour of several African states, including Benin, Liberia, Tanzania, Rwanda, South Africa, Ghana, and

Nigeria, proclaiming American friendship with Africa and highlighting the new AFRICOM as vital to both the war against terrorism and the security and prosperity of African states. The Bush administration drew attention to programs aimed at fighting malaria and the HIV/AIDs epidemic. Bush was unable to garner support or willingness on the part of his African hosts to allow AFRICOM headquarters to be located in their countries, with the exception of Liberia. At this juncture, most African leaders were not willing to exchange economic neoliberalism for military neoliberalism. The United States' war with and occupation of Iraq have cast a broad shadow over AFRICOM, and African leaders are seeking to avoid pitfalls of military neoliberalism in the war on terrorism and new accumulation by dispossession or appropriation.

The strategic interests of the United States include not only access to cheap and reliable low-sulfur oil imports, but also keeping the Chinese (for example in Sudan) and South Koreans (for example in Nigeria)—aggressive new actors in the African oil business—as well as Islamic terror at bay. In this new scramble for Africa that is unfolding, the Chinese and others have deep pockets in comparison to the debt-stricken United States.

Perhaps a major objective of the new AFRICOM is to guarantee that Nigeria and other African petroleum producers' oil fields are secure and open for business. Regardless of the conflict in the Niger Delta and other oil-producing areas, the potential for deep-water drilling in the Gulf of Guinea is high, and Africa may be on track to supply 25 percent of all U.S. oil imports by 2015. It is hoped that AFRICOM will protect the United States' vital stake in the lucrative oil industry. Once again, American policy makers are placing profits over people and are thoroughly engaged in empire building.

NOTES

1. See Patrick Karl O'Brien and Armand Clesse, ed., *Two Hegemonies: Britain 1846–1914 and the United States 1941–2001* (Aldershot, U.K.: Ashgate, 2002); and Niall Ferguson, ed., *Empire: The Rise and Demise of the British World Order and the Lessons for Global Power* (New York: Basic Books, 2003).

2. Niall Ferguson, *Colossus: The Price of America's Empire* (New York: Penguin Press, 2004).

3. See Andrew J. Bacevich, ed., *American Empire: The Realities and Consequences of U.S. Diplomacy* (Cambridge, Mass.: Harvard University Press, 2002); and Walter Meade,

ed., *Special Providence: American Foreign Policy and How It Changed the World* (New York: Routledge, 2002).

4. See Robert Kagan, ed., *Of Paradise and Power: America and Europe in the New World Order* (New York: Vintage Books, 2004).

5. See Charles Kupchan, ed., *The End of the American Era: U.S. Foreign Policy and the Geopolitics of the Twenty-first Century* (New York: Knopf, 2003); and Joseph S. Nye, ed., *The Paradox of American Power: Why the World's Only Superpower Can't Go It Alone* (New York: Oxford University Press, 2003).

6. See Immanuel Wallerstein, ed., *The Decline of American Power* (New York: New Press, 2002); Giovanni Arrighi, Beverly J. Silver, and Iftikhar Ahmad, *Chaos and Governance in the Modern World System* (Minneapolis: University of Minnesota Press, 1999).

7. Giovanni Arrighi, Beverly J. Silver, and Iftikhar Ahmad, Chaos *and Governance in the Modern World System* (Minneapolis: University of Minnesota Press, 1999).

8. David Harvey, ed., *The New Imperialism* (New York: Oxford University Press, 2003).

9. James H. Cone, "Martin Luther King, Jr.," in Peter J. Albert and Ronald Hoffmann, ed., *We Shall Overcome* (New York: Pantheon, 1990), 208.

10. Charles Henry, ed., Foreign Policy and the Black (Inter)national Interest (Albany: SUNY Press, 2000), 7.

11. Sidney Lens, *The Forging of the American Empire* (New York: Cromwell, 1971), 204.

12. Cedric Robinson, *Black Movements in America* (New York: Routledge, 1997), 134.

13. Chalmers Johnson, ed., *The Sorrow of Empire: Militarism, Secrecy, and the End of the Republic* (New York: Metropolitan Books, 2004), 2.

14. Ivan Musicant, ed., *The Banana Wars: A History of United States Military Intervention in Latin America from the Spanish-American War to the Invasion of Panama* (New York: Macmillan, 1990), 3.

15. Ibid.

16. Lens, *Forging of the American Empire,* 206.

17. Harold Molineu, *U.S. Policy toward Latin America: From Regionalism to Globalism* (Boulder, Colo.: Westview Press, 1986), 40.

18. Johnson, *Sorrow of Empire*, 2.

19. Ibid., 3.

20. Kupchan, *End of the American Er*a, 13.

21. Johnson, *Sorrow of Empire*, 3.

22. Kupchan, *End of the American Era,* 16.

23. Ivo H. Daalder and James M. Lindsay, ed., *America Unbound: The Bush Revolution in Foreign Policy* (Washington, D.C.: Brookings Institution Press, 2003), 2.

24. Cedric J. Robinson, *Black Movements in America* (New York: Routledge, 1997), 134.

25. Franz Fanon, ed., *The Wretched of the Earth* (New York: Grove Press, 1965), 22–33.

26. Robinson, Black Movements in America, 135.

27. Henry, *Foreign Policy*, 6.

28. Ibid., 2.

29. Ibid., 3.

30. Arthur S. Banks, Thomas C. Muller, and William R. Overstreet, ed., *Political Handbook of the World, 2000–2002* (New York: CSA Publications, Binghamton University, 2003), 1420.

31. Darryl C. Thomas, *The Theory and Practice of Third World Solidarity* (Westport, Conn.: Praeger, 2001), 225–28.

32. Banks, Muller, and Overstreet, *Political Handbook of the World*, 1420.

33. See Department of Defense Office of International Security Affairs, *United States Security Strategy for Sub-Saharan Africa, August 1995*.

34. The National Security Council, *The National Security Strategy of the United States*, September 17, 2002

35. The National Security Council, The National Security Strategy of the United States, 2006

36. Mutegi Njau, "An Incentive to Clamp Down: U.S. Prodding, 3 East African Nations to Get Tough with Terrorist Suspects," *Center for Public Integrity*, May 22, 2007, 1.

37. Ibid., 3

38. Alan Lallamand, "Profiteering on Location: Djibouti's Repressive Regime, Not Its Peoples, Has Prospered since 9/11," Center for Public Integrity, May 25, 2007.

39. Ibid., 1

40. Lauren Ploch, "CRS Report for Congress, Africa Command: U.S. Strategic Interests and the Role of the U.S. Military in Africa," updated version, July 2007, 18–19.

41. Ibid., 19–20.

42. Ibid., 1.

43. See J. Peter Pham, "Africa Command: A Historic Opportunity for Enhanced Engagement, If Done Right," testimony before the U.S. House of Representatives Committee on Foreign Affairs, Subcommittee on Africa and Global Health, August 2, 2007, 5. Dr. J. Peter Pham is director of the Nelson Institute for International and Public Affairs, James Madison University.

44. Ibid., 6.

45. See Ramakant Dwivedi, "China's Central Asia Policy in Recent Times," *China and Eurasian Forum Quarterly* 4, no.4 (2006): 139–159.

46. Frida Berrigan, "The New Military Frontier: Africa," Foreign Policy in Focus, September 19, 2007, 2.

47. See Danielle Langton, "CRS Report RL31772, *U.S. Trade and Investment Relationship with Sub-Saharan Africa: The African Growth and Opportunity Act and Beyond.*"

48. *New York Times*, September 24, 2007.

PART 2

Immigration and Race

4

Latino Growth and Latino Exploitation: More Than a Passing Acquaintance

ROBERT APONTE

Latinos, or Hispanics, are persons of Latin American origin. Despite varying national origins, they are widely seen as a singular group and have been much in the news of late.[1] Due largely to record-breaking immigration, Latinos have recently surpassed African Americans in sheer numbers, even though they trailed the latter group by over 20 million persons some three and a half decades ago.[2] Hence, Latinos have become the nation's largest minority, a widely heralded "achievement."

Drawing on a vast array of literature and U.S. Census Bureau data, this chapter explores one major contributor to this dramatic growth and examines several indicators of well-being for Latinos, with an eye toward discerning any connection between the two items. The effort appears warranted. The findings suggest that Latinos' rapid growth is fueled, to a significant extent, by direct or indirect employer recruitment of immigrants, primarily of Mexican origin. Following this, it is shown here that Latinos' ascension to the status of the nation's "top minority" comes at a dear price. It comes at the cost of sustaining an inordinate amount of exploitation and deprivation, if not outright oppression. Of critical importance, the associated burdens are primarily shouldered by immigrants of Mexican origin.

The largely workplace-related troubles endured by these Latinos stems from a number of interrelated factors. First, they are likely to take low-paying positions

that nonimmigrants avoid because such earnings appear lucrative when compared with the opportunities in their places of origin. But more important, many
enter the United States without authorization, which undercuts their rights and
yields substantial power to the employers who hire them. This accounts for their
desirability as workers, which in turn underlies their recruitment and fuels further migrations. The resulting rise in the pace and scope of migration propels the
Latino count upward. Hence, they quickly reach and maintain the top position
among minorities. Bluntly put, were it not for the various forms of exploitation
they endure, Latinos would not have so rapidly reached the minority "top spot."

BACKGROUND

Immigrants from Latin America come to the United States for many reasons,
but most come to obtain more lucrative employment. This is clearly true for
Mexicans, the fastest growing and largest of the Latino groups. Such migrants
typically earn far more in the United States than they can in their home countries, despite their relative concentration in the least desirable sectors of the U.S.
labor market. Indeed, hundreds die annually attempting illegal entries, usually
to obtain such positions.

However, it is also well known that better opportunity structures alone do
not suffice to entice or enable large numbers of people to immigrate. Such conditions are better deemed as necessary, but not sufficient, causes. Rather, major
migrations can usually be traced to inducements, of one variety or another, that
initiate the pioneering flows (Portes and Borocz 1989). Subsequent migrants are
steered to these same destinations via social networks or, more simply, by their
ties to the earlier movers, via a process known as chain migration (Massey 1986).
Indeed, the great European migrations of a century ago were also largely organized through such social networks (e.g., Moretti 1999).

A general prerequisite to the process is the establishment of some manner
of connection between the sending and receiving societies. Two key ways of
forging such ties are political/military intervention and labor recruitment. The
former way tends to generate refugee streams, as occurred with El Salvador and
Vietnam, the two best-known cases, while labor recruitment, best exemplified in
the case of Mexico, will directly induce "economic" or "labor" migrants.

While chain migration will often continue without benefit of continual inducements, recurring bouts of recruitment will undoubtedly increase the flow
of migrants. Moreover, it is clear that while the recruitment of foreign workers

to the United States has been highly restricted for decades, illegal recruitment is almost certainly carried out with some frequency. In the recent past, for example, the corporate giant Tyson Foods and some of its executives were indicted by a federal grand jury on charges relating to the illegal recruiting of Mexican workers during the 1990s (Grimsley 2001). As will be shown, areas specified in the Tyson indictment have witnessed Latino growth (primarily Mexican) at a rate that was nothing short of astounding.

It is clear that without continued recruitment efforts, whether direct or indirect, significantly fewer migrants would come, though migration would not simply end. The exploitability of these workers, particularly those who are undocumented, is what makes them so highly desirable and sought after (see Holzer 1996; Johnson-Webb 2003; Kirschenman and Neckerman 1990). If these generalizations are correct and it can be shown that such workers are indeed poorly paid, hold undesirable jobs, endure dangerous worksites, turn up in areas where illegal recruitment has occurred (often risking their very lives in the process), then solid support is provided to the essay's opening argument: the sheer exploitability of the Hispanic immigrants has contributed significantly to the fueling of Latinos' phenomenal population growth.

BECOMING NUMBER ONE

The contours of recent Latino migration to the United States can be seen in figure 1. It compares the relative sizes of the nation's African American and Latino populations from 1980 to 2005. The reversal in rankings is remarkable. Whereas in 1980 African Americans outnumbered Latinos by nearly 12 million persons (26.1 million to 14.6 million), by 2005 the advantage had reversed. At that time, Latinos led African Americans by 7.5 million persons (41.9 million to 34.4 million). More important, the rise in Latino numbers could not have resulted from natural increase (excess of births over deaths) alone. The near tripling of the size of the group (14.6 million to 41.9 million) in less than thirty years indicates that rapid immigration is clearly also at play. Moreover, the figures do not tell the whole story, as they omit the sizable undercounts for both groups. However, the Latinos' undercount is almost certainly greater than that for African Americans for the obvious reason that millions within the Hispanic group are undocumented.

Indeed, the latest Immigration and Naturalization Services (INS) estimates for the nation's total undocumented population, as of 2000, peg the Mexican

FIGURE 1. AFRICAN AMERICAN* AND HISPANIC POPULATIONS: 1980–2005

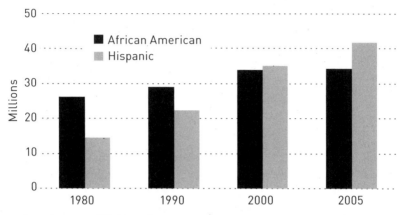

Source: CensusScope 2000. U.S. Census Bureau 2006a
* Non-Hispanic

contingent at 4.8 million persons (69 percent of the nation's total), with five additional Latin American nations (El Salvador, Guatemala, Colombia, Honduras, and Ecuador) contributing between 100,000 and 200,000 such persons apiece, along with China (INS 2003). A significant portion of the undocumented people from Latin America are almost certainly also working-class migrants who bear more than a passing resemblance to Mexican immigrants (Chavez 1996). A more recent estimate by a top researcher at the PEW Hispanic Institute pegged the Mexican contingent at 6 million persons in 2004 and noted that some 80 to 85 percent of all migration from Mexico in recent years has been undocumented. The idea that Latino growth is fueled to a considerable extent by immigration, especially from Mexico, is strongly supported by these data, as is the idea that they likely sustain a larger undercount than do African Americans.

Figure 2 shows the pattern in Latino growth from 1980 to 2005 by nationality group (Mexican, Puerto Rican, Cuban, and "Other"). The pattern is clear: Mexicans are the largest group and dominate the growth by a substantial margin. Their growth during this twenty-five-year stretch more than tripled in size (8.7 million to 26.8 million). In 2005, Mexicans outnumbered all other Latinos combined by nearly 12 million persons. The residual category of "Others," which consists of numerous Latino nationalities combined (excluding Mexicans, Puerto Ricans, and Cubans), also shows very rapid growth between 1980 and 2000, though little growth afterward.[3] The growth in both of these latter cases is also unlikely

FIGURE 2. HISPANIC IN THE U.S. BY TYPES: 1980–2005

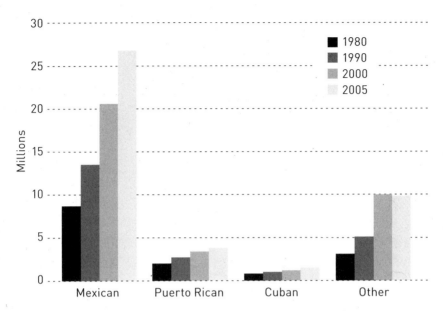

Source: U.S. Census Bureau 2002, 2006a

to stem from natural increase alone. Thus the idea that immigrants, especially Mexican immigrants, are disproportionately contributing to the phenomenal Latino growth is further supported here.

Figure 3 shows the skewed pattern of Latino settlements in the United States by presenting the group's growth between 1990 and 2000 by individual state. Most of the states with the most Latinos in 1990 have increased their leads over the others by 2000. This is mainly because having more people in place facilitates generating more natural increase as well as drawing more newcomers via social networks.

However, a close inspection of some of the lower-ranking states reveals a number of surprising shifts. Specifically, two states (Georgia and North Carolina), which ranked at the very bottom of the group in 1990, have shifted upward in ranking by 2000. Indeed, their status as upstarts in Latino population ranking is further supported in figure 4. There, the top ten states in absolute Latino growth over the 1990s (without regard to the number of Latinos currently in residence) are rank ordered. Georgia and North Carolina are shown to rank eighth and tenth, respectively. This compares with rankings of only eleventh place and fifteenth place, respectively, in figure 3.

FIGURE 3. LATINOS BY SELECTED STATES: 1990 AND 2000

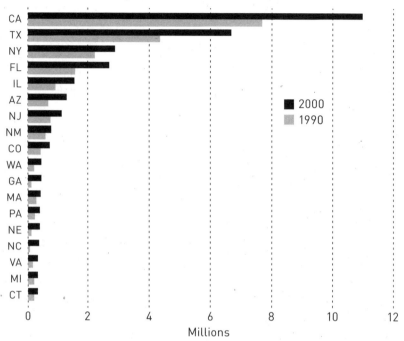

Source: U.S. Census Bureau, 20

FIGURE 4. TOP 10 STATES BY HISPANIC CHANGE: 1990–2000

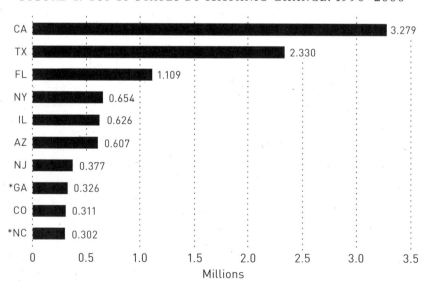

Source: U.S. Census Bureau, 20

The remarkable showings by Georgia and North Carolina are further but-tressed by the recent INS report (2003) that provides estimates on the nation's undocumented population. In that report, among other things, the states are ranked by the absolute increases in undocumented persons they are estimated to have sustained between 1990 and 2000. Georgia and North Carolina ranked fifth and sixth, respectively, in the index. Subsequently, a closer look at them is provided, for they appear to exemplify places with truly new, but significantly large, Latino communities.

MEAT PROCESSING AND LATINO GROWTH

Among other well-publicized trends about Latinos in recent years has been the finding that immigrants within the group have been drawn by meat-processing firms to nontraditionally Latino areas in the South (chicken) and the Midwest (beef and pork), largely due to recruitment (Stull et al. 1995; Schlosser 2001). Not surprisingly, such meat-processing firms are notorious for the safety viola-tions they have accumulated over the years and the dangers they pose to workers. Indeed, many believe that meat processing is the most deadly of the manufactur-ing industry categories. While Latinos have been taking even lower-paying and comparably dangerous jobs in numerous other fields (Greenhouse 2003; Maier 2001), the meat-processing industry exemplifies the key ideas of this essay.

The meat-processing industry underwent a massive restructuring in recent years that witnessed numerous changes in the nature of work. Firms abrogated union contracts, cut wages, migrated away from the major cities where they initially concentrated (for example, Chicago, Minneapolis), and set up shop in small towns of the Midwest and South (Stanley 1992; Stull et al. 1995).

Table 1 tells the story of the massive decline in wages experienced in the indus-try. It shows that average pay in the industry dropped from a point significantly higher than the manufacturing-wide average around 1970, to a level significantly below average by 1990. It is not surprising that during this period, industries began their drive to recruit the most vulnerable sources of labor they could find, which increasingly came to include (or consist largely of) immigrants, and most especially Hispanic or Mexican ones (Stull et al. 1995).

The impact of sizable shifts in the ethnicity or race of workers in any indus-try, to the settlement patterns in the areas where the industry's jobs are located, is usually not easily discerned. This is so for a variety of reasons. For example, the populations of the areas may be too large for such group shifts to have a

TABLE 1. MEATPACKING WAGES: 1969–1989

| YEAR | PRODUCTION WORKERS | AVERAGE HOURLY WAGES | | MEATPACKING WAGES AS % OF MFG. WAGE |
		MEATPACKING	MANUFACTURING	
1969	143,500	$3.66	$3.19	115
1971	145,600	4.17	3.57	117
1973	137,600	4.71	4.07	116
1975	134,500	5.61	4.81	117
1977	137,000	6.44	5.63	114
1979	134,300	7.73	6.69	116
1981	129,200	8.89	7.98	113
1983	115,400	8.58	8.84	97
1985	123,300	8.10	9.52	85
1987	115,300	8.37	9.91	84
1989	121,100	8.63	10.47	82

Source: Stanley 1992.

discernable impact. In the case of meat processing, however, such a shift is actually quite possible and eye-opening. It is possible because the communities in question are relatively small and the population shifts relatively rapid. Indeed, the remarkable growth of Latino communities in areas where meat processors have attracted Hispanic workers, despite the near-total absence of Latino residents in these places prior to 1990, is astounding.

In this regard, figures 5–7 examine communities where Tyson Foods (in the South) had meat-processing plants that were specified in the federal indictment of the firm, along with midwestern communities where IBP (a major beef and pork producer) and other meat-processing firms have relocated in recent years (see Gouveia and Stull 1995; Grey 1995; Stull et al. 1995; Grimsley 2001).

The data in figures 5–7 make clear the impact of the recruitment drives: in every case, virtually nonexistent Latino communities in 1990 exhibited astounding growth rates. Figure 6, for example, features population figures from Monroe City, North Carolina, one of the towns specified in the Tyson indictment. There, the number of Latinos rose from 215 in 1990 to 5,611 in 2000, an increase of 5,396 persons. The comparable rise in Union County, North Carolina, where Monroe is located (not shown), was nearly 7,000 persons.

Of obvious significance, these two places are in the state of North Carolina, earlier distinguished as being an upstart state in Latino population growth, along

Figure 5. Latinos in Selected Cities: 1990–2000

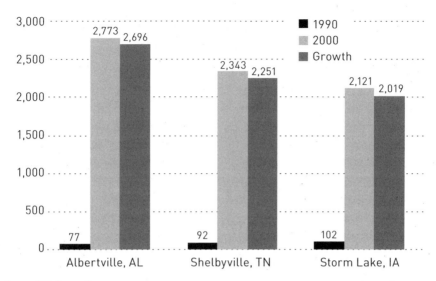

Source: U.S. Census Bureau, 20

Figure 6. Latinos in Selected Cities: 1990–2000

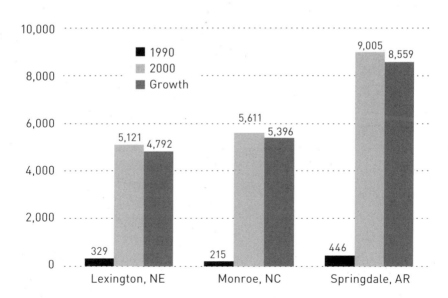

Source: U.S. Census Bureau, 20

FIGURE 7. LATINOS IN SELECTED CITIES: 1990–2000

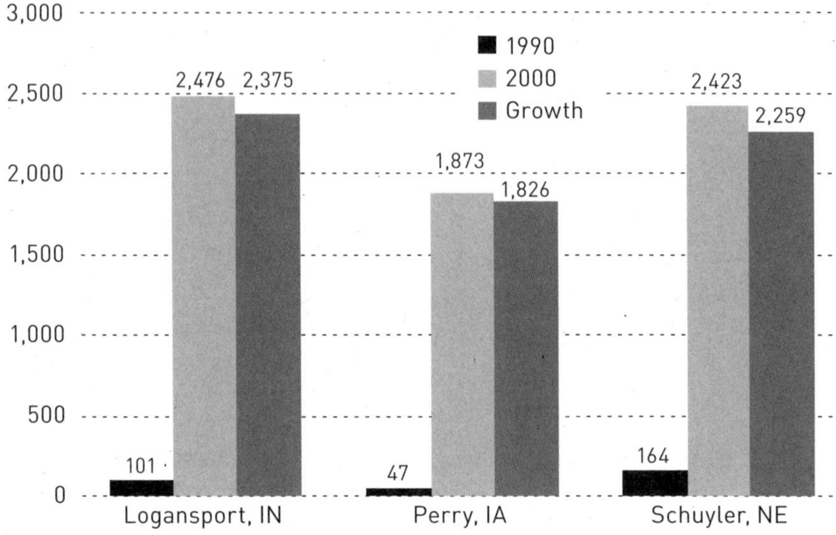

Source: U.S. Census Bureau, 20

with being highly ranked among states in the (estimated) absolute growth of undocumented persons. The population changes in a number of additional communities where Tyson or IBP maintained plants were also examined and found to exhibit similar patterns.

It is not always possible to show the specific characteristics of the Latino workers. Many of the details have to be inferred. While 1990 data on the Latinos in the places designated in figures 5–7 provided by the census did not disaggregate the category into the distinct nationality backgrounds of the residents, such data were provided in 2000.

Table 2 provides the Latino populations of the cities in figures 5–7 subdivided by Mexican, Guatemalan, and Salvadoran origin. The table clearly shows the vast majority of the Latinos in these areas are indeed of Mexican origin. Guatemalans and Salvadorans were the only other Latinos who were of sufficient numeric strength (100 persons or greater) to have their count recorded by the census in these areas.[4] These two Latino groups were also among the four such groups that each accounted for at least 100,000 of the nation's undocumented persons, as of 2000, according to government estimates (INS 2003). As shown in table 2, it is only in places where sizable numbers of Guatemalans and Salvadorans were

TABLE 2. HISPANIC POPULATION BY SELECTED TYPES IN SELECTED MIDWESTERN AND SOUTHERN CITIES: 2000

CITY	TOTAL HISPANIC	MEXICAN	% MEXICAN	GUATEMALAN	SALVADORAN	% COMBINED
Albertville, AL	2,773	2,222	80.0	306	NA	91.2
Lexington, NE	5,121	3,754	73.3	490	157	85.9
Logansport, IN	2,476	1,998	80.1	NA	NA	NA
Monroe, NC	5,611	4,741	84.5	NA	NA	NA
Perry, IA	1,873	1,165	62.2	156	232	82.9
Schuyler, NE	2,423	1,575	65.0	313	NA	77.9
Shelbyville, TN	2,343	2,054	87.7	NA	NA	NA
Springdale, AR	9,005	6,877	76.4	NA	676	83.9
Storm Lake, IA	2,121	1,708	80.5	NA	NA	NA

Source: U.S. Census Bureau, 20

present that the Mexican portion of the total Latino presence slipped to around two-thirds of the total. It is likely, however, that Guatemalans and Salvadorans were drawn to these areas in ways similar to those that lured Mexicans.[5] Taken together, these patterns provide support to the hypothesized inferences.

It is clear that a detailed analysis of other key industries absorbing Latinos would provide greater insights than those available from the mere analysis of only one (meatpacking), however important the one. Nevertheless, it can easily be demonstrated that relatively few of the additional employment alternatives available to Latinos provided lucrative livelihoods. This can be shown in a number of ways, but among the most important is earnings data. However, care must be attached to how such data are interpreted. When appropriately assembled, the requisite data show just how poorly Latinos are faring at the present. But they also show how easily the true picture can be obscured–in some circumstances—because of how data tend to be assembled.

NUMBER ONE IN EXPLOITATION

It is doubtlessly reasonable to assume that African Americans have traditionally been the poorest and most oppressed of the minority groups in the United States.

Thus, the African American group provides a useful reference point for gauging Latinos' well-being or lack thereof. Such a comparison, provided below, reveals the dismal circumstances engulfing the Hispanic group. Not only does the comparison show Latinos to be worse off in many respects, but all the figures in question are often aggregated across all Latinos. If we could disaggregate the figures so that the Latino or Mexican immigrant contingents, the truly exploited groups, could be isolated from other Latinos, their indicators would be much worse (while those for the native-born Hispanics and Mexicans would be significantly more favorable). Fortunately, enough disaggregation is possible to allow for a strong inferential case to be made in support of the basic theme of the essay.

Figure 8 compares the well-being of African Americans with that of Hispanics and, within that aggregation, of Mexicans, the largest of the Hispanic groups. The comparison for 2005 examines perhaps the most standard of measures, median household income. On that measure, figure 8 shows that Latinos and Mexicans ($36,200 and $35,500, respectively) are significantly better off than African Americans ($30,900), consistent with conventional wisdom.

However, figure 9, which depicts per capita income amounts from the very same data set, reveals a vastly different picture. There, it seems clear that African Americans ($16,700) are actually better off than either Latinos as a whole or Mexicans taken individually ($14,500 and $12,800, respectively), despite the latter groups' leads in household income. Moreover, separating out the Mexicans shows how poorly they fare when compared with other Hispanics as well as with blacks. Clearly, the incomes of Mexican immigrants taken separately would be lower still, but these cannot be shown here.

The apparent inconsistencies in the relative rankings between the African Americans and the Hispanics shown in these charts are easily explained with the help of figures 10 and 11. As shown in figure 10, Latinos have far larger households (3.7/3.4 persons, respectively, for Mexicans/Latinos) than do African Americans (2.6 persons) or whites (2.4 persons). The larger households include additional adult workers as well as more children. Hence, while such households thereby generate higher earnings, those higher earnings must provide for many more persons. On balance, therefore, the higher earning group actually ends up less well off. The same relationship held in 1989, but at the time, the per capita income gap was far smaller (Aponte 1999). The gap has widened in the interim, no doubt, because of the increases in immigration that underlie it.

An even more damning revelation on the same theme is shown in figure 11. There, the percentages of low-wage workers among whites, African Americans, and Latinos during 2003 are shown. As shown in the chart, nearly one-third of

FIGURE 8. MEDIAN HOUSEHOLD INCOME BY RACE
AND HISPANIC ORIGIN: 2005

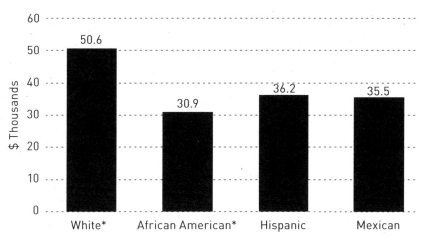

Source: U.S. Census Bureau, 2006
• Non-Hispanic

FIGURE 9. PER CAPITA INCOME BY RACE
AND HISPANIC ORIGIN: 2005

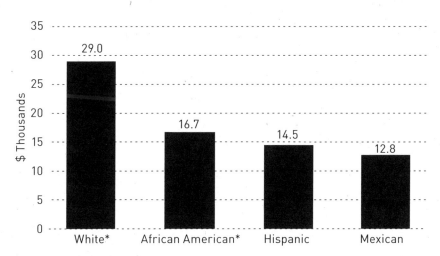

Source: U.S. Census Bureau, 2006
• Non-Hispanic

FIGURE 10. AVERAGE HOUSEHOLD SIZE BY RACE
AND HISPANIC ORIGIN: 2005

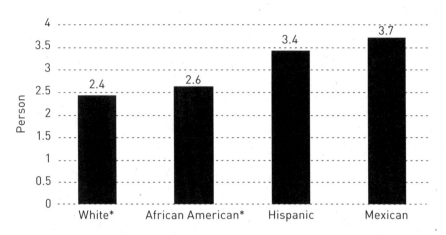

Source: U.S. Census Bureau, 2006
• Non-Hispanic

FIGURE 11. LOW INCOME EARNERS AS PERCENTAGE
OF FULL-TIME, YEAR-ROUND WORKERS, AGE 15 AND OVER,
BY RACE AND HISPANIC ORIGIN: 2005

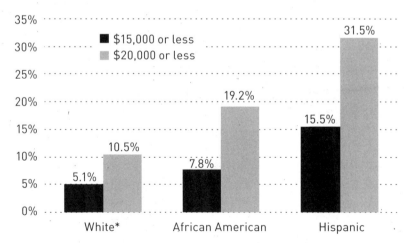

Source: U.S. Census Bureau, 2006
• Non-Hispanic

the Latino, full-year, full-time workers earned $20,000 or less. The corresponding proportion among blacks was less than 20 percent; it was less than 10 percent for whites. Unfortunately, the data for Latinos are not disaggregated. Yet when juxtaposed with the immediately preceding data shown above, it stands to reason that the Mexican portion of the Latinos, particularly the immigrants among them, are well represented among the low-income workers shown in the figure.

The data in these charts reveal shortcomings in drawing conclusions about the relative well-being of groups under comparison solely from such standard economic series as household income. However, in this instance, the misreading is further compromised, indirectly, by an unusual set of circumstances. Specifically, Latino immigrants are well known to remit to their families back home significant portions of their earnings. Hence, the earnings shown in the income series overstate the levels of living they actually afford their respective earners, at least while they maintain residence in the United States.

Indeed, the total dollar amounts that are accounted for by such remittances are known to provide substantial portions of the national incomes of some Latin American countries, and the amounts increase yearly. In the case of Mexico, the nation that has sent the most migrants to the United States, the figures have been staggering. Nearly $10 billion is estimated to have been remitted to that nation in 2002 alone. Indeed, the figure for 2003 reached an astounding $12 billion well before the year was out (Lugo 2003).

Beyond earnings, there are other workplace-related forms of exploitation or exclusion that affect Latinos more than others. No doubt, the clearest example of this concerns health coverage. In the United States, health insurance is obtained through employment in the vast majority of cases. However, not all jobs provide health coverage, and some require voluntary employee contributions that the employees cannot afford. Hence, aside from the unemployed, most adults (and their dependents) lacking coverage are connected to jobs where coverage is nonexistent or is beyond their ability to pay.

The population lacking coverage has grown to record numbers in recent years, and the issue has been the subject of many headlines (e.g., Connolly 2003; Pear 2003; Staff and New Service Reports 2003). What such headlines do not often divulge is that the Latino group is by far the least covered of the three major racial or ethnic groups. As figure 12 shows, while some 12 percent of whites lack coverage, along with 17 percent of African Americans, fully one-third (34 percent) of Latinos do so. More important, the largest figure of all, 38 percent, is that for Mexicans. Moreover, a recent analysis of survey data for California, the state with the most Mexicans, showed that Hispanic immigrants

FIGURE 12. NON-ELDERLY UNINSURED BY RACE
AND HISPANIC ORIGIN: 2005

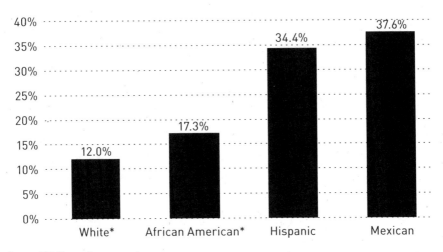

Source: U.S. Census Bureau, 2006
• Non-Hispanic

were more likely than U.S.-born Hispanics to do without insurance (Greenwald et al. 2005).

No form of exploitation sustained by Latinos, however, surpasses that of the dangers they often endure at their job sites. As suggested earlier, they are likely to be offered the least desirable jobs in terms of pay and difficulty. However, as shown by Maier (2001), among others, Latinos are often provided with work considered quite dangerous, even by the veterans of such occupations. In addition, they often receive insufficient training for such jobs and are additionally ill prepared for them because of language barriers. The results are as predictable as they are tragic: Latinos lose their lives on the job far more frequently than do others, and the gaps separating the implicated fatality rates are increasing. Figures 13 and 14 provide the grisly details.

Figure 13 shows the recorded number of fatalities on the job sustained by Latino workers in select years from 1992 to 2005. Over that period, their deaths increased from a low of 533 in 1992 to a high of 917 in 2005. Ironically, this was a period when the overall number of deaths on the job was actually decreasing (U.S. Department of Labor 2007). Unfortunately, figures on these deaths by the nationality backgrounds of the specific Latino workers are not available.

However, an important item, with particular relevance to the argument of this essay, is revealed in figure 13. There, the upward shifts in Latino deaths are

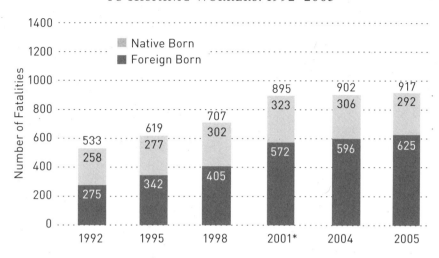

FIGURE 13. NUMBER OF FATAL WORK INJURIES
TO HISPANIC WORKERS: 1992–2005

Source: U.S. Department of Labor 2007
• Excludes fatalities resulting from the September 11 attacks.

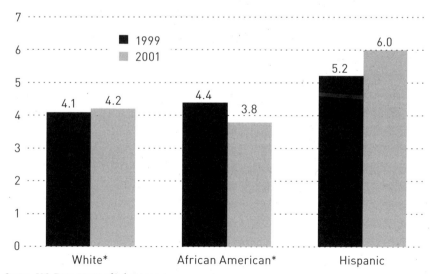

FIGURE 14. WORKPLACE FATALITY RATES IN THE U.S.,
1999 AND 2001, PER 100,000 WORKERS

Source: U.S. Department of Labor 2007
• Non-Hispanic

divided by nativity between U.S. born and foreign born. While both categories of workers are shown to have experienced increases in their yearly number of deaths on the job, that of the foreign born has more than doubled (275 to 625) in a straight upward direction. By contrast, the equally tragic deaths of the native-born workers have increased more modestly and erratically. Considering that Mexican workers clearly account for a significant majority of all Latino workers as well as accounting for the majority of Latino immigrants, it stands to reason that they are well represented among the denoted fatalities.

Perhaps more devastating than the increase of deaths in absolute numbers has been the increase in the death rates of Latino workers. Figure 14 provides a comparison of the workplace fatality rates of non-Hispanic whites and African Americans, along with those for Latinos in 1999 and in 2001. Whereas African Americans show a decrease in fatality rates from 4.4 per 100,000 in 1999 to 3.8 per 100,000 in 2001, whites show a slight increase in fatality rates (4.1 per 100,000 to 4.2 per 100,000). In sharp contrast to those figures, the death rate for Latino workers rose considerably during the two years. Their fatality rate is shown to have risen from 5.2 per 100,000 in 1999 to a phenomenal 6.0 per 100,000 in 2001.

Figure 15 provides fatality information on Latinos for just one state, Georgia. This state was earlier noted as being one of the few where sudden drastic increases in the Latino population were in evidence between 1990 and 2000. As shown in figure 16, whereas Latinos accounted for some 5.3 percent of the Georgia's population in 2000, they accounted for a staggering 33.2 percent of the state's deaths on the job that year. The rapid influx of Latinos into that state, many of whom are both undocumented and of Mexican origin, is doubtlessly related to their overrepresentation in workplace fatalities.

Although Georgia's residents include numerous Latinos with national origins outside of Mexico, Mexicans clearly accounted for most of the growth in the state during the 1990s. Whereas Mexicans accounted for less than half of the state's Latinos in 1990 (44.5 percent), they accounted for almost two-thirds of the aggregated group in 2000 (63.3 percent). In addition, areas where they are concentrated showed patterns of growth similar to those of the meatpacking towns featured earlier.

One such area is Dalton. Known as the "carpet capitol of the world," Dalton hosted a nearly eightfold growth in Latinos (1,422 persons to 11,219 persons) over the decade. Clearly, many of the Latino newcomers migrated there to work in the carpet factories. Moreover, many were necessarily of Mexican origin since Mexicans accounted for 84.1 percent of the area's Hispanics in 2000. Similar

FIGURE 15. PERCENT HISPANIC OF GEORGIA'S POPULATION AND ITS JOB FATALITIES: 2002–2005

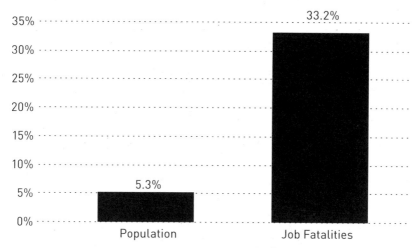

Source: U.S. Census Bureau 2003: Warren and Golbery 2001

growth was recorded in another area of Latino concentration, Gainesville, which is known as the "poultry capital of the world." There, Latino growth was slower, but still brisk (1,415 persons to 8,484 persons). Mexicans, doubtlessly drawn by the poultry industry, accounted for some 83.5 percent of that area's Latinos in 2000 (U.S. Bureau of the Census 2003).

Figure 16 reveals data on yet another form of death that uniquely affects Latino immigrants, most particularly those from Mexico. It shows the number of officially recorded deaths to potential migrants occurring along the U.S.-Mexican border from about 1996 to about 2001. Every single year shown in the series has been marked by well over 300 such tragedies. Such are the hazards faced by the workers desperate enough to take the jobs that provide enough income to barely stave off starvation, but will also often kill them. But their troubles do not end there.

If Latino immigrants crossing the border manage to safely navigate the harsh terrain and climate, there is still one additional danger to be avoided: vigilantes. The following passage, reported by Reuters (2003), notes the item:

Phoenix (Reuters)—March 6, 2003. A Mexican man who was found shot to death in a rural area outside Phoenix appears to be the ninth victim in a string

Figure 16. Officially Recorded Deaths across Mexican Border of Potential Migrants

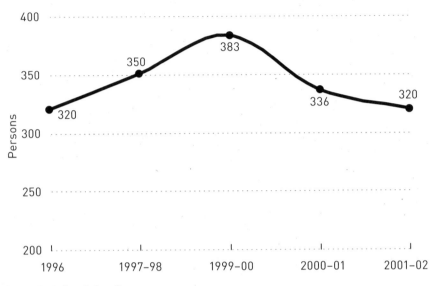

Source: Rozemberg & Carroll 2002

of execution style murders of illegal immigrants, police said on Wednesday. The body of the unidentified man . . . who was in his 30s, had been shot at close range, his hands bound behind his back. "We're positive that all the murders are related . . ." [stated the sheriff].

Conclusion

It has been argued here that the explosive growth of the Hispanic population in the United States has been accompanied by heightened exploitation. The data presented here are consistent with this interpretation. It was further argued that in the absence of the exploitation, the population explosion would not have occurred. The explanation for this is simple. If the implicated entrepreneurs, from the small contractors to the large corporations involved, were unable to obtain the immigrants' labor at the meager wages and questionable conditions currently in place, they would almost certainly not have hired them in the first place, much less recruited them over long distances. This would clearly reduce the size and pace of the migrations. But however much at fault, the workers' exploiters are not the only guilty parties here.

The federal government, or more specifically, certain components therein, are virtual co-conspirators in the depicted tragic drama. While certain agencies (and individuals within them) of government, such as the investigators of the Department of Labor and Occupational Safety and Health Administration (OSHA), do attempt to enforce standards of wages and safety, sometimes heroically, their efforts are often thwarted by other government entities.

Examples abound of unconscionable indifference by officials to workplace abuses involving loss of life and limb, along with examples where officials actively undermine the ability of others to address these problems (Barstow 2003; Barstow and Bergman 2003). For instance, since 1982, over 170,000 workers have lost their lives on the job, yet fewer than 25 percent of those deaths were investigated by OSHA, according to a New York Times study. Of those deaths examined by the agency, 2,197 were deemed to have been caused by "willful" violations of the law—the most serious degree of violation. These were cases that top officials at OSHA described as "intolerable outrages, 'horror stories' that demanded the agency's strongest response" (Barstow 2003). Despite that, more than nine out of ten from that group were not prosecuted. Even "repeat" violators who caused additional deaths were rarely prosecuted.

As far back as the 1980s, OSHA was greatly understaffed. The agency's 1,300 inspectors at the decade's start were charged with overseeing safety standards for over five million workers. Yet the Reagan administration cut the staff by about 20 percent and enacted regulations curtailing the ability of investigators to make unannounced inspections under a policy known as "voluntary compliance." According to a subsequent congressional investigation, the policy encouraged companies "to understate injuries, to falsify records, and to cover up accidents" (Schlosser 2001). At the current time, the number of OSHA inspectors (1,123) remains lower than at the start of the Reagan administration, despite the substantial increase in the nation's labor force.

When employers are sanctioned for causing workers' deaths, the sanction is usually a comparatively minor fine. For example, between 1982 and 1991 the median dollar amount of fines levied for such offenses was a mere $5,800. In more recent years, that number has risen to only about $32,000 (Barstow 2003). In a number of cases, the sanctions levied appear unbelievably inconsequential. For instance, as Eric Schlosser has written, at one particular meat plant, "Homer Stull climbed into a blood-collection tank to clean it, a filthy tank thirty feet high. Stull was overcome by hydrogen sulfide fumes. Two coworkers climbed into the tank and tried to rescue him. All three men died. Eight years earlier, Henry Wolf had been overcome by hydrogen sulfide fumes while cleaning the very same tank; Gary Sanders had tried to rescue him; both men died" (2001: 178). In the end, OSHA fined the company a mere $480 for each victim.

The reluctance at OSHA to pursue prosecution appears to reflect policy at the highest levels of the agency, according to the painstaking set of interviews and analyses in the Times's study (Barstow 2003). Rank-and-file agents or supervisors who push too hard for prosecutions are neither encouraged nor rewarded, and they are sometimes even penalized for their efforts. As Barstow (2003) notes:

> When people at OSHA explain their reluctance to pursue criminal prosecutions, they sometimes begin by pointing to the example of Ronald J. McCann. Mr. McCann, acting regional administrator in Chicago during the early 1980's, was an early champion of criminal prosecutions. He had a simple, no-nonsense approach: If a death resulted from a willful violation, it should be referred to the Justice Department without delay.
>
> But in the early days of the Reagan administration, he said in a recent interview, that policy brought a clear rebuke from OSHA's new political appointees. Twelve times he sought prosecutions. "They were all thrown out." Soon after, he said, he was removed from his job and transferred so often that he ended up living in a tent to avoid moving his family again.

In this way, and countless others beyond the scope of this essay, governmental authorities facilitate, encourage, and even abet fundamentally criminal conduct. For example, according to Chavez-Thompson (2003), executive vice president of the AFL-CIO, the Bush administration has further hindered the plight of Hispanic workers. While Bush's secretary of labor claims a commitment to addressing the Latino on-the-job death rate, in fact, the Bush administration cut training and related programs for Latino workers, quashed an ergonomics regulation that would have improved working conditions, and refuses to require employers to provide the protective gear necessary for employee safety. Such flagrant injustices cannot forever be tolerated. One way or another, they must be stopped. While the best solution to the problem cannot easily be specified here, one clear step forward is to alert a wide readership to these conditions. Such a step is taken here. But it is only the very first of many such necessary steps.

NOTES

1. The notion that "Latinos" or "Hispanics" constitute a meaningful collectivity is not without controversy. A full discussion of the issues is beyond the scope of this essay. Suffice to say that this author accepts the designation as sufficiently meaningful for the purpose at hand. Moreover, the individual nationality groups in question are sufficiently identified in the essay to avoid any misrepresentations or misinterpretations of any key issues.

2. All references to African Americans and whites refer to non-Hispanics, except where noted.

3. Slowed growth since 2000 by some of the contributors to the rapid growth earlier may reflect the diminution of the numerous Central American conflicts (e.g., in El Salvador, Nicaragua, Guatemala, and Columbia) that generated substantial refugee streams during the previous decades. It may also reflect the greater difficulty of managing unauthorized entries after 9/11. Mexican migration would be unaffected by the first item and less vulnerable to the post-9/11 constraints because Mexican ties to the United States are far more extensive and have deeper historical roots. Mexicans are also more likely to be recruited.

4. The one exception to this is Monroe, North Carolina. There, 122 Puerto Ricans were enumerated. Since that number is dwarfed by the corresponding number of Mexicans in the city (4,741), and the latter group alone accounted for around 85 percent of the area's Latinos, the Puerto Rican group was not included in the table.

5. Stanley (1992) suggests an alternative way for the Central Americans to have been steered to such places. In her review, Stanley notes that numerous refugee groups have been steered to meat-packing jobs by the government agencies overseeing their integration or by subcontractors for such agencies.

REFERENCES

Aponte, Robert. 1999. "Towards the 21st Century: Latinos in the U.S. at the Century's End and Beyond." Latino Studies Journal 10(2): 3–27.

Barstow, David. 2003. "U.S. Rarely Seeks Charges For Deaths in Workplace." New York Times, December 22.

Barstow, David, and Lowell Bergman. 2003. "Deaths on the Job, Slaps on the Wrist." New York Times, January 10.

CensusScope. 2000. "U.S. Population by Race and Ethnicity Selections, 1980–2000." Census Scope–Population by Race. Retrieved from http://www.censusscope.org/us/print_chart_race.html.

Chavez, Leo R. 1996. "Borders and Bridges: Undocumented Immigrants from Mexico and Central America." In Origins and Destinies: Immigration, Race, and Ethnicity in America, ed. Silvia Pedraza and Ruben G. Rumbaut. New York: Wadsworth.

Chavez-Thompson, Linda. 2003. "Too Many Hispanic Workers Are Dying on the Job." Hispanic Vista, April 27. Retrieved from http://www.hipanicvista.com.

Connolly, Ceci. 2003. "Census Finds Many More Lack Health Insurance." Washington Post, September 30.

Gouveia, Lourdes, and Donald D. Stull. 1995. "Dances with Cows: Beefpacking's Impact on Garden City, Kansas, and Lexington, Nebraska." In Any Way You Cut It: Meat Processing and Small-Town America, ed. Donald Stull, Michael Broadway, and David Griffith, 85–107. Lawrence: University Press of Kansas.

Greenhouse, Steven. 2003. "Illegally in the U.S., and Never a Day Off at Wal-Mart." New York Times, November 5.

Greenwald, H. P., S. O'Keefe, and M. DiCamillo. 2005. "Why Employed Latinos Lack Health Insurance: A Study in California." Hispanic Journal of Behavioral Sciences. 27(4): 517–32.

Grey, Mark A. 1995. "Pork, Poultry and Newcomers in Storm Lake, Iowa." In Any Way You Cut It: Meat Processing and Small-Town America, ed. Donald Stull, Michael Broadway, and David Griffith, 109–28. Lawrence: University Press of Kansas.

Grimsley, Kristin Downey. 2001. "Tyson Foods Indicted in INS Probe: U.S. Says Firm Sought Illegal Immigrants." Washington Post, December 20.

Holzer, H. J. 1996. What Employers Want: Job Prospects for Less-Educated Workers. New York: Russell Sage.

Immigration and Naturalization Services (INS). 2003. Estimates of the Unauthorized Immigrant Population Residing in the United States: 1990–2000. Washington, D.C.: Government Printing Office. Retrieved from: http://uscis.gov.

Johnson-Webb, K. 2003. Recruiting Hispanic Labor: Immigrants in Non-Traditional Areas. New York: LFB Scholarly Publishing.

Kirschenman, J., and K. Neckerman. 1990. "We'd Love to Hire Them But. . . ." In The Urban Underclass, ed. C. Jencks and P. Petersen. Washington, D.C.: Brookings Institution.

Lugo, Luis Alonso. 2003. "Fox Says U.S.-Mexico Remittances Hit High." Washington Post, September 24. Retrieved from http://www.washingtonpost.com.

Maier, Thomas. 2001. "4 Part, Award Winning Investigative Series on Immigrant Worker Deaths and Related Issues." Newsday, July 22–25. Retrieved from Center for Public Integrity site http://www.publici.org.

Massey, Douglas S. 1986. "The Settlement Process among Mexican Immigrants to the United States." American Sociological Review 51 (October): 670–84.

Moretti, Enrico. 1999. "Social Networks and Migrations: Italy 1876–1913." International Migration Review 33 (Fall): 640–57.

National Center for Health Statistics (NCHS). 2006. "Health United States, 2006." Retrieved from http://www.cdc.gov/nchs/data/hus/hus06.pdf.

Passel, J. 2005. Estimates of the Size and Characteristics of the Undocumented Population. Washington D.C.: Pew Hispanic Center.

Pear, Robert. 2003. "New Study Finds 60 Million Uninsured during a Year." New York Times, May 13.

Portes, Alejandro, and Jozsef Borocz. 1989. "Contemporary Immigration: Theoretical Perspectives on Its Determinants and Modes of Incorporation." International Migration Review 23 (Fall): 606–30.

Reuters. 2003. "Border War Heating Up? Slain Immigrant Called 9th Victim in Arizona Spree: Killers Not Known but Speculation Includes Armed Vigilantes as Potential Suspects." March 6. Retrieved from http://www.cnn.com.

Rozemberg, H., and S. Carroll. 2002. "45% of Crossing Deaths Occur along Arizona Border." Arizona Republic and Tucson Citizen, October 3. Retrieved from http://azcentral.com/arizonarepublic.

Schlosser, Eric. 2001. Fast Food Nation: The Dark Side of the All-American Meal. New York: Houghton Mifflin.

Staff and News Service Reports. 2003. "43 Million Uninsured in America." Indianapolis Star, September 30.

Stanley, Kathleen. 1992. "Immigrant and Refugee Workers in the Midwestern Meatpacking Industry: Industrial Restructuring and the Transformation of Rural Labor Markets." Policy Studies Review 11 (Summer): 107–17.

Stull, Donald D., Michael J. Broadway, and David Griffith, eds. 1995. Any Way You Cut It: Meat Processing and Small-Town America. Lawrence: University Press of Kansas.

U.S. Census Bureau. 2002. "Historical Census Statistics on Population Totals by Race, 1790–1990, and by Hispanic Origin, 1970–1990, for the U.S. Regions, Divisions, and States." Retrieved from http://www.census.gov/population/www/documentation/twps0056.html.

———. 2003. Censuses of 1990 and 2000. Retrieved from http://www.census.gov/.

———. 2006a. 2005 American Community Survey. Retrieved from www.census.gov/acs/www.

————. 2006b. "2005 Poverty Tables. CPS." 2006 Annual Social and Economic Supplement, Annual Demographic Survey. Retrieved from http://pubdb3.census.gov/macro/032006/pov/toc.htm.

U.S. Department of Labor. 2002. "Census of Fatal Occupational Injuries Summary." Washington, D.C.: Government Printing Office. Retrieved from http://www.bls.gov/.

————. 2007. "Census of Fatal Occupational Injuries Charts, 1992–2005." Census of Fatal Occupational Injuries (CFOI)–Current and Revised Data. Retrieved from http://stats.bls.gov/iif/oshcfoi1.htm#2005.

Warren, Beth, and David Golbery. 2001. "Latino Work Deaths Climbing: A Third of Georgia's Job Fatalities Last Year Were Hispanic." Atlantic Journal Constitution, December 17.

5

Race, Immigration, and the Limits of Citizenship

H. L. T. QUAN

I crossed the border and went to Wenatchee in August to pick apples. In January 2000 I saw the flyer in a laundromat and called the number. The guy told me to wait until he had fifteen people signed up, then he would send us to Nebraska on a Greyhound bus. When we got fifteen guys, he met with us to have us sign work contracts and give us bus tickets. A couple of guys said they didn't have any documentation. The recruiter said, "It doesn't matter, the important things is that you work."

We rode fifty-four hours to Omaha. They gave us a $100 loan to get through the first few days, but we had to repay it from payroll deductions after we started working. When we went to the office to start work, they had us fill out more papers and talked to us for thirty minutes. Then they sent us out on the line. There was no training. They told us, "Do what the person next to you is doing."

—A worker at Nebraska Beef, quoted in Human Rights Watch, *Blood, Sweat, and Fear: Workers' Rights in U.S. Meat and Poultry Plants*

In spring 2006, several million residents took to the street demonstrating solidarity with immigrants and calling for humane immigration reforms in the United States. Dozens of U.S. cities had never witnessed such an outpouring of popular participation in such large numbers until the immigrant marches of that spring.[1] On May Day, the day of the nationwide boycott, one landscaping business in Indiana reported that 90 percent of its workforce (twenty-five workers) did not show up for work.[2] Rural Homestead, Florida, a town of fewer than 50,000 people, saw more than 1,200 people marching through its historic district. The world's largest meat producer, Tyson Foods Inc., closed more than a dozen of its 100 plants. It was apparent to most people that there was a contentious debate on what to do about immigration in the United States, especially concerning the thirteen million men, women, and children who reside and work in the country without legal recognition. That spring, the hundreds of thousands of marchers signified a quiet riot exposing the inhumane treatments of migrant workers and residents in the United States.

The spring before, little notice was given to a report, *Blood, Sweat, and Fear: Workers/Rights in U.S. Meat and Poultry Plants*, compiled and released by Human Rights Watch, a premier human rights organization, documenting human rights abuses by an industry that features immigrant workers as the majority of its workforce. Among its many abuses, the U.S. meat and poultry industry effectively created a "huge underclass laboring in substandard employment conditions."[3] Accordingly,

> millions of fearful, vulnerable non-citizens work in our nation's most dangerous, dirty and demanding conditions. Abuses such as failure to prevent serious workplace injury and illness, denial of compensation to injured workers, interference with workers' freedom of association, are all directly linked to the vulnerable immigration status of most workers in the meat and poultry industry and the willingness of employers to take advantage of that vulnerability.[4]

In 2004, at the Smithfield hog processing plant in North Carolina, a labor board investigation found merit in employee charges that Smithfield and its contractors unlawfully violated half a dozen labor practices, including physical assault, false arrest, failure to pay, and threats and intimidation of workers.[5] Indeed, Human Rights Watch argues that it is at the nexus between labor rights and human rights abuses that we find most common violations and general maltreatment of immigrants living in the United States. Ironically, most participants in the debate about U.S. immigration reform neglect to address the human rights dimensions of immigrant life. This chapter argues that as a framework for livable life and work with dignity, human rights standards have much more to offer than the limited discourse of citizenship.[6] It is so because historically U.S. citizenship itself has not guaranteed humane or equal treatment due to racialization and racism. For we must ask the following question: If citizenship is politically salient for immigrants and refugees, what can we actually say about how profoundly it does not provide protection or aid to Native Americans, African Americans and the racial others? As Cedric J. Robinson points out in *Black Movements in America*, "America had been and is still a nation of freedom *and* injustice." This, according to Robinson, is our fundamental paradox, and as a nation, it is yet to be resolved. From the moment of the American Revolution, Robinson explains: "In the same place, at the same time, and in the same minds, the utopian dreams of liberty and justice competed for right of place and with the reality of slavery."[7] More than 200 years later and in the age of corporate globalization, capital is reified and its mobility celebrated, while mobile human beings are garrisoned as "illegal."[8]

I will examine research by Samuel P. Huntington to show how the immigration debate, at one level, has as much to do with economics as it does with the nature of antidemocratic politics in this country. In many ways, Huntington's controversial attack on Latino immigration reveals the fundamentally political and racial dimensions of the debate. Huntington's work is instructive because his scholarship is essentially a cipher for an antidemocratic politics embracing a white supremacist ideology that has endured and defined the terms of our social contract.[9] I also borrow Charles W. Mill's language of the "global racial contract" to show that because "white supremacy is the unnamed political system that has made the modern world what it is today," especially when considering the contemporary immigration debate, we need to make visible a political system that regulates "the differential distribution of wealth and opportunities, benefits and burdens, rights and duties," including those of citizenship.[10] Further, I argue that beyond the immediate and progressive responses to xenophobic attacks on undocumented immigrants in the form of vigilante violence as well as legislative action, there is a need to reframe the debate on immigration such that questions about race, citizenship, and democracy can be properly assessed. My basic conclusion is that embracing a human rights framework, with its guidelines, standards of protection, and humane treatment grounded in a commitment to global justice, promises a greater theoretical and practical space than the neo-liberal agenda that seeks to capitalize on cheap labor and capitulate on the possibility of livable lives.

THE HISPANIC PANIC

As a nation, we are experiencing a Hispanic panic and are in denial about our dependency on migrant labor—an endless desire for cheap and docile labor and a deep-seated fear of power sharing and democratic control. In an article in *Foreign Policy*, a magazine funded by the Carnegie Foundation, Samuel P. Huntington writes:

> The persistent inflow of Hispanic immigrants threatens to divide the United States into two people, two cultures, and two languages. Unlike past immigrant groups, Mexicans and other Latinos have not assimilated into mainstream U.S. culture, forming instead their own political and linguistic enclaves—from Los Angeles to Miami—and rejecting the Anglo-Protestant values that built the American dream. The United States ignores this challenge at its peril.[11]

Huntington then proceeds to whitewash American history, deracinate its multi-cultural heritage, and distill all experiences to that of a white, specifically, Anglo, Protestant creed. He calls this "the creed." Apparently, "the creed" has been a "crucial element" for the making of an American identity. Huntington warns that the Anglo-Protestant culture and "the creed" have come under attack by the forces of globalization and multiculturalism. He then argues: "In this new era, the single most immediate and most serious challenge to America's traditional iden-tity comes from the immense and continuing immigration from Latin America, especially from Mexico and the fertility rates of these immigrants compared to black and white American natives."[12]

One can audibly hear nativists panicking over countless brown babies crying. Huntington identifies the current socioeconomic status of Latinos and Chicanos as factors contributing to their failure to assimilate, most notably, economic status, educational attainment, and rates of home ownership and in-terracial marriages. Interestingly, he points out that "no other immigrant group in U.S. history has asserted or could assert a historical claim to U.S. territory. Mexicans and Mexican Americans can and do make that claim."[13] This sense of "one's own turf" presumably contributes to their inability to assimilate. Pointing to Latinos' comfort with their own culture and so-called contempt for "American culture," Huntington concludes that left unimpeded, we might see "the end of the America we have known for more than three centuries." In a sidebar, he also comments on the threat of white nativism and argues that its "most powerful stimulus . . . will be cultural and linguistic threats whites see from the expanding power of Hispanics in US society."[14] For Huntington, "the end of America" is not only the imagined identity becoming unglued but also that America's prestige and global positioning are under direct threat caused by multiculturalism in general, and Latino immigrants in particular. As such, immigration is not simply a domestic dilemma but a global crisis, one that has the potential of shifting U.S. international priorities.

To be sure, such anemic coverage of the making of contemporary America and the impoverished understanding of the complexity of American cultural politics, not to mention generally poor science, coming from one of our most preeminent political scientists and policy analysts, earned Huntington a fair share of criticism. But close readers of Huntington recognize that this latest panic, the twenty-first century's updated and modified version of the yellow peril, is actually a recycled argument advanced in Huntington's earlier work, *The Clash of Civilizations and the Remaking of World Order.*[15]

Eight years prior to the *Foreign Policy* publication, Huntington was broader in his reach. He posited that ideological contestations disappeared with the end of the Cold War (a public congratulatory note to Francis Fukuyama's capitalist self-aggrandizement). Accordingly, in the post–Cold War era, and are the primary sources of in world affairs. To quote Huntington:

> It is my hypothesis that the fundamental source of conflict in this new world will not be primarily ideological or primarily economic. The great divisions among humankind and the dominating source of conflict will be cultural. Nation states will remain the most powerful actors in world affairs, but the principal conflicts of global politics will occur between nations and groups of different civilizations. The clash of civilizations will dominate global politics. The fault lines between civilizations will be the battle lines of the future.[16]

Indeed, this same thesis was advanced in his earlier article, "Clash of Civilization?" published in *Foreign Affairs* in 1993. So eleven years after his initial foray into the parlance of cultural politics, Huntington brought his "clash of civilizations" thesis to the forefront on the question of immigration, with decidedly racial and domestic dimensions. It is not hard to see correlations between his treatment of Latinos in the discussion of immigration and his treatment of Islam in *Clash of Civilizations*. Though much more significant is his equal insistence that it is culture, not ideology or economics, that defines the nature of these conflicts. It is culture that makes Islam (and not only

Islamic fundamentalism) a threat to Western civilization, so it is culture that makes Latinos the greatest threat to Anglo-Protestant American identity and nationhood.

It is not insignificant that in the 1960s, Huntington redefined studies of popular mobilization and provided a paradigm shift in American political science to privilege "political order in changing societies," also the title of his most important work. It is also not insignificant that as a Cold War warrior, Huntington, while at Harvard, preached that it was the job of American political scientists to advance an anti-Communist, pro-America, and prowar stance in their scholarship.[17] His nativist stance and his antidemocratic prejudice are important clues to my inquiry into the question of race and immigration. The immigration marches of spring 2006 raise a number of issues for nativists, not least among which was the fear that U.S. cities and towns would be overrun by immigrants, particularly undocumented immigrants participating in the political process through mass demonstrations and political mobilizations. Nativism precludes any notion of political participation by foreigners, and as such, immigrants, documented or otherwise, are not considered legitimate actors in the political process. Indeed, in his seminal work on political development, Huntington argues that when the mass is "prematurely activated," a nation risks chaos and ungovernability.[18]

The fear of popular mobilization is central to Huntington's and the modernization school of thought. It was their antidemocratic biases that allowed them to privilege military and authoritarian regimes in Latin American over democratic ones.[19] How ironic it is then, almost forty years after the publication of *Political Order in Changing Societies*, that Huntington would have to confront Latino mobilization, not in South America and Central America, but in the United States. If nothing else, corporate globalization has ensured that people who once participated in demonstrations themselves or were witnesses to demonstrations in the streets of Latin America against authoritarianism would one day be moved to take to the streets of Atlanta, Los Angeles, San Francisco, New York, Chicago, and even Homestead, Florida, against human rights abuses in the United States. Huntington's fear of "the cult" of multiculturalism is fueled by his antidemocratic bias and predisposition against the mass public as evidenced by his scholarship. Huntington's America is an elitist one, a white Protestant country that would deem all others inconsequential, regardless of its own dependency on the labor or love of the inconsequential other. Huntington, however, cannot claim to be a pioneer in his conflation of citizenship, political participation, and nativism. That practice has a much longer history.

CITIZENSHIP AND THE LIMITS OF AMERICAN DEMOCRACY

Contemporary Western democracies credit ancient Greece for their lineage, but few are aware of the fact that Solon, whom many credit as one of the "founding fathers" of Athenian democracy, codified Athenian citizenship as nonslave. Faced with mass economic dislocation, popular discontent, and civil strife and in a time of war, Solon's first act after he took office in 594 B.C. was to "strike at the fundamental evil in the state, the debt situation."[20] In a single move, Solon, by decree, liberated debtors who were Athenians and forbade the practice of securing loans by the borrower's person. The decree prevented the enslavement of poor Athenians who, with no possessions beyond their personhood, would otherwise be forced to use their own bodies as collateral. According to Aristotle, foremost in Solon's mind was the need to mend the tensions between the powerful rich and powerless poor, "for they happened, so to speak, to have a share in nothing."[21] Solon's constitutional reform was credited as a fundamental feature for the development of the future Athenian democracy.[22] It was this provision that helped conflate Athenians with citizenship and nonslave status and led Aristotle to designate Solon the father of Athenian democracy. For the first time, then, one could not enslave an Athenian in Athens. More important, being a male Athenian entitled one to be a full citizen; namely, one who could directly participate in the democratic political process. Foreigners or *metics* could own property but not participate in the Athenian democracy.

Not coincidentally, one of the first laws passed by the newly formed Congress of the United States was the Naturalization Act of 1790, which specified that only a "free white person" could begin the process of naturalization leading to citizenship. This act granted citizenship to "free white persons" and deliberately excluded white indentured servants, slaves (including indigenous people), free people of color, and later, Latinos and Asian Americans. The racial restriction clause was not suspended until 1952. Within this framework, whiteness and nonslave status translate to citizenship.

Since 1790, there is ample evidence suggesting we have not moved very far from this white supremacist model of citizenship, not least among which is the history of the exclusion of Asian immigrants. Interestingly, most theories on democracy, even when limited to only white personhood, are about the mechanics of election or procedural rather than direct participation. Even proportional representation, however limited it is as a procedure compared to direct democracy, continues to be censured and is frequently perceived as naive and "quota proned."[23] In fact, direct democracy is not even considered by mainstream theorists as a viable concept.[24] Ironically then, while we retain the nativist dimension of Athenian democracy, historically we have limited popular participation in our democratic polity.

Given the fundamentally pronativist and antidemocratic prejudice inherent in contemporary political thought, citizenship, as it is constructed here, provides little assurance that genuine political incorporation and democratic politics will take place. Moreover, the history of the political exclusion of people of color in the United States, as a result of legal and extralegal measures, including racial terrorism as a means to discipline nonwhite residents against participating in the political process, suggests that even when people of color achieve nominal citizenship, democratic participation and political incorporation are not guaranteed. Put differently, racism has precluded and continues to preclude an automatic relationship between citizenship and participation, and any assurance that citizens would be treated equally. The humanitarian crisis and the public policy failure in the Hurricane Katrina disaster help us further appreciate this dilemma.

ALL BUT IN NAME

While it is not the scope of this chapter to provide a systematic comparison of the treatment of immigrants and antiblack racism, Katrina is a remarkable lesson against historical amnesia about racialization and racism in the United States. In this instance, citizenship provides little comfort (physical and otherwise) for those who were systematically excluded from the global racial contract.

Hurricanes Katrina and Rita (September 2005) caused extensive damage to southern Louisiana and parts of Mississippi and Alabama, as well as the displacement of hundreds of thousands of mostly poor and black residents from the region—constituting the greatest exodus of black people in contemporary American history. The resulting "evacuation" produced the depopulation of the region. What is most remarkable is the fact that in the city of New Orleans, the black community accounted for 80 percent of the total population lost. Significantly, more than 73 percent of blacks (counted in the 2000 census) are no longer there. Put differently, less than 27 percent of the black population in New Orleans remains in the city.[25] Even as it was unfolding, Katrina debunked the notional and paradigmatic claims of color blindness as a fact and an epistemological standpoint. The crisis of legitimacy was visible, and we, as a nation, can no longer deny what we have always known; namely, some people in arguably the richest nation on earth actually go to bed hungry, that depending on where you are and who you are, you might not have food or water even though as a country we produce enough *waste* to feed nations, that there is a color to poverty, and that racism is the engine of the American social contract.

In the aftermath of Katrina, in addition to the horrors of having lost loved ones, watching sick people die needlessly, and having been forced to evacuate with the knowledge that all their worldly possessions were likely to be destroyed, the displaced persons from the Gulf States, most of whom were poor black people, also had to deal with the fact that their "border status" in the words of cultural critic Valerie Smith, "illuminate[d] the silences upon which consensus depends" and "implicate[d] viewers more directly in the effects of the specific constructions of race and gender and relations."[26]

A debate emerged about whether to categorize these displaced individuals as refugees, internally displaced people, evacuees, or simply victims. Ultimately, the idea of an internally displaced people or refugees did not find traction in the United States, yet what actually occurred demonstrates in fact that they were internally displaced from their homes and communities, and all most all of whom are citizens. A greater difficulty perhaps has to do with the persistent denial in mainstream consciousness that uneven urban development, unequal treatment, and political disenfranchisement contributed to this natural and human-made disaster.[27]

Some voiced their outrage against the bureaucratic and official bankrupt handling of the crisis by simply stating the fact that these are citizens of the United States, and thus, pathetic response was a national disgrace. The long track record of political and economic disenfranchisement of the poor and people of color in the United States reveals this view to be naive at best. This is especially so when we consider the following facts: pre-Katrina New Orleans had a rate of poverty that doubled the national average rate (at 27.9 percent); 91.2 percent of the poor families in New Orleans were black; and 35 percent of the black population in the city lived in poverty. Therefore, it is not difficult to conclude that uneven urban development engendered a particular pattern of federal, state, and local responses (both during the immediate crisis and in the rebuilding effort).

But New Orleans is not unique. It shares a pattern of uneven urban development with Atlanta, Chicago, Detroit, Washington, D.C., and other large American urban centers, where there is a sizable population of people of color, citizens and noncitizens. This uneven development is caused in part by the combined effects of neo-liberal economics, racism, globalization, and the greater entrapment of young people into the correctional system. Within this context, citizenship itself seems inadequate as a mechanism for securing even bodily safety. Indeed, vulnerability and "premature death" more accurately characterize the plight of the displaced people in the region.[28]

One wonders if a majority of the displaced people would have received better treatment had they been Chinese or British nationals, with predictable diplomatic pressure from powerful national governments. We can only speculate on that hypothetical, but we do know that two years after Katrina, the majority of the displaced people have not received adequate support.[29] According to an American Civil Liberties Union (ACLU) report, "Broken Promises: Two Years after Katrina," the ACLU has been "inundated with reports of racial injustice and human rights violations that have taken place in Louisiana and Mississippi." The complaints came from people of diverse backgrounds and were documented in the report, which "details the increase in police abuse, racial profiling, housing discrimination, and other civil liberties violation."[30] So it seems that Katrina simply exacerbated what was already a well-established pattern of uneven development, concentrated poverty and racialized public policies.

If we deem humane treatment and political enfranchisement by immigrants as essential to democratic politics, then the Katrina example is instructive in that it shows citizenship itself to be an empty trope. If citizenship does not guarantee equal treatment or political incorporation, as empirical evidence clearly suggests, what then is the recourse for immigrants in this country? At a minimum, this essay argues that the racist limitations of American democracy require immigrant rights advocates to look beyond national boundaries and beyond the state. Doing so is not ignoring the limits of the United Nation and the conventional global justice framework, and campaigners for another possible world would assuredly appreciate the necessity of having the persistent of visions and alternative spaces for political mobilization. As the historian Howard Zinn has pointed out, social movements have forced the political process to include, rather than exclude, new groups of people in this country.[31] Cedric Robinson concurs. He argues that it has been the case that "domination and oppression [have inspired] that spirit in ways we may never fully understand."[32] If Robinson is right about the irresistible and persistent "human impulse" to imagine a different existence, and what Jacques Derrida calls "a matter of an ethical and political imperative, an appeal as unconditional as the appeal of thinking from which it is not separated,"[33] then state-sanctioned citizenship within the context of white supremacy is fundamentally anemic compared to other traditions.

A CODA

In 2000, the U.S.-born population of Asian descent was 4.5 million people, less than half of the Asian American Pacific Islander (AAPI) population. The total AAPI population is at 11.2 million. AAPIs make up a quarter of all foreign-born Americans. More than 40 percent of this total population does not speak English as a primary language. And in the Southeast Asian community, close to 40 percent of the population lives in or near poverty. Many of those living in poverty are immigrants.[34] Asian Americans have the distinction of being a group that was most systematically excluded from legal immigration.[35]

When the first Asians arrived in this country, they faced hatred, discrimination, and exclusion. They also found a friend in Frederick Douglass, one of the most well known abolitionists and freedom fighters in American history. More than 135 years ago, in defense of Chinese and Japanese immigrants, Douglass wrote in his "Composite Nation" speech that beyond the struggle for civil rights, we must look toward a framework that functions outside of the racial contract and that would appeal to "higher principles." To quote Douglass at length:

> In a composite nation like ours as before the law, there should be no rich, no poor, no high, no low, no white, no black, but common country, common citizenship, equal rights and a common destiny.
>
> Do you ask, if I favor such immigration, I answer *I would*. Would you have them naturalized, and have them invested with all the rights of American citizenship? *I would*. Would you allow them to vote? *I would*. Would you allow them to hold office? *I would*.
>
> I submit that this question of Chinese immigration should be settled upon higher principles than those of a cold and selfish expediency. There are such things in the world as human rights. They rest upon no conventional foundation, but are external, universal, and indestructible. Among these, is the right of locomotion, the right of migration, the right which belongs to no particular race, but belongs alike to all and to all alike. It is the right you assert by staying here, and your fathers asserted by coming here. It is this right that I assert for the Chinese and Japanese and for all other varieties of men equally with yourselves, now and forever. I know of no rights of race superiority to rights of humanity, and when there is a supposed conflict between humanity and national rights, it is safe to go to the side of humanity.[36]

More than a century later, these are still precious lessons of freedom *and* justice. Within the framework of global human rights, there are nearly two dozen articles and guidelines that are potentially available. They are located in the International Convention on the Protection of the Rights of All Migrant Workers and Members of their Families (1990), the International Labor Organization (1949, 1975), the Inter-American Court of Human Rights, and the United Nations Universal Declaration of Human Rights. These include provisions to protect against inhumane working conditions, labor intimidation and harassment, and unfair detention and deportation, as well as provisions to protect the right to work, associate, and freedom of conscience.[37] Douglass not only anticipated the contemporary discourse on human rights but also presciently understood that fundamentally the American creed, as articulated then by an American plantocracy, was bankrupt. The creed has now been retooled in the pages of *Foreign Policy* and on CNN to limit the parameters of public discourse on immigration.[38] Just as the antilynching campaign of the nineteenth and twentieth centuries looked abroad for social solidarity, so perhaps the immigrant movement in the twenty-first might look toward the global community for guidance.[39] Indeed, the chief spokesperson of the earlier centuries and one of the most astute students of antiblack racism and American imperialism, Ida B. Wells, knew then that an elitist, racist democracy cannot and should not police itself. Wells understood that the antilynching campaign needed a transnational stage to properly expose what she called "nineteenth century barbarism."[40]

While Douglass did of course champion the cause for naturalization and citizenship rights for immigrants, the "higher principles" he evoked are "superior" to both race and nation. The terms he employed "rest upon no conventional foundation, but are external, universal, and indestructible." They come closest to the language of the Universal Declaration of Human Rights, and thus operate outside of national or racial boundaries. It is also the language used by Malcolm X when he appealed to the United Nations to act on behalf of black people in their struggles for freedom and justice.[41] As Malcolm X understood then, citizenship, within the matrix of a global racial contract and empire, as advanced by ciphers like Samuel P. Huntington and Lou Dobbs, is simply a mirage and not a promise for a livable life.

NOTES

A version of this chapter was presented at the Race in 21st Century America conference at Michigan State University (East Lansing, Mich., April 2007). I want to acknowledge Curtis Stokes, Darryl Thomas, C. A. Griffith, and Tiffany Willoughby Herard for their comments and suggestions.

1. Cities in all regions of the continental United States saw mass protests in April and May 2006. Local newspapers such as the *San Diego Union-Tribune* and the *Arizona Republic* reported "historic" numbers of public demonstrations in San Diego and Phoenix respectively.

2. "Immigration Marches Across U.S.," May 1, 2006, http://www.msnb.msn.com/id/12573992.

3. "Immigrant Workers in the United States Meat and Poultry Industry," submission by Human Rights Watch to the Office of the United Nations High Commissioner for Human Rights Committee (UNHCHR) on Migrant Workers, December 15, 2005. Based on the findings of the report *Blood, Sweat, and Fear: Workers' Rights in U.S. Meat and Poultry Plants*, Human Rights Watch offered this case study for UNHCHR for consideration in December 2005.

4. Human Rights Watch, *Blood, Sweat, and Fear*, 2. It is important to note that clearly "vulnerability is more acute for undocumented workers." Nevertheless, in the age of deregulation and union busting, all workers experience some forms of work insecurity and vulnerability.

5. Ibid., 98–99.

6. I want to be clear in noting the limits of the human rights discourse itself, with its over-emphasis on individualism and individual rights, not to mention its Western grand narrative of universal humanism. The use of human rights rhetoric to discipline peoples and states by governments in the Global North, especially by the United States, should also be noted. Precisely because of the historical abuse of such rhetoric and the accompanied double standards, the human rights framework is seen as a suspect. Standards of human decency and social life, however, are not the exclusive province of Western civilization or modernity. While I do not believe that the liberal framework of human rights or a Global North controlled United Nation adequately addresses the racialization of the Latino immigrant population and many racialized others as targeted bodies for cheap and docile labor, I believe that human rights standards, not

citizenship, should be a starting point for a sensible dialogue about human dignity, livable life and the treatment of undocumented workers in the United States.

7. Cedric J. Robinson, *Black Movements in America* (New York: Routledge, 1997), 1.

8. For a discussion of the U.S. economy's dependence on immigrant labor and the violent realities of "border control" see Justin Akers Achon and Mike Davis, *No One is Illegal: Fighting Violence and State Repression on the U.S.-Mexico Border* (Chicago: Haymarket Books, 2006).

9. Employing the Rousseau-Lockean conceptualization of the social contract, I am referring to the implied "consent" that serves as an organizing principle in the making of modern United States. For further reference to the global racial contract, see Charles W. Mills, *The Racial Contract* (Ithaca, N.Y.: Cornell University Press, 1997).

10. Ibid., 3.

11. Samuel P. Huntington, "The Hispanic Challenge," *Foreign Policy* (March/April 2004): 30.

12. Ibid., 32.

13. Ibid., 36, 37.

14. Ibid., 41.

15. Samuel P. Huntington, *The Clash of Civilizations and the Remaking of World Order* (New York: Simon and Schuster, 1996).

16. Samuel P. Huntington, "The Clash of Civilizations?" *Foreign Affairs* (Summer 1993): 22

17. John Trumpbour, ed., How Harvard Rules: Reasons in the Service of Empire (Boston: South End Press, 1989).

18. Samuel P. Huntington, *Political Order in Changing Societies* (New Haven, Conn.: Yale University Press, 1968).

19. Mark Kesselman, Order or Movement? The Literature of Political Development as Ideology," *World Politics* 26, no. 1 (1973).

20. John V. A. Fine, *The Ancient Greeks: A Critical History* (Cambridge, Mass.: Harvard University Press, 1983), 198.

21. Cited in ibid., 194.

22. It is important to note that *demokatia* (rule by the demos) did not come into use until after Solon's time (ibid., 208).

23. The controversy over the nomination of Lani Guinier as assistant attorney general for civil rights and the grotesque mischaracterization of her work is well documented but nevertheless reveals the fundamental bias against the demos within mainstream democratic thinking. Attacked as "quota queen," Guinier never had an opportunity to explain her views on proportional representation, and her nomination was ultimately

withdrawn. For further reference, see Lani Guinier, *The Tyranny of the Majority: Fundamental Fairness in Representative Democracy* (New York: Free Press, 1994).

24. For further reference on democratic theory and practice, see Carole Pateman, *Participation and Democratic Theory* (Cambridge: Cambridge University Press, 1970). It is still one of the most cogent critiques of modern democratic thought and politics.

25. 2006 Louisiana Health and Population Survey Report.

26. Valerie Smith, *Not Just Race, Not Just Gender: Black Feminist Readings* (New York: Routledge, 1998), 30, 41.

27. For further reference, see Krin A. Bates and Richelle S. Swan, *Through the Eye of Katrina: Social Justice in the United States* (Durham, N.C.: Carolina Academic Press, 2007); and Michael Eric Dyson, *Come Hell or High Water: Hurricane Katrina and the Color of Disaster* (New York: Basic Civitas, 2006).

28. Ruth Wilson Gilmore, in "Race and Globalization," defines racism as premature death as a result of the "fatal coupling of power and difference." From R. J. Johnston et al., *Geographies of Global Change: Remapping the World* (Malden: Blackwell, 2002), 261–74.

29. See the ACLU report, "Broken Promises, Two Years after Katrina," August 2007.

30. Ibid., 7. The ACLU report and others employ the language of human rights to enumerate and expose various abuses.

31. Robinson, *Black Movements in America*; Howard Zinn, *A People's History of the United States: 1492–Present* (New York: HarperCollins, 1999).

32. Cedric J. Robinson, *An Anthropology of Marxism, Race and Representation* (Aldershot: Ashgate, 2001), 157.

33. Cited in ibid.

34. U.S. Census 2000.

35. Gary Y. Okihiro, *The Columbia Guide to Asian American History* (New York: Columbia University Press, 2005).

36. Frederick Douglass, "Composite Nation" (Boston, 1869).

37. See Appendix D in Human Rights Watch, *Blood, Sweat, and Fear*, 156–60. It is important to reiterate that I am not arguing that the human rights discourse itself is unproblematic. I am merely suggesting that immigration is a global issue, and therefore it would be fruitful to look beyond national boundaries for political solutions in addition to domestic ones.

38. Lou Dobbs, anchor and managing editor of the *Lou Dobbs Tonight*, the second-most popular CNN evening show (after *Larry King Live*), has articulated one of the most xenophobic and virulent strands of nativism on mainstream media.

39. See Allison Parker, "Inalienable Rights: Can Human Rights Law Help to End U.S. Mistreatment of Noncitizens?" *American Prospect*, January 10, 2004.

40. Ida B. Wells, *The Reason Why the Colored American Is Not in the World's Columbian Exposition* (1893).

41. Malcolm X, with the assistance of Alex Haley, *The Autobiography of Malcolm X* (New York: Ballantine Books, 1965).

6

African Americans and Immigration: The Economic, Political, and Strategic Implications

ROBERT C. SMITH

In 2002, at a forum on globalization at the City College of San Francisco I presented a paper coauthored with Steven Shulman on the economic impact of immigration on African Americans. Shulman, an economist at Colorado State University who has written extensively on immigration and ethnic inequality, and I came together because of our shared concern that illegal immigration–especially from Mexico–was having deleterious effects on the well-being of low-income African Americans and that African American leaders had been derelict in their responsibilities to address the problem (Shulman and Smith 2005). To our surprise, fellow panelists (Latino and Anglo) accused us of racism. In the course of the discussion, the pro-immigration panelists of course disputed our conclusion about the negative effects of immigration on African American well-being. (I say "of course" because the literature on the impact of immigration on the economy generally and on the black community specifically is not unambiguous.) Agreeing to disagree on the meaning of the empirical research, I asked a Latino respondent, if it could be shown that immigration did have the negative consequences we suggested, would he be prepared to consider restrictive policies? His response was that he had not thought about it, but he would probably nevertheless oppose efforts to restrict the flow of immigration and would consider those who supported such policies racist.

Subsequently, Manuel Pastor, a professor of Latin American studies at the University of California at Santa Cruz, and Enrico Marcelli, a professor of economics at the University of Massachusetts at Boston, wrote a thoughtful response to our paper (Pastor and Marcelli 2004). In this essay, I want to review their response in the context of my understanding of the social, economic, political, and strategic implications of immigration on the well-being of the African American community and the responsibilities of African American leadership in light of these implications.

The debate at City College in San Francisco in 2002 foreshadowed the national debate on immigration in 2006. In late 2005 the House of Representatives passed an immigration bill that made illegal immigration a felony, imposed new penalties on illegal immigrants, required groups giving assistance to individuals to check their legal status, and proposed erecting fences along large portions of the Mexican-U.S. border. This action sparked mass protests by immigrants (mainly Latino) throughout the United States. In Los Angeles, more than half a million protested, and there were massive protests in other cities, including Chicago, Denver, and Washington, D.C. While marching in opposition to the House bill, protest leaders endorsed legislation supported by President George W. Bush and passed by the Senate that would establish a guest worker program and provide a "pathway" to possible citizenship for the estimated twelve million illegal immigrants in the United States. The Congressional Black Caucus, the National Association for the Advancement of Colored People (NAACP), Senator Barack Obama, and most other African American leaders and organizations joined the opposition to the House bill while supporting some version of the legislation passed by the Senate.

Although immigration has not been a central item on the agenda of black civil rights and political organizations, during the course of the 2006 debate, the NAACP released a set of principles for revision of the nation's immigration laws (Cottman 2006). These principles generally track those of Latino and other immigrant advocacy groups. They include, among other things, support for family reunification, protections for agricultural workers, legal permanent residency and citizenship for college students, and support for due process rights for immigrants facing deportation. The NAACP also expressed opposition to the mandatory detention of undocumented immigrants as well as efforts to penalize persons for providing "humanitarian" assistance to illegal immigrants. Also, the NAACP devoted the July/August 2006 issue of its magazine, the *Crisis*, to a generally sympathetic symposium on immigration. In addition, the Leadership Conference on Civil Rights (LCCR), a coalition of nearly 200 civil rights organizations, has taken a leadership role in lobbying on the issue, including support for a "pathway" to citizenship for the estimated twelve million illegal persons in the United States (LCCR 2007). Thus, in general there is a consensus in the African American leadership group in favor of liberal immigration reform notwithstanding the possible negative consequences for low-skill, low-income workers who are disproportionately African American.

African American leaders tend to discount the negative consequences of immigration on the well-being of low-income blacks. In addition, many argue that the issue should not be allowed to disrupt the black–brown coalition, which is viewed as indispensable to the long-term prospects for the building of a sustainable, progressive coalition in the United States. In addition, black leaders are wary of joining anti-immigration forces because some opponents of immigration are clearly racists and white supremacists (see Swain 2002).[1] Nevertheless, there are, as I discuss below, reasons to question this "presumed alliance" and to be wary of the long-term prospects for an enduring black-brown coalition.[2] And while the evidence is ambiguous, I conclude from my review that widespread illegal immigration has had and will continue to have negative consequences for low-income black workers and their communities.

A PERSONAL NOTE

I should begin by indicating that my concern about immigration as a problem in black politics is a rather recent development, occurring only after I returned to California in 1989 after living since 1972 in New York City and Washington, D.C. Thus, my initial concern was a result of experience rather than research. For example, in a 1998 review of my *We Have No Leaders*, the late Hugh Davis Graham, the author of the definitive work on civil rights policy making during the 1960s (1990) as well as a major work on how immigration negatively impacted black access to affirmative action (2003), wrote "[Smith] largely ignores other state policies, such as US immigration policy, which arguably have been enormously damaging to the black underclass" (Graham 1998: 2004).

Initially, I found Graham's observation a rather minor criticism given my advocacy of policies such as full employment, national health insurance, full funding for education, and higher taxes on wealthy individuals and corporations. However, the force of Graham's observations came home after I returned to California and experienced the impact of immigration on Los Angeles in general and black Los Angeles in particular.

I migrated from rural Louisiana to Los Angeles in 1965. At that time, there were distinct ethnic enclaves in the city: Jewish, black, and Latino. When I returned almost two decades later, black Los Angeles as a space had almost disappeared, having been transformed into either Latino or multiethnic communities. Pastor and Marcelli (2004: 131) report that while blacks in Los Angeles remain relatively segregated from whites, they saw the probability of having a Latino neighbor rise from 11 percent in 1970 to 41 percent in 2000. Meanwhile, many of the traditional black economic, recreational, and cultural institutions had disappeared, and residents spoke of intense competition between blacks and Latinos for space, jobs, housing, and education. Los Angeles, Pastor and Marcelli write (2004: 120), is the "acknowledged heart of undocumented immigration." Thus, the dramatic displacement of blacks there is unusual; however, witnessing this transformation led me to pay more attention the problem of immigration and its impact on African Americans than I had when researching and writing *We Have No Leaders*.

In the following sections, I examine the economic impact of immigration on African Americans, its political consequences, and the strategic implications for African American political leaders.

ECONOMIC IMPACT

The literature, econometric and qualitative, on the economic impact of immigration on African Americans is problematic, with widely different methodologies, data sets, and ambiguous and noncumulative findings (for a collection of papers that provide a balanced summary and overview of the literature, see Shulman 2004). My reading of the literature suggests the following is a rough consensus: illegal immigration has increased the supply of low-wage labor, which tends to reduce employment and wages for American citizens as well as legal immigrants. This would, of course, have a disproportionately negative impact on the black community since blacks tend to be concentrated in the low-wage sector. There is also a reasonably good body of evidence that shows that employers may prefer to hire illegal immigrants, who are viewed as harder working and more compliant than blacks. Yet it is also clear that immigrants likely contribute to economic growth overall, which benefits blacks generally. Finally, it is also probably the case that immigrants do certain kinds of work (largely agricultural) that native-born citizens are unwilling to do at the prevailing wages for the labor.

Historically, African Americans have been skeptical about immigration, fearing competition for jobs (Daniels 1990: 76, 323). As Frederick Douglass said in the 1880s referring to the waves of immigrants from Europe, "The old employment by which we have heretofore gained our livelihood, are gradually and it may seem inevitably passing into other hands. Every hour sees the black man elbowed out of employment by some newly arrived immigrant whose hunger and color are thought to give him a better title to the place" (quoted in Shulman and Smith 2005: 199). After the closing of the door to immigration from eastern and southern Europe as a result of passage of the racist Immigration Restriction Act of 1924, African Americans did gain some access to jobs previously unavailable. Yet the reforms that ended racism in the nation's immigration laws were partly an outgrowth of the civil rights movement. As Briggs writes, "It was the passage of the Civil Rights Act of 1964 . . . that created the national climate needed to legislatively end the discriminatory national origins system the following year with the adoption of the Immigration Act of 1965" (2004: 12). And polls show that African Americans, although uneasy, are generally supportive of immigration and immigrant rights (Pantoja 2005; Pastor and Marcelli 2004; Swains 2006). In California, for example, blacks rejected the anti-immigrant Proposition 187 by a margin of 53 to 47 percent, while whites voted for it 63 to 37 percent. Pastor and Marcelli suggest the generally tolerant opinions of blacks on immigration are rooted in politics. That is, "African Americans are ambiguous in their views of immigrants as economic competitors but view them as potential political allies" (Pastor and Marcelli 2004: 108).

POLITICAL CONSEQUENCES

The political consequences of immigration for African Americans are ambiguous. There is competition for political offices and resources between blacks and Latinos throughout the United States (McClain and Karning 1990). However, there is also cooperation between blacks and Latinos and the possibility of a long-term progressive "rainbow coalition" (Jennings 2003).

The competition for political offices is not a major problem. In California, as a result of the out-migration of blacks from the central cities and the influx of Latinos, there is no majority or even plurality black legislative or congressional districts (all three of the Los Angeles–area congressional districts represented by blacks have Latino pluralities ranging from 35 to 43 percent). As a result, according to the Joint Center for Political and Economic Studies data, the number of black elected officials in the state declined from about 300 in the 1980s to 230 in 2006.

Thus, black representatives in the next decade in the state are likely to be replaced by Latinos, or they will have to balance black and Latino interests. This probably will lead either to a dilution of black officeholding in the state or the dilution of the representation of black interests. (Increasingly, I should note, in California, blacks are being elected in majority white suburban places, as mayors and to city councils, school boards, and the state legislature.) However, in California and in Washington, it is becoming increasingly difficult to distinguish black interests, and black representatives have not articulated a distinctive black agenda for some time (Raspberry 2001). And thirty years after the beginnings of the incorporation of blacks into the political system, we now know that simply having black faces in high office–Congress, the cabinet, mayors' offices, and local and state legislative bodies–does not have much policy payoff for blacks, especially low-income blacks.

There is, however, some evidence that immigration may depress mass or grassroots political engagement by blacks. In the first longitudinal study (1973–94) assessing black political activism nationally, immigration "was found to have consistently negative effects on black civic behavior during the time period under study" (Harris et al. 2006: 123). Indeed, the authors conclude–strikingly–that levels of immigration were a more consistent predictor of black civic disengagement than inflation, unemployment, criminal activity, or the degree of income inequality in the black community. The authors speculate, "The increased entry of low-skilled and semiskilled laborers into the workforce economically dislocates black workers, which may, in turn, leave blacks with fewer material resources to engage in civic activities beyond voting" (Harris et al. 2006: 123).

RAINBOW COALITION?

The idea of a rainbow coalition of people of color is based on the assumption that the new immigrants of color tend to be poor and may face discrimination or racism from the white majority, and therefore there is an objective or material basis for a coalition with blacks in terms of support for civil rights and social welfare legislation. Blacks and the leaders of Asian American and Latino communities are part of the broad LCCR, but this coalition has been marked by tensions and conflicts (Pinderhughes 1992). At the mass level, while majorities of both Latinos and Asian Americans believe they face discrimination from the white majority, they think they have more in common with whites than they do with blacks (National Conference of Christians and Jews 1994: 7). Latinos in general tend to embrace the same negative stereotypes about blacks as held by whites (Hernandez 2007; McClain et al. 2006). These negative stereotypes regarding blacks constitute a "serious barrier" to cooperation and coalitions between blacks and Latinos (National Conference Christians and Jews 1994: 7).

The advocates of a coalition between blacks and Latinos should not be Pollyannaish about its prospects because "the fact is that racism–and anti-black racism in particular–is a pervasive and historically entrenched reality of life in Latin America" (Hernandez 2007). On arriving in the United States, many Latinos easily embrace the racist stereotypes about blacks that are pervasive here, thus reinforcing the social distance from blacks that is a part of Latin American culture. At the same time, survey after survey (see Hernandez 2007) documents that African Americans have substantially more positive views of Latinos and are more willing to have them as neighbors, spouses, and coalition partners. Hernandez writes: "Ironically, African Americans, who are often depicted as being averse to coalition-building with Latinos, have repeatedly demonstrated in their survey responses that they feel less hostility toward Latinos than Latinos feel toward them."

STRATEGY

Given this brief overview of the economic and political consequences of immigration, how should blacks and their leaders approach the issue of immigration? As I indicated in the essay with Shulman, I think black leaders were derelict in their responsibilities to address this problem with reasonable proposals to restrict the flow of immigration before it became a tidal wave in the 1980s and 1990s. In 1994 Barbara Jordan, the nationally renowned African American congresswoman from Texas, chaired a commission that recommended, among other things, substantial reductions in the annual level of legal immigration, limits on the admission of unskilled adults, and a concerted effort to stop illegal immigration (U.S. Commission on Immigration Reform 1994). The entirely reasonable recommendations of the Jordan Commission were ignored by the Congressional Black Caucus, the NAACP, and the rest of the established black leadership. Shulman and I contend that black leaders ignored the Jordan report and the immigration issue generally for fear of antagonizing Latinos and their leaders, prioritizing the interests of a rainbow coalition over those of low-income blacks.

It is still not too late for black leaders to address the issue. Shulman and I discussed a number of proposals, including policies to improve the economic conditions in Mexico that might reduce the incentives to immigrate, tougher sanctions on businesses that hire illegal immigrants, and a national ID system. These proposals would offer some promise of slowing down the flow of illegal immigration from Mexico. However, it is estimated that as many as twelve million illegal immigrants are already in the country. Since there is no realistic way to remove them, the only alternative is to embrace policies that would better incorporate them into the economy and political process.

Pastor and Marcelli argue that it would be a strategic error for African Americans to support restrictionist policies because the Latino population is growing and "memory matters" (2004: 129).[3] Pastor and Marcelli recognize that blacks may have legitimate concerns about the impact of immigration on their communities and that to raise them is not racist. They nevertheless maintain that blacks should subordinate those concerns and focus on the things that could bring African Americans and Latinos together in a broad, progressive social change coalition. To do otherwise is, they believe, strategically foolish because it risks alienating the nation's fastest-growing segment of the population, which they contend in the long run would undermine African American interests and power. However, they caution their fellow immigration advocates that "all of us should be particularly concerned with the fate of African Americans in the contemporary economy. This is partly for reasons of historic redress and fairness but also because of the central role African Americans have played in the history of progressive change in the United States, including around the liberalization of immigration legislation itself" (2004: 132).

Pastor and Marcelli offer reasonable suggestions for managing black–Latino differences on immigration and rightly place the strategic dilemmas confronting blacks at the center of their analysis. They do not, however, in my view pay sufficient attention to the attitudinal barriers to a sustainable Latino-black coalition that exists among rank-and-file Latinos. It is clear that black leaders are not going to embrace the restrictionist policies that Shulman and I propose. They have not done so in the past and are even less likely to do so in the future. In the long run, this may be the correct strategic calculus. However, in the long run it may also result in the further isolation, stigmatization, and exclusion of African

Americans as Latinos become white (Yancey 2003). History suggests that there is little reason for African Americans to be sanguine about the outcome.

NOTES

1. Swain's study of right-wing racist and neo-fascist leaders finds that immigration and affirmative action are the two issues that most drive their mobilizing efforts. To appease them and thereby blunt what she perceives to be their growing influence, Swain proposes the abolition of affirmative action and an end to immigration (see Swain 2002).

2. Nicolas Vaca (2004) uses "presumed alliance" as the title of his book, which, from the perspective of a Latino, challenges the idea of common interests as the basis of a black-brown coalition.

3. By 2050, the U.S. Census Bureau estimates that nonwhites will constitute half the U.S. population. Latinos are projected to constitute 24 percent, African American 14 percent, Asians 8 percent, and Native Americans, Hawaiians, and Pacific Islanders and mixed race 4 percent (U.S. Bureau of Census 2001).

REFERENCES

Briggs, Vernon. 2004. "The Economic Well Being of Black Americans: The Overarching Influence of U.S. Immigration Policies." In Steven Shulman, ed., *The Impact of Immigration on African Americans*. New Brunswick, N.J.: Transaction.

Cottman, Michael. 2006. "NAACP, Barack Obama Call for Earned Citizenship for Illegal Immigrants," April 3, backamericanweb.com.

Daniels, Rogers. 1990. *Coming to America: A History of Immigration and Ethnicity*. New York: Harper Collins.

Graham, Hugh Davis. 1990. *The Civil Rights Era: Origins and Development of National Policy, 1960–1972*. New York: Oxford.

———. 1998. Review of *We Have No Leaders: African Americans in the Post Civil Rights Era*, by Robert C. Smith. *Ethnic and Racial Studies* 21: 803–4.

———. 2003. *Collision Course: The Strange Convergence of Affirmative Action and Immigration Policy in America*. New York: Oxford.

Harris, Frederick C., Valeria Sinclair-Chapman, and Brian McKenzie. 2006. *Countervailing Forces in African-American Civic Activism, 1973–1994*. New York: Cambridge University Press.

Hernendez, Tanya. 2007. "Roots of Latino/Black Anger." *Los Angeles Times*, January 7.

Jennings, James. 2003. "Political Coalitions Between Communities of Color." In Curtis Stokes and Theresa Melendez, eds., *Racial Liberalism and the Politics of Urban America*. East Lansing: Michigan State University Press.

Leadership Conference on Civil Rights (LCCR). 2007. "Statement of Wade Henderson," President and CEO. Subcommittee on Immigration, Committee on Judiciary, House of Representatives, May 3.

McClain, Paula, and Albert Karning. 1990. "Black and Hispanic Socioeconomic and Political Competition." *American Political Science Review* 84:571–84.

McClain, Paula, et al. 2006. "Racial Distancing in a Southern City: Latino Immigrant Views of Black Americans." *Journal of Politics* 68:571–84.

National Conference of Christian and Jews. 1994. *Taking America's Pulse: The Full Report of the National Conference Survey on Inter-Group Relations*. New York: National Conference of Christians and Jews.

Pantoja, Adrian. 2005. "Friends or Foes: African American Attitudes toward the Political and Economic Implications of Immigration." In William Nelson and Jessica Lavariega Moniforti, eds., *Black and Latino/A Politics: Issues in Political Development in the United States*. Miami, Fla.: Barnhardt and Ashe.

Pastor, Manuel, Jr., and Enrico A. Marcelli. 2004. "Somewhere Over the Rainbow? African Americans, Unauthorized Mexican Immigration, and Coalition Building". In Steven Shulman, ed., *The Impact of Immigration on African Americans*. New Brunswick, N.J.

Pinderhughes, Dianne. 1992. "Divisions in the Civil Rights Community." *PS: Political Science and Politics* 25:485–87.

Raspberry, William. 2001. "The Incredible Shrinking Black Agenda." *Washington Post*, January 9.

Shulman, Steven, ed. 2004. *The Impact of Immigration on African Americans*. New Brunswick, N.J.: Transaction.

Shulman, Steven, and Robert C. Smith. 2005. "Immigration and African Americans." In Cecilia Conrad et al., eds., *African Americans in the U.S. Economy*. Lanham, Md.: Rowman and Littlefield.

Swain, Carol. 2002. *The New White Nationalism in America*. New York: Cambridge University Press.

Swains, Rachel. 2006. "Growing Unease for Some Blacks on Immigration." *New York Times*, May 4.

U.S. Bureau of the Census. 2001. *Projected Change in the United States, by Race and Hispanic Origin: 2006–2050*. Washington, D.C.: U.S. Bureau of the Census.

U.S. Commission on Immigration Reform. 1994. *Legal Immigration: Setting Priorities.* Washington, D.C.: U.S. Commission on Immigration Reform.

Vaca, Nicolas. 2004. *The Presumed Alliance: The Unspoken Conflict between Latinos and Blacks and What It Means for America*. New York: Rayo.

Yancey, George. 2003. *Who Is White?: Latinos, Asians, and the New Black/Nonblack Divide*. Boulder, Colo.: Lynne Rienner.

PART 3

Affirmative Action as a Human Rights Tool

7

Historicizing Affirmative Action and the Landmark 2003 University of Michigan Cases

PERO GAGLO DAGBOVIE

Transcending and moving beyond the various, at times complex political and legal definitions of affirmative action that surfaced between the 1935 National Labor Act and the political and social reforms of the 1960s and 1970s, how can we more holistically understand and contextualize affirmative action in the new millennium? How can the "core black studies" discipline, history, inform our interpretations of affirmative action? How can we better understand the deeper implications—historical, contemporary, and future—of the 2003 Supreme Court decisions about affirmative action at the University of Michigan? Using Ira Katznelson's *When Affirmative Action Was White: An Untold History of Racial Inequality in Twentieth-Century America* (2005) and especially Philip F. Rubio's *A History of Affirmative Action, 1619–2000* (2001) as revealing case studies and points of departure, this essay stresses the significance of historicizing contemporary expressions of and debates surrounding affirmative action within the broader African American struggle for equality, advancement, social justice, and basic human rights. Katznelson's and Rubio's studies are important because unlike many presentist-thinking scholars of affirmative action, they not only place post–civil rights movement debates and variations of affirmative action within the broader context of the experience of blacks in the United States, but, equally important, they also conceptualize affirmative action as a mechanism that has historically benefited various classes of white Americans. In analyzing affirmative action, this essay embraces "contextualized (historical) thinking."[1]

Affirmative action is arguably among the most controversial, emotionally and politically charged, racially divisive, and misinterpreted issues and phenomena in twenty-first-century American culture. Though various groups of historically discriminated against peoples have benefited in diversified manners from formal and informal affirmative action legislation and programs, compensatory actions, and reform since the pivotal 1960s and 1970s, affirmative action has been oversimplified, politicized, hyperracialized, and "blackened" by whitestream American political and popular culture. It has become the modern-day version of the turn-of-the-twentieth-century mislabeled "Negro Problem." In this process, blacks have often been demonized and transformed into unworthy recipients of government-funded and -mandated handouts, especially in higher education, who reap the benefits of so-called reverse discrimination.

On the eve of June 23, 2003, did the American general public realize that the University of Michigan's highly contested "Point System" for prospective undergraduate students—a perfect score being 150—was determined by many elements, including their grade point averages, their test scores, where they were born and raised, their relationships with alumni, the content of their personal essays and achievements, their leadership and service attributes, and other "miscellaneous" factors? How many people who advocated any particular stance on the debates over affirmative action knew that the twenty points that were granted to African American applicants (by nature of the fact that they belong to an "underrepresented/racial ethnic minority identification or education") fell under the category of "miscellaneous," which included other elements that could award applicants potential points?

More specifically, from this "miscellaneous" category, applicants could potentially accumulate twenty points for being a racial/ethnic minority, socioeconomically disadvantaged, or a scholarship athlete. In this "miscellaneous" category, applicants could also get twenty points at the "Provost's discretion" or five points for being a male student studying nursing. It must be stressed that applicants to University of Michigan undergraduate programs could only get a maximum of twenty points in the "miscellaneous" section. Based upon these realities, why did the debate over the University of Michigan's "Point System" and affirmative action policies focus on race and ethnicity, especially blackness, and not on, for instance, the twenty points granted to many scholarship athletes and whites who could claim a "socioeconomic disadvantage"? The fundamental

answer to the above queries is quite simple: the social construction of race persists to significantly characterize and influence American society, and affirmative
action has been turned into a "black thing" by the U.S. white majority. The "black-
ening" of affirmative action is part of a larger historical process and is particularly misleading and displaced because numerous scholars have highlighted and
documented how white women have been among the historically disadvantaged
groups in America who have benefited the most from modern, post–civil rights
movement affirmative action policies and programs.[2] On another note, imagine,
for fun, if the University of Michigan did not actively employ affirmative action
in granting their scholarship athletes, especially football players, admission.

"The two Michigan cases, *Jennifer Gratz v. Lee Bollinger; President of the
University of Michigan*, and *Barbara Grutter v. Bollinger* (2003), argued for the
petitioner undergraduate and law school students by the Center for Individual
Rights, began in 1997 and resulted in two of the most complex and yet revealing
affirmative action cases that the U.S. Supreme Court has decided."[3] The historic,
landmark, and precedent-setting Supreme Court decision on June 23, 2003, has
heightened scholars', activists', politicians', and the general U.S. public's interest
and stakes in affirmative action. The Supreme Court ruling was also critically
covered in international media outlets, especially in London and Canada. More
than any other decision since *Bakke v. California Board of Regents* (1978), the
Court's ruling in the University of Michigan cases will have an enormous impact on American universities' future admissions policies that seek to promote
racial and ethnic diversity. The debate concerning the University of Michigan's
affirmative action policies has been showcased in countless popular media and
scholarly venues and publications, the most exhaustive and perceptive of these
being Barbara A. Perry's *The Michigan Affirmative Action Cases* (2007). Perry
historicizes the Supreme Court's 2003 decision and thoroughly explores its par-
ticulars and aftermath.

In his provocative and informative study, *Affirmative Action: Racial Preference in Black and White* (2005), Tim J. Wise has offered a straightforward sum-
mation of the University of Michigan cases that Perry intricately dissects. Wise
observes that

> the Supreme Court handed down a split decision, upholding affirmative ac-
> tion in the law school while striking down Michigan's undergraduate admis-
> sions plan. The College of Literature, Science, and the Arts had been using
> a weighted point system, which automatically gave twenty points (out of an
> overall maximum of 150) to anyone who was a member of an underrepresented

minority group, known as URMs. At Michigan, URMs are blacks, Latino/as, and American Indians, all of whom are statistically underrepresented, relative to their numbers in the potential applicant pool. Referred to as a de facto quota system by the plaintiffs and their attorneys, the point scheme was struck down as an unfair preference that placed an undue burden on white applicants, as well as Asian Pacific Islanders, who were not underrepresented at the University of Michigan. The law school program, although it considered race as one of many factors in admissions in an attempt to promote a diverse student body, had never operated with a point system. Because there was no explicit weighting on behalf of URMs in the law school, the Court upheld the constitutionality of the program, although narrowly, by a five to four vote. Because the Court allowed schools to continue using race as a factor in admissions and yet struck down systems that use precise weighting for the purpose of expanding campus racial diversity, the controversy over affirmative action in higher education is sure to continue.[4]

What are the deeper implications of the Supreme Court's 2003 "split decision"? Fundamentally, "the court banned mechanical formulas that take race into account, but endorsed the concept of affirmative action." The Court concluded that colleges and universities can indeed consider applicants' race and/or ethnicity in the quest for diversifying their campus cultures, "provided that they do so in a narrowly tailored fashion that guarantees each applicant full consideration." The "split decision" essentially left the issue of affirmative action a bit unresolved and open for dynamic future debate: colleges and universities still have the right to use race-based affirmative action admission policies as long as they do not include a point system, or other "mechanical formulas," that automatically grants blacks, and other underrepresented ethnic groups, points by nature of their ethnic background. As a staff writer for the *New York Daily News* insightfully observed and predicted in the aftermath of the decision, colleges and universities now face the challenge of developing "more nuanced" approaches to attaining racial diversity, indeed "a labor-intensive process." How have colleges and universities responded to the Supreme Court's decision? Schools with point systems have been forced to abandon such practices. Others have decided to modify and revisit their strategies and policies. The bottom line is that colleges and universities throughout the nation must now look more seriously at their affirmative action admissions policies. The state of Michigan provides a particularly interesting case. Impacted by the Supreme Court's 2003 ruling, in November 2006 Michigan voters "approved a state-wide ban on affirmative action in public education, public employment, and state contracts." As of early 2007, "seventeen states have approved either constitutional amendments or legislative enactments barring any consideration of applicants' race in public education or professional school admissions." While the exact future ramifications of the Supreme Court's 2003 decision and Michigan's controversial Proposal Two cannot be predicted with certainty, it is clear that these cases, like previous monumental cases, will significantly affect future debates and provosts' and administrators' attitudes concerning affirmative action.[5]

The scholarship on affirmative action is vast, encompassing, and mul-tileveled, especially during the last several decades. Certainly influenced by California's Proposition 209, since the 1990s countless diatribes, newspaper and journal articles, monographs, and anthologies and collections have been written and published on affirmative action.[6] "Many scholarly and popular onlookers have disputed how affirmative action has shaped our schools, workplaces, and government, civil and military. Advocates and detractors have developed power-ful arguments about key moral, constitutional, and practical issues." "These by now," an affirmative action scholar has recently observed, "are familiar."[7] Besides the ongoing, ever present, and publicized injustices against African Americans, such as the recent, nationally publicized "Jena 6" case in Louisiana, affirmative action has polarized white and blacks, and continues to do so. According to a 2003 *Newsweek* poll, "the idea of making decisions on racial grounds is unpop-ular—especially among whites, who oppose preferences for blacks by 73-22 per-cent margin."[8] A 2003 *USA Today* poll indicated a similar trend, indicating that approximately 44 percent of whites and 70 percent of blacks favored affirmative action programs for racial minorities.[9]

With the exception of a cohort of black neo-conservatives like Shelby Steele, Armstrong Williams, John McWhorter, Ward Connerly, Clarence Thomas, and others, the vast majority of African American intellectuals, scholars, leaders, spokespersons, and rank and file believe that some form of affirmative action, reparations being the most fundamental and extreme expression, makes sense, is justified, would help address the mounting disparities between whites and blacks, and, at a minimum, deserves consideration and productive, critical discourse. On the other hand, it seems that "most whites believe racial discrimination has declined so much that affirmative action's challenge to competition and mobility based on individual merit, effort, ambition, and color-blind equal opportunity is needed no longer. Others dislike it for uglier reasons."[10]

Departing from the methodologies of most affirmative action scholars whose arguments are often limited by their presentism, Ira Katznelson and Philip F.

Rubio offer history-centered approaches to critically theorizing and exploring affirmative action. While Rubio traces the roots of affirmative action to early-seventeenth-century North America in an effort to demonstrate how America's past social and racial policies are connected to contemporary American society, Katznelson begins his historical analysis of affirmative action in the 1930s and 1940s, showing "how inequality, in fact, increased at the insistence of southern representatives in Congress, while their congressional colleagues were complicit." For Katznelson, embracing a historical and proactive prescriptive perspective is a necessity. "I propose that affirmative action focus on antidotes to specific harms that date back to national policies in the 1930s and 1940s as remedies for the deep, even chronic dispassion that continues to afflict a large percentage of black America." He continues, "I propose . . . a change in our historical attention span. Discussions of affirmative action . . . usually begin with events and debates that took place four, rather than seven, decades ago. . . . By contrast, I look back as well as forward from the vantage of the mid-1960s. As a result, a mainly neglected earlier history of race and public policy comes into view, allowing us to see, think, and act about affirmative action in fresh ways."[11] Highlighting the inequality of government-sanctioned affirmative action programs in racial terms as well as the "series of forgotten early experiments in affirmative action" during the New Deal, 1940s, and 1950s, *When Affirmative Action Was White* demonstrates that the 2003 University of Michigan cases have undisputable twentieth-century antecedents. Though he prioritizes the events of the proto–civil rights movement, he also pinpoints the significance of President Lyndon B. Johnson's 1965 commencement address at Howard University, "To Fulfill These Rights," the only document in his study's appendix.

Probing deeper into the history of America's race relations than Katznelson's study, and building upon the theoretical frameworks of "whiteness" studies by David R. Roediger and Theodore Allen, among others, while also directly responding to California's controversial 1996 Proposition 209, Rubio's work on affirmative action is refreshing in that he intricately weaves this concept, both as a "compensatory civil rights program" for African Americans and as a concrete expression of white privilege, into an encompassing narrative of U.S. "social, cultural, labor, political, and intellectual" history and into the historical experiences and protest strategies of African Americans since the early seventeenth century. Rubio's conceptualization of affirmative action is essentially rooted in an effective historical framework. Like others, he defines the classic expression of affirmative action as "a state-sanctioned social reform and control mechanism" that "came into being in the late 1960s." At the same time, he underscores that affirmative action is "a product of years of black-led protest against what might be called 'white affirmative action' (or better put: 'white-affirmative action')." For Rubio, whites have benefited from concrete forms of affirmative action that privileged their whiteness since the founding of the "New Nation." "The earliest uses of 'preferences and quotas,' as affirmative action is often characterized today, emerged with slavery itself and were embellished with the legislated protection of white labor." Rubio adds that "affirmative action in reality represents a compromise fusion of disparate social and legal elements brought into being by the black protest tradition against white privilege" and that "affirmative action sums up the story of the United States: the struggle for justice, equality, and self-determination and whether African Americans will or even should be able to enjoy chosen labor and increased life chances. It represents the history of white supremacy, privilege, and guilt verses black protest, militance, and demands for compensation and reparations."[12] Complex and history centered, Rubio's study is original and unique.

Highlighting the overarching oppression endured by blacks, the concept of white solidarity, and the invention, social construction, and evolution of "whiteness," Rubio traces the roots of the contemporary debates over affirmative action and white privilege by exploring periods, events, and issues such as colonization, slavery, the Civil War, Reconstruction (the first major antecedent of modern affirmative action programs), the "nadir" (defined by Rayford W. Logan as the period from 1877 until 1923), the 1920s, the Great Depression and the New Deal, the 1941 March on Washington, the Cold War era, the 1950s, the civil rights movement, the Black Power era, and Proposition 209.

Rubio surmises that since America's colonial experience and the founding of the United States, the badge of white skin granted white Americans, regardless of class status, specific privileges, opportunities, and social positions that were denied to blacks because of their blackness, and clearly placed whites above African Americans along social, political, and economic lines. Many examples stand out in his useful paradigm for understanding and historicizing affirmative action. In describing the evolution of white citizenship rights during the antebellum era, Rubio notes that the enfranchisement of whites and simultaneous disenfranchisement of blacks was "a mass white movement as much as is today's white anti-affirmative action backlash." During the period of slavery, "white privilege is implicated in black subordination." Reconstruction, in Rubio's estimation, represented "the first attempt to rectify the effects of slavery and white supremacy and in that sense serves as the first antecedent to affirmative action." Rubio offers illuminating comparisons between the debates over blacks' social equality during the 1860s and 1870s with those debates over affirmative action and blacks' civil rights one hundred years later and ultimately contends that the Reconstruction era "established precedents for today's affirmative action debate."[13]

The "nadir" period represented a direct attack on any affirmative action–like policies initiated during Reconstruction. "The most salient characteristics of this *American* nadir," Rubio observes, "was the white affirmative action of race riots and lynchings."[14] He makes the same observation about the race riots and anti-black violence of the 1940s and 1950s. According to Rubio, many incidents in the twentieth century served as antecedents to modern expressions of affirmative action. Foreshadowing Katznelson, Rubio argues that the "pro-black revolt against the reconstruction of whiteness that emerged with the advent of the New Deal in 1933 gives us the most immediate context for today's affirmative action debate." Rubio then suggests that "the actual origins of modern affirmative action advocacy and policy" were the byproduct of A. Philip Randolph's 1941 March on Washington movement. He also posits that the New Deal and the Roosevelt administration "saw demands for compensatory justice" that were reminiscent of affirmative action. While Rubio acknowledges the deep historical origins of the contemporary affirmative action debates, he also firmly locates the "prelude to the modern civil rights movement" in the 1950s and 1960s.[15]

Central to Rubio's argument is his belief that affirmative action was the byproduct of blacks' protest, most concretely during the 1960s and 1970s. Many black leaders of this era, from Martin Luther King Jr. to the Black Panther Party, demanded compensation for the historical discrimination endured by African Americans. To Rubio's dismay, at the dawning of the new millennium, "little" research had been completed on the 1960s black student movement's impact on affirmative action. Rubio prioritizes this movement's impact. "It can be fairly stated that without Black Power at the workplace, in the communities, and on the college campuses there would be no such thing as affirmative action today."[16] Rubio's call for a focus on African American affirmative action activists is important. While many historians have chronicled how African Americans' efforts and demands have resulted in dramatic changes in the collective status of African Americans, fewer scholars have explored the struggles and contributions of pioneering African American affirmative action activists. In detailing the activism of ex-slave, washerwoman, and leader of the National Ex-Slave Mutual Relief, Bounty and Pension Association, Callie House (1861–1928), in *My Face Is Black Is True: Callie House and the Struggle for Ex-Slave Reparations* (2005) Mary Frances Berry has challenged us to recognize the predecessors of the modern reparations movement, indeed a pro–affirmative action movement.[17] Several other new publications have also revisited and highlighted the monumental efforts of early African American activists for reparations and affirmative action, the most recent being *Redress for Historical Injustices in the United States: On Reparations for Slavery, Jim Crow, and Their Legacies*, edited by Michael T. Martin and Marilyn Yaquinto.[18]

The last part of Rubio's exhaustive study examines the recent history of, and series of presidential attacks on, affirmative action from the early 1990s until 2000. Rubio concludes his work in a historically reductionist/deterministic manner:

> The more one studies the past, the clearer it becomes that the forces opposed to affirmative action and antidiscrimination measures will continue to have the upper hand in the debate until proponents acknowledge affirmative action's historical roots in black-led protest to end white supremacy and achieve substantial compensation—whatever the name. . . . The essence of the struggle remains the same; only the particulars keep changing. The historical precedents and parallels are both canny and instructive.[19]

Historians must be a bit cautious with the fundamental thrust of Rubio's and, to a lesser degree, Katznelson's central and completely logical argument: that the contemporary state of affirmative action is a manifestation of past events, movements, and developments. While the present is certainly inextricably bound to the past, as historian Gerda Lerner has warned: "History is not a recipe book; past events are never replicated in the present in quite the same way. Historical events are infinitely variable and their interpretations are a constantly shifting process. There are no certainties to be found in the past."[20] At the same time, Rubio and Katznelson do not fall prey to simply arguing that because something happened in the past, the same, or similar, thing manifested itself in the future. Their history-centered analyses seriously challenge scholars, policy makers, and the American public to acknowledge, at minimum, that the issue of affirmative action, despite the fact that the use of this exact terminology and slogan did not enter the mainstream American public's vocabulary until the 1960s, is nothing new. Indeed, in order to understand the recent Supreme Court decision concerning affirmative action at the University of Michigan and its future implications and ramifications, it would be wise to revisit crucial developments, events, personalities, and phenomena in the United States' intriguing and complex past.

NOTES

1. For a discussion of how I envision "contextualized thinking," see Sam Wineburg, *Historical Thinking and Other Unnatural Acts: Charting the Future of Teaching the Past* (Philadelphia: Temple University Press, 2001). Wineburg defines this concept throughout his study. This approach dictates that we confront our inherent presentism ("the act of viewing the past through the lens of the present," a tendency of affirmative action scholars); attempt to view history through the experiences of others; "go beyond the fleeting moment in history into which we have been born"; and essentially place historical phenomena within their proper contexts.

2. For instance, a perusal of the nation's leading, mainstream newspapers reveals that the vast majority of mainstream journalists focused on affirmative action and African Americans. Though the University of Michigan cases surround race-based affirmative action practices, they are best understood within the broader context of affirmative across racial/ethnic, class, economic, and gender lines.

3. Barbara A. Perry, *The Michigan Affirmative Action Cases* (Lawrence: University Press of Kansas, 2007), x.

4. Tim J. Wise, *Affirmative Action: Racial Preference in Black and White* (New York: Routledge, 2005), 2.

5. Karen W. Arenson, "The Supreme Court: Affirmative Action; Impact on Universities Will Range from None to a Lot," *New York Times*, June 25, 2003; "Reaffirmative Action," *Washington Post*, June 24, 2003; Alison Gendar, "Admissions Costs Will Skyrocket," *New York Daily News*, June 24, 2003; "Michigan Votes to Ban Affirmative Action," *Feminist Daily News Wire*, November 6, 2006, //F:Majority Foundation US Daily News Wire.htm (accessed September 25, 2007); "Editor's Preface," in Perry, *Michigan Affirmative Action Cases*, ix.

6. In part triggered by the 1996 Proposition 209 in California, since the mid-1990s there have been many studies published on affirmative action. See, for instance, Joan Nordquist, *Affirmative Action: A Bibliography* (Santa Cruz, Calif.: Reference and Research Services, 1996); Carol Lee Bacchi, *The Politics of Affirmative Action: "Women," Equality and Category Politics* (Thousand Oaks, Calif.: Sage, 1996); Robert Emmet Long, ed., *Affirmative Action* (New York: H. W. Wilson, 1996); Mari J. Matsuda, *Where Is Your Body?: And Other Essays on Race, Gender, and the Law* (Boston: Beacon Press, 1996); Bryan J. Grapes, ed., *Affirmative Action* (San Diego, Calif.: Greenhaven Press, 2000); Giradeau A. Spann, *The Law of Affirmative Action: Twenty-five Years of Supreme Court Decisions on Race and Remedies* (New York: New York University Press, 2000);

Kul B. Rai and John W. Critzer, *Affirmative Action and the University: Race, Ethnicity, and Gender in Higher Education Employment* (Lincoln: University of Nebraska Press, 2000); Dennis Doverspike, Mary Anne Taylor, and Winfred Arthur Jr., *Affirmative Action: A Psychological Perspective* (Huntington, N.Y.: Nova Science, 2000); Jo Ann Ooiman Robinson, ed., *Affirmative Action: A Documentary History* (Westport, Conn.: Greenwood Press, 2001); Patricia M. Nelson, *Affirmative Action Revisited* (Huntington, N.Y.: Nova Science, 2001); Benjamin Baez, *Affirmative Action, Hate Speech, and Tenure: Narratives about Race, Law, and the Academy* (New York: Routledge Falmer, 2002); Norma M. Riccucci, *Managing Diversity in Public Sector Workforces* (Boulder, Colo.: Westview Press, 2002); Rachel Kranz, *Affirmative Action* (New York: Facts on File, 2002); Carl Cohen, *Affirmative Action and Racial Preference: A Debate* (New York: Oxford University Press, 2003); James A. Beckman, ed., *Affirmative Action: An Encyclopedia* (Westport, Conn.: Greenwood Press, 2004); Faye J. Crosby, *Affirmative Action Is Dead: Long Live Affirmative Action* (New Haven, Conn.: Yale University Press, 2004); Thomas Sowell, *Affirmative Action Around the World: An Empirical Study* (New Haven, Conn.: Yale University Press, 2004); *Affirmative Action: An Annotated Bibliography* (New York: Nova Science, 2004); Leora Maltz, ed., *Affirmative Action* (Farmington Hills, Mich.: Greenhaven Press, 2005); Edward J. Kellough, *Understanding Affirmative Action: Politics, Discrimination, and the Search for Justice* (Washington, D.C.: Georgetown University Press, 2006); Kevin L. Yuill, *Richard Nixon and the Rise of Affirmative Action: The Pursuit of Racial Equality in an Era of Limits* (Lanham, Md.: Rowman and Littlefield, 2006); Helen Lipson, *Talking Affirmative Action: Race, Opportunity, and Everyday Ideology* (Lanham, Md.: Rowman and Littlefield, 2006).

7. Ira Katznelson, *When Affirmative Action Was White: An Untold History of Racial Inequality in Twentieth-Century America* (New York: W. W. Norton, 2005), xi.

8. Howard Fineman and Tamara Lipper, "Affirmative Action: Race in the Spin Cycle," *Newsweek*, January 27, 2003, 28.

9. Joan Biskupic and Mary Beth Marklein, "Court Upholds Use of Race in University Admissions," *USA Today*, June 24, 2003.

10. Katznelson, *When Affirmative Action Was White*, 167.

11. Ibid., x, xi.

12. Philip F. Rubio, *A History of Affirmative Action, 1619–2000* (Jackson: University Press of Mississippi, 2001), xiv, 3, 9, 191.

13. Ibid., 9, 24, 55.

14. Ibid., 58.

15. Ibid., 89, 92, 95.

16. Ibid., 160.

17. Mary Frances Berry, *My Face Is Black Is True: Callie House and the Struggle for Ex-Slave Reparations* (New York: Alfred A. Knopf, 2005).

18. Raymond A. Winbush, ed., *Should America Pay?: Slavery and the Raging Debate on Reparations* (New York: Amistad, 2003); Michael T. Martin and Marilyn Yaquinto, eds., *Redress for Historical Injustices in the United States: On Reparations for Slavery, Jim Crow, and Their Legacies* (Durham, N.C.: Duke University Press, 2007).

19. Rubio, *History of Affirmative Action*, 192, 193.

20. Gerda Lerner, *Why History Matters: Life and Thought* (New York: Oxford University Press, 1997), 204–5.

8

A New Coalition: Reaching the Religious Right to Deal with Racial Justice

George A. Yancey

A white woman changes her hiring prac-
tices to engage in "affirmative recruitment," and so she works hard to recruit as
many people of color as possible for open positions in her organization (Harris
and Schaupp 2004, 159). White members of a church join a march of solidarity in
response to a drive-by shooting of a black teen (Hodges 2006). A white friend of
mine observes a situation in a store in which a person of color is ignored by the
salesperson, and my friend utilizes his racial status to make sure that this person
is treated right. By themselves these examples do not mean much. However, in
each situation the white individuals involved in these real life events are conservative Christians. Such actions are counterintuitive to what most of us expect
from white conservative Christians. Yet these individuals have had encounters
with people of color that have altered their perceptions and actions on racial issues. Individuals in a subculture not known for being sensitive to issues of racial
justice may become advocates under the right conditions. Obtaining more allies
is important to those who seek to advocate racial justice. Learning how to gain
such allies among what may be called the Religious Right is an important way to
strengthen support for racial justice.[1]

Emerson and Smith's (2000) now classic study of evangelicals documents
the racial divide that runs between black and white Christians. The authors build

on the well-known social fact that whites and blacks in the United States have contrasting perspectives on racial issues. Basically, whites have a more individualistic approach to racial issues, while blacks possess a more structuralist understanding (Bonilla-Silva and Lewis 1999; Kluegel 1990). This divide, as big as it is among white and black nonevangelicals, is even greater among white and black evangelicals. Thus white evangelicals are even more individualistic than whites in general, while black evangelicals are even more structuralist in their societal interpretation than blacks in general (Emerson and Smith 2000). This difference in racial perception continues even though white and black evangelicals share a great deal of theological beliefs.

The results of this divide can readily be seen in racial politics. For example, Michigan recently passed Proposition 2, which ended affirmative action. This proposition was passed over the objections of many black clergy, who understand affirmative action as a way for dealing with structural racism. Such clergy worked mightily toward the defeat of this proposition. They did so generally without the aid of white evangelicals. Had the conservative white evangelicals, an important part of what is known as the Religious Right, lent their support to the black clergy, it is quite possible that Proposition 2 could have been defeated.

Many are hesitant to believe that members of the Religious Right would develop a supportive attitude on issues of racial justice. The adherence of members of this subculture to the Republican Party seems to work against the possibility that the Religious Right can become a potent force for progressive racial change. But such doubts, while understandable, are miscalculations. It is possible to recruit members of the Religious Right to develop a more powerful coalition for racial justice. This possible coalition will not happen by accident. It will not happen if the current political and social atmosphere in the United States does not change. But my experience and research strongly suggest that it is a possibility. The purpose of this chapter is to approach this question and offer some ways in which a more powerful coalition for racial justice can be built.

I come at this problem having worked a great deal on racial issues with Christians who are either members of the Religious Right or are sympathetic to the aims of this group. I do not write this chapter as a representative of the Religious Right, as I am not. My previous public work has not promoted the sort of conservative political agenda central to the aims of the Religious Right. To the degree that my previous work has promoted any political agenda, it has been an agenda that calls Americans to take seriously the continuing racial alienation in our society.[2] However, I do contend that, contrary to the belief of many activists, this group can be recruited to aid in the struggle for civil rights if they are approached wisely. In fact, I believe that it is imperative to use activism to not merely "preach to the choir" (pun intended), but such efforts must recruit individuals who usually may not have a great deal of interest in dealing with racial issues. For this reason, I argue that seeking an alliance with a group that normally would not support progressive racial aims is a vital part of building a working consensus in the United States that can lead to altering the racial status quo.

WHO ARE THE RELIGIOUS RIGHT?

Many people tend to think of only well-known political conservatives such as Pat Roberson or Michael Medved when they think of the Religious Right. However, I conceptualize a more expansive understanding of that group. I envision members of the Religious Right simply as individuals who have a conservative political orientation and a high degree of religiosity within a traditional religion. Whites are more likely than non-whites to be part of this group, as they are more likely to use their faith to justify a conservative political ideology. My experience is that these individuals often legitimate their political orientation with their religious beliefs. Because of this religious justification, it is quite difficult for them to entertain alternatives to their current political vision. The intrinsic source of their political support provides them with a level of conviction that makes them valued allies for conservative political groups.

It is a mistake to look only to well-known political leaders of the Religious Right to understand this group. According to my definition, anyone with conservative political ties and traditional religious beliefs is part of the Religious Right. Many individuals in this group are not highly politically active. Historically, traditional religiosity has not been a steady source of support for political conservatism. It is only relatively recently that we can document traditional religiosity as buttressing conservative ideology. In fact, most individuals who fit into the Religious Right are not highly active in politics. They often vote, because they believe it to be their religious duty to vote. They also tend to vote Republican, as the party fits with their political beliefs. But their priorities generally are focused on their family, local communities, and living out their religious beliefs. There are not always centralized organizations for such individuals, except for their local conservative church, and thus there is a de-centralized attribute to this group, even as they tend to vote in lockstep for conservative causes.

I direct my attention to this average person in the pew. These individuals are sympathetic to the aims and goals of groups such as the Christian Coalition and

Focus on the Family, but political endeavors do not rule their lives. They are often seen as enemies to progressive causes because of their traditional perspective on social issues. However, it is a large group that generally has conservative political and religious values reinforced in their religious and community organizations. If they can become allies for challenging our racial structures, then activists of color will have much to gain from courting such individuals.

A Brief History of the Religious Right

Because of the prevalence of the Religious Right today, it is tempting to think that religion is generally used to maintain conservative, traditional political and social norms. In reality, religion has often been used to challenge social and political structures. For example, many of the early abolitionists (Harrill 2000; Howard 1990; Speicher 200) and women suffragists (Grimke 1988; Bordin 1981; Swartley 1983) utilized religious legitimization in their challenges to racism and sexism. However, recently a subculture known as the Religious Right has emerged to take an important role in the political environment of the United States. Rather than providing a radical challenge to social structures of oppression, this social movement fought to maintain notions of traditional social order (Brown 2002; Martin 1996; Wilcox 2000).

It is hard to pin down when the modern Religious Right movement began. Perhaps it emerged as the Reverend Billy Graham developed an anti-Communism strain to his preaching in the late 1940s. This emphasis was part of the larger challenge of Graham and other evangelicals against the social forces of modernism that threatened the exclusivity claims found within those religious groups. Ironically, Graham and some of these evangelicals also were concerned about issues of racial justice and offered support for school desegregation (Martin 1996). Other evangelicals, especially those who lived in the southern states, were less inclined to support efforts to overcome racism. Rev. Jerry Falwell preached against desegregation and the civil rights movement in general (Martin 1996). But Graham's willingness to encourage Christians to alter political and social norms set the stage so that Falwell could emerge as a political player.

The emergence of the Religious Right has led many majority-group individuals of faith into the Republican Party. The political development of the Religious Right that created this movement did not occur in a smooth, linear transition. Falwell became somewhat hesitant to become active nationally until 1973. In that year, the Supreme Court rendered its influential decision about a woman's right to have a legal abortion in *Roe v. Wade*. This decision brought first Catholics and then conservative Protestants into the political realm. Once they were there, other social forces cemented the emergence of the Religious Right as a political force. Francis Schaeffer's famous work (1976) argued for the need of Christians to become involved in the public arena in general and in the political arena in particular. The Eagle Forum, formed by Phyllis Shlafly, was used to fight against passage of the Equal Rights Amendment, which was seen as an attack on traditional family values. By the late 1970s, the Religious Right had become a social movement that was in full force.

The consequences of this movement became immediately clear. Falwell founded a group called the Moral Majority in 1979 in an effort to deal with the social and moral issues that members of this subculture found important. This group surprised progressive political groups and contributed to the electoral landslide enjoyed by President Ronald Reagan in 1980 (Moen 1989). The Moral Majority eventually gave way to the formation of Rev. Pat Robertson's Christian Coalition. This organization has been instrumental in maintaining the "pro-life" plank in the Republican Party platform. For example, the movement has a built-in media system of megachurches and religious television and radio stations to promulgate its message (Liebman 1983). With such institutional advantages, there is little wonder that the Religious Right has continued to possess a significant amount of influence. Thus what has been called the "New Right" developed as a confluence of economic and social conservatism, with both aspects playing an important role in the emergence of this political group (Himmelstein 1983).

The Religious Right has developed a powerful political focus on certain social issues. Specifically, issues of abortion and the Equal Rights Amendment first animated conservative Christians (Brown 2002; Moen 1989; Wilcox 2000), and lately the issue of same-sex marriage has also served as a powerful motivator for members of this subculture (Diamond 1998; Posner 2005; Smith 2001). Members of this subculture have fashioned "moral" reasons for their stance on these issues. While a claim of adherence to the Bible is often used to justify these stances, abortion and same-sex marriage are not mentioned in the Bible. Rather, members of the Religious Right use principles they attached to their religious beliefs to develop their political positions. For example, although the Bible is silent on abortion, there are many passages in it that can be used to justify protection of innocent life.[3] Thus many members of this subculture have developed "pro-life" positions based upon the principle of protecting innocent life. Because the Republican Party has adopted political positions that oppose abortion and same-sex marriage, members of the Religious Right found a comfortable political home with it. This adherence seems largely based upon such moral issues, and members of the Religious Right do not always agree with Republicans on economic and racial issues. But support of moral issues appears to be enough motivation for members of the Religious Right to stay faithful to the Republican Party.

Of course, one has to be careful not to place all people of faith into the same political spectrum. The media's treatment of religion can lead one to believe that all individuals of faith support every conservative political tenet. Even ignoring the fact that people of color who have faith tend to be politically progressive (Emerson and Smith 2000; Stevens-Arroyo 1998), there are plenty of white Christians and Jews who embrace a more progressive political agenda. Such individuals often are active in dealing with issues of racial justice. Generally, they belong to organizations with a more theologically liberal perspective, such as mainline Protestantism, Catholic congregations that embrace liberation theology, or Reform Judaism. These are not the individuals I am talking about reaching. Rather, I am talking about reaching whites of faith who have married elements of their faith to certain politically conservative philosophies. Such individuals are more likely to be part of organizations with a more conservative theology, such as evangelical/fundamentalist Protestants, traditional Catholics, or conservative Jews. These individuals often are the most loyal supporters of a general political conservatism that works against public policy solutions to institutional racial structures. Yet their basis for political conservatism generally has little to do with notions about racial inequality and more often is focused on their definition of "moral issues," such as abortion and same-sex marriage. There is the opportunity for such individuals to be convinced that racial justice is also a moral issue worth their time and effort.

Work on white racial identity has illustrated how the racial perceptions of majority group members help to maintain the racialized status quo (Bonilla-Silva and Lewis 1999; Carr 1997; Lipsitz 1998; Wildman and Davis 2002). An important component of this racialized white identity is individualism. The Religious Right has built upon this individualism to emphasize the "sins" of the individuals rather than to focus on societal failings. This emphasis has led to criticism of members of the Religious Right as being overly focused on issues of abortion and same-sex marriage (Simon 2007; Wallis 2006). Indeed, dealing with issues of individual morality is the core of the political activism of the Religious Right. As stated above, the association of this group with the Republican Party is largely due to the party's position on these issues.

For members of the Religious Right, racial issues are also issues of personal morality. Publicly, they decry any overt individual racism. But among members of the Religious Right there is general criticism aimed at the perceived moral failings of people of color for their lack of economic and academic success. Like the results of the Emerson and Smith research, my experience with members connected to the Religious Right is that many have not even considered issues of institutional racism, and when they are told about its existence, they perceive arguments of institutional racism as a copout to cover individual shortcomings.

Can such individuals be reached through educational institutions? As I have taught courses in race and ethnicity, I realize that the understanding of many majority group members about institutional discrimination comes from their exposure to these ideas in classrooms.[4] However, I am skeptical that educational institutions will be very effective in dealing with the racial perspectives of members of the Religious Right. Previous research has suggested that individuals in the Religious Right do not trust educational institutions (Berliner and Biddle 1995; Gribbin 1995; Reichley 1986; Stacey and Shupe 1984). My experience confirms this research. They resent much of the secularized philosophy that is part of the contemporary educational system. Attempts to produce racial awareness among members of the Religious Right through our educational system are likely to be met with charges of political correctness.

Traditional social activism is also unlikely to persuade members of this group of the importance of racial justice. Members of the Religious Right may also be busy engaging in their own local activism. Activism connected to racial justice may prove to be a competitor to the socially conservative activism in which members of the Religious Right participate. These members are not necessarily opposed to the agenda of racial justice, but they do not yet prioritize these issues highly enough to take them seriously. A second issue that has to be considered is the association of social activism with the Democratic Party. For reasons that I go into later, this often provides an insurmountable barrier toward gaining support of members of the Religious Right through social activism.

In short, members of the Religious Right are not likely to be influenced by the mechanisms that many activists for social justice use to promote a vision of racial egalitarianism. The tragedy of this is that some members of this subculture can be persuaded into seeing racial justice as an important issue to fight for. What is necessary to achieve this potential is to find new ways to communicate to members of the Religious Right the importance of racial justice.

Reaching the Religious Right

To recruit members of the Religious Right to the cause of racial justice, it must first be remembered that desires for morality play an important role in the thinking of these individuals. Basically, their motivation is based upon a desire to make society a better place. They are not as motivated by economic gain as other political conservatives. Because of this desire for a better society, members of this subculture can be motivated to deal with issues of racial justice. They fail to be so motivated because many of them believe that racism has largely been eliminated. They have bought into the idea of color blindness that is a prominent feature of white racial identity (Ansell 1997; Bonilla-Silva 2001; Carr 1997). For members of the Religious Right to become involved in issues of racial justice, they have to believe that racism is still an important feature of our society.

Why do members of the Religious Right accept notions of color blindness? Is it because they want to ignore the evidence of structural racism that is around them? It is not my experience that such ignorance is self-imposed. Rather, the philosophy of freewill individualism popular among members of the Religious Right makes it difficult for them to appreciate the ways social structures affect the life chances of nonwhites. Their acceptance of freewill individualism allows them to deal with overt individualized racism, but blinds them to the existence of institutional racism. They are aware that the type of overt individualistic racism that was once common has been greatly reduced, which provides them with even more evidence that racism is not a serious problem. Thus majority group members of the Religious Right have to be shown evidence that they can comprehend that institutional racism still profoundly affects the lives of minority group members.

This evidence can be obtained through the interpersonal relationships that white members of the Religious Right develop with people of color. Recent work on interracial contact in religious institutions has indicated that majority group members in racially integrated organizations are more likely to have progressive racial attitudes than other majority group church attendees (Yancey 1999; Yancey 2001). Evidence suggests that interracial contact effects are not entirely due to self-selection (Dixon and Rosenbaum 2004; Ellison and Powers 1994; Pettigrew and Tropp 2000). Anecdotally, I have talked with several politically conservative white Christians who have developed progressive racial perspectives because of the interaction they have with people of color. The empirical research, and my experiences, indicates an important way in which members of the Religious Right may be convinced of the importance of racialized social structures. This way is interaction and meaningful dialogue between members of the Religious Right and minority group members, most notably people of color who also possess high religiosity and can communicate to members of the Religious Right in their own spiritual language. The lack of a dialogue between religious people of color and members of the Religious Right is one of the pressing barriers that inhibit the ability of Religious Right advocates to understand structural racism. White religious conservatives are less likely than others to have a high number of close friends of color, especially since they are most likely to find their close friendships from those of their same religious tradition (Emerson and Smith 2000). Because of the importance members of the Religious Right place on personal experiences, they learn best about social reality through interaction with individuals who have experienced the reality of racism. Without dialogue with people of color, it is very difficult to see how many members of this subculture will gain the motivation necessary to address racial injustice.

To engage in this dialogue, activists for racial justice are going to have to change their approach to the Religious Right: they are going to have to engage in a respectful and meaningful dialogue. This means listening to the concerns of members of the Religious Right as well as communicating concerns of racial justice to them. This does not mean that such activists have to agree with all of the social concerns of members of the Religious Right. However, there are mutual concerns for both religious conservatives and religious liberals. For example, the coarsening of our culture is not merely the concern of religious conservatives, but of many religious liberals as well. When it is possible for advocates of racial justice to do so, working with members of the Religious Right can provide a valuable way to develop the relationships that can prove useful in recruiting them into movements for racial justice.

Listening to some of the concerns of the Religious Right will show the type of respect that can lead to gaining a voice among members of this subculture. The next step will be to use that voice to gain support from that subculture for issues of racial justice. To be successful, it is important to talk in the language of the hearer. For conservative Christians, this means that two types of arguments are needed. First, there needs to an understanding about racial justice based upon recent books written by progressive Christians that deal with racial issues (Anderson 2007; DeYoung 1995; Usry and Keener 1996; Woodley 2001). The argument from the Bible is key, as the Scriptures are the basis for all social activism promoted by Christians in the Religious Right.[5] Thus if there is any hope that members of the Religious Right will engage in activism that promotes racial justice, it is important to find a biblical basis for that activism.

Bradley Christerson teaches sociological courses in race and ethnicity at a conservative Christian university. He has found that many of the white conservative students tend to ignore racial issues unless they are given biblical scriptures that address these issues (Christerson 2002). Once they are given such biblical support, they become open to the sociological and empirical evidence that he can provide about institutional racism. Motivating majority group members with a traditional religious orientation to develop a concern about racial inequality may be difficult, but it is not impossible.

The second important piece of evidence that needs to be provided to members of the Religious Right is experiential. Many members of this subculture have a difficult time believing that racism still affects the lives of people of color. They are unimpressed by empirical evidence of institutional racism, as they place a high priority on individual effort and experience. Thus hearing the stories from people of color who are troubled by the continuing racism in the United States can have a profound effect upon members of the Religious Right, especially if they have relationships with those individuals. It is not an accident that Bill McCartney took what was at the time an extraordinary step of intentionally including people of color in the leadership in his Christian organization—PromiseKeepers. As coach of the University of Colorado Buffaloes, he interacted with many college football players who were racial minorities, and his daughter had become pregnant with the child of one of those players. He had been forced to hear the experiences of people of color who were in his intimate social networks. Likewise, my previous research of interracial marriages (Yancey 2007) found several white Christians who developed racial awareness because of what they either learned from their spouse of color or from friends of color that their marriages brought into their lives. Finally, I was struck by an interview of a white pastor of a multiracial church who recounted learning about how his African American congregants had developed a mistrust of the police force because of incidents of police brutality. Being a small man himself, he had always looked up to the police for the protection they provided him. But he became more racially aware as he learned about the problems that the criminal justice system created for individuals of color.

The racial isolation of their social networks prevents many members of the Religious Right from engaging in the type of introspection that can lead them to more robust support for issues of racial justice. Nonetheless, these individuals possess a moral legitimization system that can be tapped into. This is different from political conservatives with a nonreligious basis for their conservatism. Such individuals are unlikely to be persuaded by moral arguments, for issues of justice and interracial interaction may not motivate them to abandon principles of limited government and freewill individualism. It is in the interest of those who are concerned about racial justice to make use of the moral systems within the Religious Right by developing the social networks with such members that can activate those systems.

POLITICAL LIMITATIONS

While I contend that there is potential gain in attempting to work with the Religious Right, it is important to be clear about what the limitations are in this type of potential alliance. I can envision an alliance whereby members of the Religious Right will become advocates for issues of racial justice through support of political activism, through support of referendums that protect affirmative action measures, through financial support of programs that serve economically marginalized people of color, and through other such programs. What is not likely to occur is that members of this subculture will be willing to leave the Republican Party in mass numbers and unite with activists of color in the Democratic Party. An expectation of such abandonment is likely to lead to the frustration of unrealized expectations.

Why am I so sure that such a movement is unlikely to occur? My experience with members of the Religious Right indicates that the issue of abortion is simply too important for them to make such an exodus. Many of them perceive abortion to be a holocaust greater than what happened in Nazi Germany.[6] They are insulted by talk of aborted "fetuses" and instead see dead babies. The same moral essence that can make these individuals open to accepting issues of racial justice also links them to uncompromising positions on the issue of abortion. In their perception, they simply cannot support an organization, such as the Democratic Party, that legitimated such needless loss of innocent life.[7] Contrary to popular belief, members of the Religious Right do not agree with the Republican Party on all issues. But they have such moral indignation at the prevalence of legal abortions that they will tend to stay with the Republican Party as long as it is seen as the pro-life party.

Activists do not have to agree with the abortion politics of the Religious Right to work with members of these groups. But they need to understand the depth of support these individuals have for this position. A failure to understand this can lead racial justice activists to believe that the support from members of the Religious Right is superficial because they remain Republicans. From the perspective of the members of the Religious Right, it is a choice of helping individuals who are victims of racial discrimination or helping those who are not even provided a chance at life. They cannot choose the former over the latter, but they may be persuaded to work at both causes if they do not have to make an exclusive decision. Furthermore, there may be value in their continued presence in the Republican Party since, if members of the Religious Right become more open to issue of racial justice, they will take that concern into the Republican Party.[8] This ultimately can lead to less overall resistance from political conservatives toward public efforts to confront the modern and institutional forms of racism that persist in the United States.

THE GREEN MOVEMENT

One can have more hope of working with members of the Religious Right if there is evidence that this group may be open to progressive initiatives. For this reason, there is an interesting trend among some members of Christian subculture that feeds much of the Religious Right. Recently, several leaders of that subculture have begun to perceive protecting the physical environment as an important moral issue and to argue that Christians must take a more proactive stance toward cleaning up the environment (Davies 2007; Harden 2005). This type of activism is contrary to the traditional conservative political schema many white Christians have accepted. To the degree that these leaders are able to persuade people of faith to accept a more progressive interpretation of environmentalism, there is insight as to how other progressive concerns may gain a hearing among conservative people of faith.

We can see the results of this emphasis more clearly by looking at an evangelical church that has adopted a more "green" policy as it shapes its activism—the Boise Vineyard Church located in Boise, Idaho. The leader of the church is Tri Robinson, and his vision helped to inspire the move of the Vineyard denomination toward more environmental activism.[9] Robinson's interaction with an environmentally conscious individual at a wedding he officiated led him to rethink much of his church's ministry. Afterward, church members began a community recycling program, collected unused cell phones, started addressing environmental concerns in their missionary outreach, sat on certain governmental boards that dealt with the environment, and addressed the inadequate disposal of plastic in the community. They also promoted learning programs within the church, and Robinson has written a book outlining their environmental efforts. Because of its efforts, the Boise Vineyard Church received a certificate of appreciation from the National Forest Service. Pastor Robinson has stated an unwillingness to become directly involved in the larger political fight around environmental issues, but clearly the efforts of the Boise Vineyard Church have helped to shape issues of environmental awareness in the larger Boise area.

It is tempting to dismiss such information by seeing this church as an outlier. Indeed, there has been some conservative backlash against this church and other Christians who have criticized making environmentalism an important issue in their ministry.[10] However, this church has not merely had an important impact on its own members, but it has also been a significant factor in helping to influence the entire Vineyard denomination.[11] Because of the work from the members of this church, there have been more efforts on the behalf of the Vineyard denomination to address issues of environmentalism. As such, the Boise Vineyard Church has received prominent support in the literature put out by the Vineyard denomination, and there have been efforts within this denomination to promote ministry that is more conscious of environmental concerns. Furthermore, there is evidence that this emphasis on environmentalism is not limited to the Vineyard denomination. A recent article in *Christianity Today*, long considered the flagship journal for conservative Protestants, indicates a green movement is occurring on Christian college campuses (Crosby 2007). This is significant given the short time in which environmentalism has become highly acceptable among conservative Protestants. This article documents that about a third of the Christian college campuses have significant green initiatives. Imagine what changes might occur if a third of the Christian colleges also had serious programs of racial justice on their campuses.

What has happened with the Religious Right's concerns about environmental issues can also happen with racial justice issues. Such traditionally conservative religious organizations may be unwilling to attack political conservatives directly, since such stances can be seen as running counter to other moral issues. But focusing on that reality misses other assets such churches can provide. They can be very active in local community issues. They can use some of their financial capital to support programs that aid people of color. Their moral presence can legitimate issues of racial justice to a larger audience, just as churches like Boise Vineyard Church influence their local community and their denomination. Perhaps most important, such churches may stop following all conservative political dictates and thus stop being barriers to issues of racial justice. Such churches would not be automatic supporters of Proposition 2 in Michigan, and discussion with the members in such churches may lead to the defeat of such propositions. If the example of the Boise Vineyard Church can be replicated in major metropolitan areas in the United States, then the balance of racial power in the United States can change, and activism supporting the racially marginalized can be strengthened.

What Needs to Be Done?

Since I have done research in this area, I have worked with Christian groups that seek to racially diversify their congregations. One of the first pieces of advice I provide for such groups is that they will have to make intentional efforts to create racial diversity. The type of racial hostility that has developed in U.S. society has made it nearly impossible for religious organizations to become racially diverse without intentional efforts. Likewise, overcoming social and philosophical barriers that manifested themselves between racial activists and members of the Religious Right will require intentional efforts from both parties. While activists for racial justice cannot force members of the Religious Right to engage in such efforts, they can do their part to lower some of the barriers and thus recruit new possible allies for racial justice issues. With that thought in mind, I outline some steps that can be taken to begin the development of such an alliance. I present these steps in a particular order, since it is my opinion that these steps are in a logical progression.

Forgo Demonizing the Religious Right

It is obvious that any sort of recruitment of members of the Religious Right into an alliance to fight for racial justice must begin by respecting these individuals. Some of the Religious Right can be persuaded by moral arguments about the rightness of racial justice. But few, if any, people are likely to be persuaded if they do not think that those persuading them have respect for them. One of the ways individuals show a lack of respect is by demonizing members of the Religious Right. Individuals striving to live a highly moral life can be instructed to engage in the sort of introspection that can lead them to challenge the racial hegemony in the United States. But attempts to demonize them will not produce that sort of introspection and instead will make members of the

Religious Right less willing to participate in social activism that supports efforts for racial justice.

One of the clearest ways in which members of the Religious Right are demonized is through accusations of racism. As most members of the Religious Right
understand racism, through their rubric of individualism, they are not racist.
Many of these members are ignorant of the way institutional racism continues to
affect people of color, and indeed many of them should take more responsibility
to learn more about the effects of institutional racism. But this type of error is
not the same as being racist in an individualistic way. In many instances, the way
charges of racism are launched toward these members denotes an image of them
being akin to white supremacists. Such charges may produce satisfaction among
those who do not like the Religious Right, but ultimately they make it harder to
convince members of Religious Right that those who fight for racial justice care
at all about them. After enduring such charges, there is little wonder that when
issues such as Proposition 2 come up, members of the Religious Right are unwilling to work with social activists. Who wants to help those whom you suspect do
not care about you?

This does not mean one must agree with members of the Religious Right
or fail to challenge them about their current racial perceptions. I know that
individuals in the Religious Right subculture can be persuaded that their previous understandings about racial issues are wrong and that they need to develop
new racial perspectives. Generally, these individuals accept an ideology of color
blindness in their attempts to understand racial issues. I have had many discussions with members of the Religious Right in which I have helped them to
see why their previous perceptions are incorrect. I have challenged them with
information that indicates that racism is still an important aspect of the United
States and that it may unfortunately be a part of their own lives. Criticism of
members of the Religious Right, in and of itself, does not dissuade members of
this subculture from revisiting some of their previous racialized perceptions. If
that criticism comes from people whom they believe actually want to dialogue
with them and who care about them, then such criticism can stimulate productive alterations of previous racial attitudes.[12] But if that criticism is done just
to "score points" among political and social progressives, then it will merely
put up more barriers toward persuading members of the Religious Right to
become active in seeking racial justice. The most basic requirement to be met
if members of the Religious Right are going to be recruited into causes of racial
justice is that there must be an effort to avoid any unnecessary demonizing of
this subculture.

Develop a Mindset of Reaching Out

The next step in the process of finding support among the Religious Right is to develop a mindset of reaching out to them. It is normal, and perhaps even natural, for individuals to develop relationships and connections with like-minded people. Thus individuals who have a powerful desire to seek racial justice are very likely to develop relationships with other individuals who seek racial justice. But the development of these social networks will do little in helping to recruit others who may be convinced that seeking racial justice and combating institutional discrimination are worthy social goals. Instead, it is important to find opportunities by which such individuals may learn about such social values and become more proactive in their desire to deal with modern forms of racism.

Many individuals active in movements for racial justice may be perfectly content to live with social barriers that limit their interaction with members of the Religious Right. Such contentment will not gain future allies for racial justice, but outreach outside of these comfortable social circles can. Outreach can only be accomplished after attempts to demonize the Religious Right have ceased. At that point, it becomes important to envision the development of cross-racial and even cross-political alliances. This means that talks, sermons, and writings have to advocate the value of talking with members of the Religious Right rather than confrontation with them. Too often, I fear, confrontation is emphasized over the sort of dialogue and relationships that may help to produce the opportunities for racial awareness among members of the Religious Right.

In the past, I have often worked with multiracial churches in an attempt to foster the development of these types of multiracial relationships. I remain convinced that such efforts are important, since I have done research suggesting that whites attending such churches are more racially progressive than other whites (Yancey 1999; Yancey 2001).[13] Black churches served, and continue to serve, an important place in the African American community. We will continue to have black churches for the foreseeable future. However, it is also clear that even black churches can do more to foster an outreach to religious conservatives. Cultural exchanges such as pastor or choir exchanges, as well as planned social fellowships with churches that serve the Religious Right, are invaluable ways of producing racial understanding and creating an atmosphere where alliance becomes possible. Unfortunately, many members of the Religious Right have distorted images of religious blacks, in part because the media tends to focus only on the conflicts that happen between majority and minority group religious organizations. Efforts to break our social patterns in hopes of creating interracial friendships can help to demystify these images and make the next step possible.

Work on Projects of Common Interest

In an ideal world, new interracial relationships will provide immediate allies for issues of racial justice. Majority group members would get to know people of color in these relationships and become concerned about the social/racial conditions that inflict the lives of their new friends. But in the real world, life is not so simple. Individuals generally need a little time to accumulate new data/ information and use it to change previously held values. As such, members of the Religious Right are not likely to have an immediate willingness to immerse themselves into issues of racial justice.

A much better tact would be to work with members of the Religious Right on issues where a consensus exists. Neither civil rights activists nor members of the Religious Right should feel compelled to become active on issues they do not have passion for, or for issues they disagree on. Individuals should only work on issues they truly believe in, and while belief among Religious Right members about the need for racial justice will grow over time, it is important not to pressure them into actions they are not ready to take. Rather, mutual support on issues that both civil rights activists and members of the Religious Right can agree upon can set the stage for similar alliances later as some of the members of the Religious Right become more convinced about the need to challenge institutional racism.

What sorts of issues might involve such common interests? I am of the opinion that individuals, such as civil rights activists and members of the Religious Right who are motivated by a sense of morality, can find such issues of agreement. For example, immediately after the controversy about Don Imus's remarks about the Rutgers University women's basketball team, the discussion moved toward some of the misogynist language and incivility that are part of contemporary music in the United States. Dealing with such language is an issue that civil rights activists and members of the Religious Right are both concerned about, but it is an issue where they generally work on different tracks instead of working together.[14] Because of their previous disposition to perceive racial issues from an individualistic perspective, I have found that members of the Religious Right are also open to dealing with instances of overt racism. Before the formation of an alliance to protect measures that challenge institutional racism, such as affirmative action, it is important to have experience already working with members of this subculture on issues of overt racism.[15] Finally, economic efforts to help the poor are not uncommon among members of the Religious Right. Merging some of these efforts with similar efforts sponsored by civil rights activists may provide for another common interest that can benefit both groups.

Finding common interest may not always be easy, but it is an important step that allows for more trust to develop between civil rights activists and members of the Religious Right. This step also establishes a habit between the two groups of working together, a habit that may become profitable as the relationships between these two groups begin to blossom. But as this working together takes place, there will be a need to deal with misunderstandings that are likely to emerge. Dealing with such potential misunderstandings can occur with the next important step.

Establish Open and Honest Dialogue

One of the hardest things to do as it concerns racial issues is to promote dialogue that is honest and open. Few people want to be labeled a racist, if they are white, or a complainer, if they are a person of color. Such fears are important barriers to the creation of a social atmosphere in which people of different races can freely express their fears and concerns. Yet without such openness, it is hard for individuals to confront those fears and to possibly deal with them.

One of the reasons why some majority group members of the Religious Right hold on to politically conservative racial ideas is to protect themselves from accusations of racism. Adherence to ideas of color blindness is useful for protecting an individual from accusations of racism, since color blindness attributes blame for racial problems at the feet of those who are paying attention to race. In this way, many members of the Religious Right argue that their willingness to ignore racial issues is part of the solution, and not the problem. An important way to deal with this tendency to hide from their racial fears is for members of the Religious Right to have honest and open dialogue with people of color, particularly those of faith, who can discuss with them the shortcomings of an ideology of color blindness. This is especially relevant to members of the Religious Right, as there is evidence that interpersonal relationships are an important way white conservative Christians may alter previously held beliefs (Emerson and Smith 2000).

But the lack of honest, open interracial communication prevents such interpersonal encounters, which hampers the potential attitudinal alterations that may occur among members of the Religious Right. This is why it is important to find venues to engage in productive interracial communication. This type of communication can develop after members of the Religious Right and people of color have worked together on common interests for a period of time. Such was the case in Jackson, Mississippi, when a predominantly white ministry worked with a black community on issues of economic development. Over time, these conservative white Christians and blacks engaged in a series of "talks" that led many of the whites to gain a new understanding about racial issues and that significantly influenced these whites' views on racial politics. At times the talks were brutal in their honesty, but because relationships had developed between the two groups, interracial understanding could blossom.[16]

Some of what is called dialogue often has not been productive. Meaningful dialogue can only take place in a situation where there is mutual respect. Activists for racial justice who merely seek to "preach" at members of the Religious Right will make no headway with members of this subculture unless there is respect for social relationships between these activists and Religious Right members. Working together on issues they hold in common can provide an opportunity for that respect to develop. But civil rights activists must follow up this opportunity by seeking respectful, honest forums that can promote meaningful communication.

Recruitment of the Religious Right into Issues of Racial Concern

It is only after these first four steps are taken that the last, important step can be walked. That step is the recruitment of members of the Religious Right into advocating issues of racial justice. This recruitment must happen with the understanding of the limitations that I have outlined in previous sections of this chapter. But indeed, we have already seen some evidence that members of the Religious Right can be influenced into supporting issues of racial justice.

The manner in which individuals of the Religious Right can be influenced into advocating issues of racial justice should not depart from the style of relationship building that brings us to this point. In other words, attempts to strong-arm members of the Religious Right into supporting certain racial concerns are likely to fail. However, appealing to their sense of morality and justice can be very effective. Using their own religious texts can also provide powerful persuasion tools. As relationships with members of this subculture develop, activists for racial justice will learn more about the spiritual and moral justifications that members of the Religious Right use to legitimate their beliefs. Similar types of arguments, and the development of interpersonal relationships that alter previous stereotypes members of the Religious Right may hold toward civil rights activists, can be powerful tools in the recruitment of members of the Religious Right into dealing with issues of racial justice.

A productive aspect about dealing with the Religious Right with this type of methodology is that there will be a mutual level of trust and good feelings between members of both groups. The agenda of racial justice does not have to be promoted by confrontation. Confrontation can create change, but rarely does it create change through consensus. Working with members of the Religious Right will produce more promoters of racial justice and do so in a way that does produce consensus. Changes that happen because of consensus, instead of confrontation, are more stable since there are fewer individuals who will seek to reverse these changes.

Conclusion

I am quite aware of how controversial the suggestions of this chapter are. There is a great deal of anger leveled at members of the Religious Right, and much of it is justified. Several members of that community have been tremendous roadblocks to the promotion of efforts to create racial justice in American society. The thought of working with members of this subculture to promote issues such as affirmative action or hate crimes legislation seems antithetical to the experience of many activists for racial justice.

Yet I am convinced that working with members of this subculture is smart and that more effective action can be taken. The reality is that there is not sufficient public support out there for stopping initiatives like Proposition 2. There is even less public support to create new initiatives for racial justice. The recent surge of political power for the Democratic Party is not going to produce much more support. Michigan is a reliable blue state, and yet Proposition 2 still passed. Previous effects that have relied upon confrontation were necessary at one point of our racial history. My fear is that now such methods are outdated and unreliable for producing social change. If we rely upon such previous efforts, we will only reproduce the same ineffective results as before.

To become more successful, it is important to find allies in realms where they do not already exist in large numbers. My experience in working with members of the Religious Right let me know that at least some of them can become such allies. Under conditions of confrontation, they will never become allies in large numbers. In part, I am writing this chapter to discourage confrontation as the principal way for dealing with the Religious Right, and to argue that there is a better way to collect allies. Ultimately, it is my hope that in time we can truly address many of the racial inequities that persists in the United States. I seek a stable solution built upon consensus, and I am critical of previous efforts based upon confrontation. I respect those who share similar concerns but do not share my ideas about the methodology of achieving them. It goes without saying that I hope that those who disagree with me will also respect my intentions. Furthermore, I hope also to engage in a meaningful conversation with such individuals as to how to best promote issues of racial justice. Such dialogue is necessary if we are going to investigate all of the possible ways to deal with institutional racism in the United States.

NOTES

1. In this chapter, I use the term "Religious Right" to denote the subculture of conservative people of faith. It is also plausible to use the term the "Christian Right," but that term eliminates from discussion religiously conservative Jews, Mormons, and Muslims. My experience has been exclusively with Christians, but I wanted to be as inclusive as possible.
2. For example, see Yancey (2002) and Yancey (2007). This is not to say that I am unsympathetic to some of the goals of the Religious Right. However, I prioritize other social/political goals over the core conservatism exhibited by the Religious Right.
3. For example, Genesis 4:10, Proverbs 6:17, Isaiah 59:7, and Matthew 27:4 all can be used to support the notion that innocent life should be valued.
4. However, it should be recognized that it is unclear that education may produce long-term alterations in the actions of majority group members. It has been documented that highly educated whites are actually less likely to send their children to racially integrated schools and to live in racially integrated neighborhoods (Sikkink and Emerson 2008), indicating that education does not necessarily lead to actions that promote racial equality.
5. My own personal work has concentrated on conservative Christians. Yet the same sacred text for them is also held in esteem, to varying degrees, by conservative Jews, Mormons, and Moslems. I suspect that these sectors of the Religious Right also need

convincing within their own religious traditions. This convincing may utilize the Bible or other sacred writings such as the Koran, Torah, and/or Pearl of Great Price.

6. If you believe that this is an exaggeration, then you only need to look at the actions of O'Connor as documented in Goldman (1992, 123–24).

7. In fact, it is not uncommon for members of the Religious Right to link their opposition to abortion to the historical opposition that many religious abolitionists had toward slavery (Dennehy 2006, Garton 1998, Kirk 2003, Olasky 1992). In both cases, they perceive people of faith fighting for the rights of marginalized others who are not perceived as being fully human in the eyes of the larger society.

8. In the recent fight concerning immigration, there were several conservative religious voices (for example, Michael Medved and Richard Land) who advocated a more progressive comprehensive solution than the "close the border" crowd that eventually killed the bill. While such voices were not enough to ensure passage of a guest worker program, they do show that Republican thought on racial issues does not have to be monolithic. It is fair to assert that it may be these types of religious voices that persuaded President Bush to attempt immigration reform, which is clearly one of his more progressive political stances.

9. Much of the information that I gained about this congregation came from an article about them in the main denominational organ of the Vineyard (Pool 2007).

10. In fact, Rev. Robinson has commented that the only individuals who have criticized this push toward environmentalism tend to be conservative Christians who sometimes attack him when he is on conservative talk shows (Pool 2007).

11. The Vineyard denomination is generally conservative theologically, but it has not been that active politically. The political views of most members in the Vineyard denomination likely match most of the views of those in the Religious Right; however, they are less likely to be as politically active as members of other conservative Protestant denominations.

12. For example, some research I have been conducting indicates that Christians are less willing to romantically date people of a different race than of a different faith (Yancey et al. 2007). I could use that information to make charges of racism against white conservative Christians. Instead, I use that information to challenge these Christians to develop a more real faith that places racial issues in a proper context relative to issues of faith. I challenge them to do that by examining the role racism still plays in their lives and in their churches. This allows me to make racial challenges without making unfair accusations and to indicate to them the importance race still plays in our society. I can do this in the context of their own religious beliefs, which is a powerful legitimating tool when it comes to producing racial awareness.

13. This research indicates that people of color in these institutions do not tend to alter their racial attitudes. Fears that people of color will lose their desire for racial justice are largely unfounded.

14. In fact, several years ago Bill Bennett, a member of the Religious Right, and C. Delores Tucker, a civil rights activist, worked together on this same issue. Both of them found common ground in their concern that some of the lyrics in rap music were detrimental to the African American community. This effort indicates that such alliances are possible when both groups in the alliance have a passionate belief in the cause, even if the sources of their beliefs differ.

15. Perhaps this is why sometimes after the Ku Klux Klan holds a rally, interfaith and/or interdenominational groups are formed for the promotion of "racial healing." I will leave it up to the reader to decide the value of such groups, but these groups do represent opportunities for multiracial, multipolitical alliances between members of faith. To the degree that such groups promote the development of alliances that can lead to relationships that develop racial awareness among majority group members, political and religious conservatives might increase their propensity to become active in pursuing racial justice. Future research may assess whether such a process does emerge from such groups.

16. Details of this encounter can be seen in Rice (2003).

REFERENCES

Anderson, David A. 2007. *Gracism: The Art of Inclusion*. Downers Grove, Ill.: InterVarsity Press.

Ansell, Amy Elizabeth. 1997. *New Right, New Racism: Race and Reaction in the United States and Britain*. Washington Square: New York University Press.

Berliner, David C., and Bruce Biddle. 1995. *The Manufactured Crisis: Myths, Fraud and the Attack on America's Public Schools*. Reading, Mass.: Addison-Wesley.

Bonilla-Silva, Eduardo. 2001. *White Supremacy and Racism in the Post-Civil Rights Era*. Boulder, Colo.: Lynne Rienner.

Bonilla-Silva, Eduardo, and Amanda Lewis. 1999. "The 'New Racism': Toward an Analysis of the U.S. Racial Structure, 1960s-1990s." In *Race, Ethnicity and Nationality in the United States: Towards the Twenty First Century*, ed. Paul Wong. Boulder, Colo.: Westview Press.

Bordin, Ruth. 1981. *Women and Temperance: The Quest for Power and Liberty, 1873–1900*. Philadelphia: Temple University Press.

Brown, Ruth Murray. 2002. *For a Christian America: A History of the Religious Right*. Amherst, N.Y.: Prometheus Books.

Carr, Leslie G. 1997. *Color-Blind Racism*. Thousand Oaks, Calif.: Sage

Christerson, Bradley. 2002. "Race at an Evangelical College." Paper presented at the annual meeting of the Society for the Scientific Study of Religion. Salt Lake City.

Crosby, Cindy. 2007. "Christian Colleges' Green Revolution." *Christianity Today*, May 25, 52-55

Davies, Frank. 2007. "Religion, Politics Mix at Warming Hearing." *San Jose (Calif.) Mercury News Weekend,* June 8.

Dennehy, Raymond. 2006. *Anti-Abortionist at Large: How to Argue Abortion Intelligently and Live to Tell About It*. New Bern, N.C.: Trafford.

DeYoung, Curtiss. 1995. *Coming Together: The Bible's Message in an Age of Diversity*. Valley Forge, Pa.: Judson Press.

Diamond, Sara. 1998. *Not by Politics Alone: The Enduring Influence of the Christian Right*. New York: Guilford Press.

Dixon, Jeffrey C., and Michael S. Rosenbaum. 2004. "Nice to Know You? Testing Contact, Cultural and Group Threat Theories of Anti-Black and Anti-Hispanic Stereotypes." *Social Science Quarterly* 85:257-80.

Ellison, Christopher, and Daniel Powers. 1994. "The Contact Hypothesis and Racial Attitudes among Black Americans." *Social Science Quarterly* 75:385-400.

Emerson, Michael O., and Christian Smith. 2000. *Divided by Faith: Evangelical Religion and the Problem of Race in America*. Oxford: Oxford University Press.

Garton, Jean Staker. 1998. *Who Broke the Baby? What the Abortion Slogans Really Mean*. Grand Rapids, Mich.: Bethany House.

Goldman, Ari L. 1992. *The Search for God at Harvard*. New York: Ballantine Books.

Gribbin, William. 1995. "Religious Conservatives and Public Schools: Understanding the Religious Right." *English Journal* 84:84-90.

Grimke, Sarah Moore. 1988. *Letters on the Equality of the Sexes and Other Essays*. Edited by Elizabeth Ann Bartlett. New Haven, Conn.: Yale University Press.

Harden, Blaine. 2005. "The Greening of Evangelicals." *Washington Post,* February 6.

Harrill, J. Albert. 2000. "The Use of the New Testament in the American Slave Controversy: A Case History in the Hermeneutical Tension between Biblical Criticism and Christian Moral Debate." *Religion and American Culture* 10:149-86.

Harris, Paula, and Doug Schaupp. 2004. *Being White: Finding Our Place in a Multiethnic World*. Downers Grove, Ill.: InterVarsity Press.

Himmelstein, Jerome L. 1983. "The New Right." In *The New Christian Right: Mobilization and Legitimation,* ed. Robert C. Liebman and Robert Wuthnow. New York: Aldine.

Hodges, Sam. 2006. "Houston Pastor Strives for Worship Diversity." *Dallas Morning News*, July 13.

Howard, Victor B. 1990. *Religion and the Radical Republican Movement, 1860-1870*. Lexington: University Press of Kentucky.

Kirk, Peggy. 2003. *You Aren't Alone: The Voices of Abortion*. Nevada City, Calif.: Blue Dolphin.

Kluegel, James R. 1990. "Trends in Whites' Explanation of the Black-White Gap in Socioeconomic Status, 1977-1989." *American Sociological Review* 55:512-25.

Liebman, Robert C. 1983. "Mobilizing the Moral Majority." In *The New Christian Right: Mobilization and Legitimation*, ed. Robert C. Liebman and Robert Wuthnow. New York: Aldine.

Lipsitz, George. 1998. *The Possessive Investment in Whiteness: How White People Profit from Identity Politics*. Philadelphia: Temple University Press.

Martin, William. 1996. *With God on Our Side: The Rise of the Religious Right in America*. New York: Broadway Books.

Moen, Matthew C. 1989. *The Christian Right and Congress*. Tuscaloosa: University of Alabama Press.

Olasky, Marvin. 1992. *Abortion Rites: A Social History of Abortion in America*. Wheaton, Ill.: Crossway Books.

Pettigrew, Thomas F., and L. R. Tropp. 2000. "Does Intergroup Contact Reduce Prejudice?: Recent Meta-Analytic Findings." In *Reducing Prejudice and Discrimination*, ed. S. Oskamp. Mahwah, N.J.: Lawrence Erlbaum.

Pool, Jim. 2007. "Caring for the World." *Cutting Edge: Association of Vineyard Churches USA* 10, no. 3, 6-9.

Posner, Sarah. 2005. "With God on His Side." *American Prospect* (November): 25-30.

Reichley, A. James. 1986. "Religion and the Future of American Politics." *Political Science Quarterly* 101:23-47.

Rice, Chris. 2003. *Grace Matters: A Memoir of Faith, Friendship, and Hope in the Heart of the South*. San Francisco: Jossey-Bass.

Schaeffer, Francis A. 1976. *How Should We Then Live?: The Rise and Decline of Western Thought and Culture*. Grand Rapids, Mich.: Fleming H. Revell.

Sikkink, David, and Michael O. Emerson. "School Choice and Racial Segregation in U.S. Schools: The Role of Parents' Education," *Ethnic and Racial Studies* 31, no. 2 (2008).

Simon, Stephanie. 2007. "Christian Leaders Promote Care for Orphans, Adoption." *Los Angeles Times*, May 13.

Smith, Anna Marie. 2001. "The Politicization of Marriage in Contemporary American Public Policy: The Defense of Marriage Act and the Personal Responsibility Act." *Citizenship Studies* 5:303-20.

Speicher, Anna M. 2000. *The Religious World of Antislavery Women: Spirituality in the Lives of Five Abolitionist Lecturers.* Syracuse, N.Y.: Syracuse University Press.

Stacey, William A., and Anson Shupe. 1984. "Religious Values and Religiosity in the Textbook Adoption Controversy in Texas, 1981." *Review of Religious Research* 25:321-33.

Stevens-Arroyo, Anthony M. 1998. "The Latino Religious Resurgence." *Annals of the American Academy of Political and Social Science* 558:163-77.

Swartley, Willard M. 1983. *Slavery, Sabbath, War, and Women: Case Issues in Biblical Interpretation.* Scottdale, Pa.: Herald.

Usry, Glenn, and Craig Keener. 1996. *Black Man's Religion.* Downers Grove, Ill.: InterVarsity Press.

Wallis, Jim. 2006. *God's Politics: Why the Right Gets It Wrong and the Left Doesn't Get It.* San Francisco: Harper.

Wilcox, Clyde. 2000. *Onward Christian Soldiers? The Religious Right in American Politics.* Boulder, Colo.: Westview Press.

Wildman, Stephanie M., and Adrienne D. Davis. 2002. "Making Systems of Privilege Visible." In *White Privilege: Essential Readings on the Other Side of Racism*, ed. Paula S. Rothenberg. New York: Worth.

Woodley, Randy. 2001. *Living in Color: Embracing God's Passion for Diversity.* Grand Rapids, Mich.: Chosen Books.

Yancey, George. 1999. "An Examination of Effects of Residential and Church Integration upon Racial Attitudes of Whites." *Sociological Perspectives* 42:279-304.

———. 2001. "Racial Attitudes: Differences in Racial Attitudes of People Attending Multiracial and Uniracial Congregations." *Research in the Social Scientific Study of Religion* 12:185-206.

———. 2007. *Interracial Contact and Social Change.* Boulder, Colo.: Lynne Rienner Publishers.

Yancey, George, Emily Hubbard, and Amy Smith. 2007. "Unequally Yoked? Using Personal Advertisements to Assess the Willingness of Christians to Engage in Interracial and Interfaith Dating." Paper presented at the annual meeting of the Southern Sociological Society. Atlanta.

9

Human Rights, Affirmative Action, and Development: An Agenda for Latin America and the Caribbean

JONAS ZONINSEIN

T he 1948 United Nations Universal Dec-
laration of Human Rights provides the moral norms and indices of achievement
for the indivisible and inalienable rights due to all individuals. Affirmative action
constitutes a set of policies and programs that specifically seek to promote the
unrealized rights and freedoms of racialized and ethnic minorities in all member
states of the United Nations. This essay proposes a research and policy agenda
that focuses on the instrumental linkages between affirmative action in higher
education and the promotion of universal human rights in Latin America and
the Caribbean (LAC).

The construction of a Latin American and Caribbean union requires a
holistic agenda beyond the development of commercial relations, investment,
infrastructure ties, and political dialogue among the national governments in the
region.[1] Region building also should focus on forging a stronger sense of identity,
solidarity, cohesion, and agency among the individuals and groups that would
benefit from an inclusive, democratic, and prosperous LAC. Of the 520 million
people living in this region today, 40 million are indigenous, and 160 million
are Afro-descendents. Available data suggests that indigenous peoples and Afro-

descendents are far more likely than whites to live in poverty, be illiterate, reside in substandard housing, and die at a younger age (Telles 2007).

Cooperation in education policy is a foundational component of region building and a prerequisite for a successful political and economic union. A focus on education policy can advance regional integration and the construction of an LAC union, providing a cultural dimension and a bottom-up approach to an inclusive and nonisolationist agenda of nation-state building. Cultural and education policy initiatives oriented toward expanding the economic, social, and political inclusion of minorities constitute a relevant priority due to their strategic influence on human capital investment, the productivity of the labor force, the accumulation of productive assets, and the legitimacy of democratic nation-states. Affirmative action in higher education contributes directly to enhancing the life aspirations and achievements of minority individuals and their socioeconomic inclusion, and opens the opportunities for social choices regarding the goals of national and regional development.

One of the main roadblocks to advancing the agenda of regional integration has been the lack of bottom-up initiatives that would make the process of integration participatory, transparent, and accountable to the peoples in the region. Minority agency and affirmative action initiatives promoting the inclusion of minorities in the mainstream process of regional development constitute a specific approach for pursuing human development priorities in LAC. They would enhance decision making regarding the goals and procedures for regional integration, thereby making region building more participatory, effective, and democratic. Racial and ethnic formations and systems operate differently in different nation-states. Although these formations and systems grew out of parallel institutions and common international discourses and regimes, 200 years of political independence and sovereign nation-state building gave birth to a multiplicity of legal and veiled practices of systematic discrimination against minorities in LAC.

The conceptual framework for strengthening minority agency in education sector development in LAC is in its embryonic phase. This conceptual framework ought to be developed as a regional and comparative undertaking, resulting from intellectual exchange and debate among cultural and education policy makers, their advisers, academics, intellectuals, and education sector activists immersed in their own specific national struggles for minority inclusion.

This essay seeks to contribute to this debate. Its main objective is to scrutinize the instrumental linkages among minority agency, affirmative action, inclusive nation-state building, and the promotion of a universal human rights regime in

LAC. In the next section, I address the foundations of the universal human rights regime, the nature of group human rights, and their synergistic interactions with individual human rights advocacy. In the section that follows, I discuss the goals of minority agency in inclusive nation-state building, and examine the various components of a public policy agenda necessary for a strategy of development that would deliver the inclusion of minorities in LAC. I then focus on affirmative action in higher education to identify the opportunities it poses for the mobilization of minority agency around the objectives of national development. Finally, I propose a regional agenda of research on affirmative action in higher education oriented to promote inclusive development and universal human rights.

Universal Human Rights and Nation-State Building

The protection of human agency is one of the key foundations of the universal human rights regime established after World War II. It is perhaps the most important right because its pragmatic nature pervades all other moral foundations enunciated in the 1948 Universal Declaration of Human Rights, such as equal dignity, free and equal personhood, equal creation or endowment, and equal brotherhood and sisterhood. A relevant controversy remains, nevertheless, regarding the nature of human agency identified in this international regime, in particular, as the precise nature and reach of collective (group) agency and its impact on individual agency within the moral universe of human rights (Ignatieff 2001; Donnelly 2003). The proper understanding of its nature and limits has practical implications for the struggle against discrimination and the exclusion of racialized and ethnic minorities in individual nation-states and globally.

Liberal political philosophy is unyielding in its argument that the proper balance between individual and group rights and interests relies on the notion that only individual rights are truly universal. Human rights principles rely ultimately on the protection of free, reasoned, and conscious agency and the consent of individuals, including their right of collective action and self-rule to enhance the international regime of universal human rights.

The complex instrumental relationship between individual rights and the collective right of self-rule, particularly the individual and collective rights of minority individuals, deserves specific attention. Individual rights covered by the universal human rights regime can be exercised and enjoyed by the collective action of these individuals. Political participation, use of common language, public education, and affirmative action are relevant examples of this collective action dimension to universal individual human rights. Group membership is essential because it enriches the life and choices of individuals. Civil society activity and the rights of individuals to participate in its multiple undertakings are protected human rights. It is, however, important to distinguish the right of individuals to collective action from the collective rights of voluntary organizations and groups. The latter are only protected by the human rights regime to the extent that they are authorized by the consent of each and every individual who belongs to these groups and organizations. If these groups infringe on the human rights of any of their members–an infringement that, of course, must be freely voiced by the individual suffering from it–these collective rights would be contrary to the universal human rights standards. Since World War II, freedom of association, of expression, of religion, and from discrimination are specific human rights that explicitly protect the rights of minority *individuals* and their agency in promoting and developing their cultural identity, as well as their civil, political, economic, and social rights.[2]

The right of peoples to self-determination recognized in the 1966 International Covenants on Civil and Political Rights and on Economic, Social, and Cultural Rights could inadvertently be interpreted as an exception to the hegemonic rule of individual rights under the universal human rights regime. A careful interpretation of the right of self-determination of a people to freely determine their political status and pursue their cultural, economic, and social development, using the lens of liberal political philosophy, indicates that the right to self-determination also should be interpreted as the collective expression of individual rights. The right of self-determination protects individuals against, for example, threats to their dignity and agency resulting from imperialist coercion by a foreign nation-state that seeks to restrict the right of a people to determine their political status and development path. However, people's self-determination to freely construct their national identity and establish their sovereign nation-state is subordinate to the assumption that sovereign nation-states would abide by the standards of the universal human rights regime and its discourse to adjudicate internal and international conflicts.

There is always the danger that nationalism and the construction of nation-states would address the demands of dominant ethnic and national groups for national sovereignty while producing new categories of oppressed minorities. Liberal internationalists assume that nation-states becoming less rigid or unitary in their national identities and adopting more inclusive economic and social policies, while maintaining their stability and economic growth, will reduce this danger. The liberal assumption that democratic and constitutional nation-states are neutral and hands-off arbiters of a civic pact among social classes and ethnic and national groups is, therefore, a shortsighted and naive approach to the required agency the nation-state needs to hold together the global edifice of universal human rights. The idea that a state is simply a passive supervisor of existing power structures removes it from its proactive duty and compensatory intervention in civil society to advance the economic power and social capital of oppressed minority groups. It must sustain a positive sum game in the competition among different interests in sovereign and democratic nation-states. To successfully check the power of majority interests and groups, and to enforce the universal civic, political, economic, social, and cultural rights of their minorities, nation-states ought to develop specific policies and instruments to promote cultural freedoms and diversity.

MINORITY AGENCY, NATIONALISM, AND INCLUSIVE DEVELOPMENT

This section addresses the goals of minority agency in nation-state building and the public policy instruments required for a process of development that will deliver the inclusion of LAC minorities. Due to the decentralized and competitive nature of the existing system of nation-states, the implementation of the universal human rights regime depends almost exclusively on sovereign nation-state policies. The influence of the universal human rights norms and standards on individual national policies, however, is contextually constrained by the cultural, political, economic, and social processes of nation-state building and accumulation of wealth that, historically, excluded minorities from the benefits of development.

The ideology of nationalism constitutes the overriding norm that guides nation-state building by integrating and coordinating three sets of individual and collective agency: the state as a sovereign political and territorial entity that connects individuals to a reciprocal system of duties and rights; the nation as a cultural and historical nexus of identities and loyalties of individuals; and the economy as an organization of production, exchange, and accumulation of assets by individuals.

According to Bhaduri (2002), this modern three-way merging of civil society disguised as the nation, the state, and the economy is problematic and unstable. In each country, the political authority of the state over a distinct territory and civil society ultimately relies on the state's ability to satisfy the standards of national self-determination and sovereignty defined by the society's most powerful and influential interest groups. When successful, the cultural and political processes operating under the umbrella ideology of national interest and nationalism integrate and mobilize the diverse social and ethnic groups around a project of nation-state building and national development. But these processes generally involve intense conflicts, since they rely on the combined agency and exercise of power by diverse social classes and ethnic groups over the allocation of resources (cultural, political, social, and economic) at the state and civil society levels. The uneven accumulation of skills by different individuals and groups, together with income concentration and asymmetrical asset ownership accumulation, intensifies the competition for resources both in civil society and state institutions. This structural conflict, involving ethnic groups and other social groups over resources, is further aggravated when radical changes in global economic integration take place and international capital mobility undermines the regulatory fiscal and financial mechanisms of the nation-state (Bhaduri 2002; Chua 2004).

The identification and interpretation of the ethnic and racialized asymmetries that accompany and support nation-state building and development processes are necessary to design the objectives and instruments of minority agency, such as affirmative action, in individual nation-states. Nationalism and nation-state building have been associated with specific class and ethnic group preferences, interests, power structures, and coalitions, which, in turn, produce manifold national forms of inclusion and exclusion. The politicization of ethnicity and racism, together with the hierarchies of social classes and gender, is part of a dynamic process that constrains the life opportunities of different individuals and groups.

Wimmer (2002) posits a "social closure" model of nationalism, centered on the image of the nation as a closed territorial, sovereign, and homogeneous community. A nation is based on the unique social, economic, political, and cultural ties that bind its members. He argues that despite the nationalist ideals of building a national community as an egalitarian space based on cultural homogeneity and common civic and political duties and rights for its citizens, as well as their fair participation in the production and distribution of economic goods, racial and ethnic exclusion are concomitant dimensions of all modern nation-states. The social borders separating minorities (racialized and ethnic groups, and immigrants) from "legitimate" majority members of the nation are key dimensions of the national order constructed by nationalism. Immigrants who have been discriminated against and racialized and ethnic minorities have always been present in all modern nation-state building. According to Wimmer

(2002), the closure of the nation-state has five instrumental dimensions: a legal system defining who are the nation's citizens; a political system representing national sovereignty; a military system established by a national army; a national community of solidarity based on the privileged access of national citizens to social security; and an imagined community of the nation.

Wimmer's social closure model, however, is only partially useful for interpreting the historical complexities of minority exclusion materialized in LAC since the early twentieth century. In the countries of this region, with the end of legal slavery in the nineteenth century, the economy, civil society, and access to state institutions and services became the main sphere where minority exclusion has been reproduced. Slowly, the individual nation-states began adopting the standards of universal human rights, and opting for a cultural policy of minority assimilation into an idealized model of national *mestizo* identity and formal republican citizenship after World War II. Concomitantly, socioeconomic discrimination against minorities continued to be pervasive. Most of the LAC nation-states are now, at least in their official discourse, engaged in functioning as a historical and cultural nexus of national identity and loyalty for their citizens. However, the available empirical evidence indicates that the cultural successes of imagining inclusive national identities in building racelessness or racial harmony in LAC societies were not robust enough to produce the effective socioeconomic inclusion of minorities.

The gaps, asymmetries, and hierarchies experienced by the ethnic and racialized groups remain markedly present in multiple socioeconomic dimensions in the region. These include gaps in educational attainment, health conditions, access to the labor market, income generation and asset ownership, social capital, and public action agency. These gaps and asymmetries, however, are neither inevitable nor unchangeable. Minority agency and participation in nationally designed multicultural policies can influence the transformation of existing power hierarchies in LAC, affecting the distribution of economic resources and the process of national and regional development. Minority politics can intervene successfully in cultural, political, social, and economic development to change public policy, nation-state building, and the economy.

Equality of human agency is a principle of public action that focuses on the capacity of social groups to form preferences, and to design and implement successful coordination mechanisms for collective action and public policy making. (Rao and Walton 2004) The United Nations Development Programme's (UNDP) *Human Development Report 2004* (UNDP 2004) proposes a multipronged strategy of domestic and international development policies that are integrated into a menu of multicultural policies to accommodate people's demands for inclusion in society and promote cultural choice, diversity, and respect for ethnicity, religion and language. The 2004 UNDP agenda provides a holistic and flexible framework within which minorities can mobilize their agency and pursue their struggle to influence nation-state building and national development in LAC, in accordance with the standards of the universal human rights regime.

The *Human Development Report 2004* is an effort to translate the *2001 Durban Program of Action*[3] to eliminate all forms of discrimination and exclusion into specific policy agendas and development strategies at the national level. Since 2001, the main challenge has been to develop new public policy initiatives to include historically excluded groups at the local, national, regional, and global levels. This essay emphasizes the potential role of affirmative action (one of the components of the multicultural agenda examined in the *Human Development Report 2004*) in promoting the socioeconomic inclusion of ethnic and racialized minorities in LAC, and to consolidate democratic nation-state building, improve economic development performance, and implement the standards of the 1948 universal human rights regime.

The 2004 UNDP agenda of multicultural policies is integrated into a multi-pronged strategy for inclusive development. This agenda searches for the recognition and support for the multiples ways in which citizens with different politics and social and cultural backgrounds can interact in civil society, in the political system, and in the economy to design and implement public policy initiatives (UNDP 2004; Sen 2006). Multicultural policies comprise two broad categories: . national multicultural policies and international multicultural policies. National multicultural policies encompass policies for ensuring the political participation of diverse cultural groups, policies on religion and religious practice, policies on customary law and legal pluralism, policies on the use of multiple languages, and policies for redressing socioeconomic exclusion, composed of investments in social programs, the recognition of legitimate claims to land and livelihoods, and affirmative action in favor of disadvantaged groups. International multicultural policies include the promotion of the rights of indigenous peoples through the regulation of extractive industries, and the recognition and defense of indigenous peoples' traditional knowledge; the promotion of the production of indigenous and local cultural goods; and the adequate management of immigration flows and the integration of foreign migrants into national societies. The objectives of these policies are to protect cultural liberty and expand people's choices regarding their identities and their demands for inclusion in society, and to promote socially inclusive and culturally diverse nation-states.[4]

Traditional approaches to social, economic, and political equality have been based on the assimilation of different ethnic groups into the dominant national culture, ignoring specific cultural traditions and socioeconomic conditions. The 2004 UNDP agenda seeks to correct this shortcoming in development policy.

To be effective, the multicultural policies proposed by the UNDP in 2004 should be integrated into three other development agendas for a strategy of inclusive national development: the promotion of democracy, pro-poor economic growth, and the equitable expansion of social opportunities. The *Human Development Report 2004* argues that these three policies are necessary but not sufficient to promote cultural liberty and the inclusion of minorities. In particular, integrating affirmative action into national development strategies may be necessary to overcome discrimination and redress past wrongs, when conventional pro-poor economic growth and social policies fail to eliminate the socioeconomic exclusion of minorities and fail to expand opportunities for their access to education, health, housing, employment, and participation in the political process. Affirmative action allocates jobs, public contracts, business loans, and admissions to higher education on the basis of membership in disadvantaged minority groups (UNDP 2004; Weisskopf 2004).

An inclusive development strategy should promote opportunities for the effective mobilization of minority agency in LAC. Forty percent of the 520,000,000 people living in this region form a large cohort of historically excluded groups–indigenous peoples and African descendents. More than half of this cohort lives in conditions of extreme poverty. National multicultural policies for redressing socioeconomic exclusion and the international multicultural policies constitute specific policy initiatives that can articulate the agency and inclusion of minorities, democratic nation-state building, and development in LAC.

The multicultural agenda identifies specific goals and policy instruments for fighting discrimination and promoting the inclusion of minorities that can be adjusted to different national and local conditions. To be successful, it must be articulated to the implementation of democratic governance procedures, pro-poor economic growth policies, and the provision of social services by nation-states and civil society. The agency of minorities, in particular, should be mobilized to promote the broader objectives of an inclusive development strategy.

Affirmative Action in Higher Education
and Development in LAC

Here, I examine affirmative action in higher education and emphasize the opportunities that affirmative action poses for the mobilization of minority agency, and the connections among minority agency, inclusive nation-state building, and development. Among the various multicultural policies discussed in the previous section, affirmative action is the one that best suits the goals of Afro-descendents' socioeconomic inclusion in LAC. Indigenous groups also can benefit from affirmative action, but they have used more intensively other components of the large menu of multicultural policy instruments. The classic republican nationalism of homogeneous citizenship and mestizo national identity implemented in many LAC countries during the twentieth century buttressed a process of nation-state building and development that, although culturally inclusive, did not deliver the socioeconomic inclusion of minority groups. Substantive inequalities in their access to economic and social resources persist as obstacles against their achieving their full contribution as citizens, producers, and consumers.

Affirmative action has been mostly absent in LAC until the end of the 1990s, except as isolated initiatives to hire minorities in the public sector. In general, the various kinds of multicultural initiatives implemented in the last two decades were constrained by their association with slow-growth economic policies and mediocre efforts to promote social development after the 1982 debt crisis. In the aftermath of the democratization of political regimes in LAC during the 1980s and 1990s, the preparations for the 2001 Durban World Conference on Racism, Racial Discrimination, Xenophobia, and Related Intolerance served as a powerful catalyst for new initiatives by individual activists, minority organizations, national governments, and the international development community to promote policies focusing on the goal of minority inclusion in the region. In particular, following the leadership of international donors such as the Ford Foundation, the World Bank and the Inter-American Bank designed specific lending and grants programs oriented to improve data collection disaggregated by race and ethnicity; promote the empowerment of excluded groups by developing their capacities to improve their livelihoods and to participate in public policy dialogues; improve access to and the quality of social services for minorities; enhance opportunities for economic development; advocate rights, regulations, and legal safeguards that would benefit minorities; and review their project portfolios to identify gaps and improve the means to respond to minority needs more effectively. (Turner 2007; Inter-American Development Bank 2006; World Bank 2003)

The programs of the international donors and multilateral financial institutions produced tangible results by supporting the mobilization of minority agency at the local level in many countries in the region, but the most recent evidence available (for early 2000s) suggests that due to the paucity of resources involved, the meager and uneven commitment by nation-states, and the more recent termination of the diversity programs by multilateral institutions (the commitment and financial support of the Inter-American Development Bank and the World Bank lasted less than a decade, declining by 2006), multicultural policies have failed, so far, either to stimulate minority agency around the national objectives of cultural liberty and inclusive development, or to generate any significant impact on the persistent socioeconomic exclusion of minorities.

In the countries where indigenous groups constitute a large proportion of the population, their social movements made significant strides in political mobilization, and succeeded in introducing multicultural policy initiatives in recent years (Langer and Muñoz 2003; Van Cott 2005). Affirmative action in higher education, however, has not yet gained prominence, except in Brazil.

In 2000, all United Nations member states adopted the Millennium Development Goals (MDGs) for social indicators by 2015. The MDGs, however, are silent on the question of race and ethnicity. If successful in reducing poverty levels in the region, the agenda of the MDGs could provide one of the necessary ingredients for addressing minority discrimination and exclusion. Assuming that constitutional democratic consolidation continues in the future, and the current successes in export-led policies are consolidated and translated into a policy of regional integration, accelerated investment, and pro-poor economic growth, the crucial area where minority agency in LAC will be tested will be in its capacity to design and implement national mixes of multicultural policies, including affirmative action.

There is a clear sense that new political and economic strategies are necessary to forge an agenda for regional integration, including higher education. This is the moment for minority actors and their supporters within the higher education system to join forces to share experiences and best practices to expand the access of Afro-descendents and indigenous peoples to higher education and leadership positions in the professional, economic, and political arenas in LAC.

A clear understanding of the scope, nature, and limits of the various instruments of multicultural policy is a precondition for their effective use. In what follows, I examine affirmative action in higher education, and its instrumental connections to a strategy of inclusive development, to illustrate the complex challenges of a development strategy linked to cultural liberty. The access of national and ethnic minorities to education at the university level constitutes a crucial dimension of an agenda of inclusion, universal human rights and democratic development in the region.

To reiterate, affirmative action is a set of regulations and policies that protects and promotes the equality of agency and educational and economic opportunities for minority individuals, and enhances their ability to participate in the construction of inclusive nation-states. Affirmative action is based on preferential rules for the access of minority individuals to specific positions in education and the economy, including opportunities for employment, participation in government procurement, and access to credit. I approach affirmative action as a method to construct inclusive nation-states and rely on minority agency to engage civil society, the government, and the economy in the implementation of the universal human rights regime initiated in 1948.

Multicultural policy initiatives by national governments, social movements, and civil society organizations have proliferated in LAC since the 1990s. However, the lack of disaggregated data on minority status and consolidated information about the impact of these initiatives constitutes a serious obstacle to implement a robust agenda of multicultural policies. Only in Brazil has affirmative action in higher education occupied a central position within this expanding framework of multicultural agency. Its implementation, analysis, and evaluation, however, remain preliminary and incomplete. (Zoninsein and Feres Jr. 2007)

Close to forty Brazilian public universities have adopted quotas for the admission of ethnic and racialized minorities since 2002. The federal government and selected state governments have declared their support for these admission quotas in public universities, but have neither provided financial resources nor developed the broad range of supplemental academic activities, financial assistance, and evaluative procedures necessary to deliver a successful outcome of education inclusion over the four or more years of undergraduate programs, including access to internships and elite professional networks. Brazilian public universities, therefore, are not fully embracing the challenges of minority inclusion. The successful creation of admission quotas (typically 20 percent for minorities) constitutes, however, a significant step forward. It also generated a useful national debate about Brazilian identity, racialized social structures, and the scope of a progressive reform program of higher education in Brazil. In theory, preferential admission policies would accelerate upward vertical mobility for those minority individuals who are capable of taking advantage of the new opportunities created by the quota regime. Such policies could enhance minority individuals' social capital; provide new opportunities for minority individuals to expand their economic entrepreneurship; and intensify the exchange of views among all the universities' academic communities regarding the challenges of national development, including racial and economic equality.

It is still too early to seriously evaluate the full impact of the quota system. Implementing the new admission procedures cost little in terms of human and financial costs for those universities that adopted admission quotas. The class of students admitted in 2002 recently graduated, and it is too early to evaluate the success of its minority cohort in the labor market. The efficacy of affirmative action should be evaluated during the next two decades using indicators regarding labor market success and the upward mobility of minorities into the ranks of middle class and selected professions such as medicine, engineering, law, and high finance. Anecdotal evidence from the State University of Rio de Janeiro (UERJ), the first public Brazilian university to adopt admission quotas for minorities, suggests that the students who were admitted under the quotas regime exhibited an academic performance on average similar to the rest of their class. It is not clear, however, whether a similar evaluation applies to the more competitive and difficult courses of UERJ.

The reform of Brazilian universities will constitute the most important factor for the success of affirmative action in higher education over the long term. Minorities constitute 50 percent of the Brazilian nation. To be successful, the reform of the university system will have to simultaneously address the challenges of social and racial inclusion and create solid partnerships with the productive sector and civil society.

The decentralized and transparent approach adopted by the public universities in designing and implementing the admission quota regime constituted a positive indication that the academic communities understand the nature of the challenges they face. The public universities (with the exception of UERJ in 2002) pursued a path of academic autonomy in relation to their main funding agencies, the federal and state governments. Minority faculty members were able to build the consensus necessary for their governance bodies to approve the admission quotas. This consensus has contributed to sustain the political legitimacy of affirmative action in the short run. It remains to be seen whether the universities will remain fully accountable and proactive regarding the academic performance of all their students in future years, both by disaggregating data about academic performance and mobilizing additional resources to improve the quality of the education currently provided.

It is therefore too early to comprehensively evaluate the social returns on Brazil's investment in affirmative action in higher education. In the short run, increased financial support for the poorest students, augmented access of minority students to graduate courses, and new faculty positions are some programmatic steps that public universities—which, coincidently form the core of the elite higher education in Brazil—could adopt in their affirmative action programs. In addition, the federal and state governments should create financial mechanisms to support and disseminate best practices in affirmative action in public universities. To succeed in the long term, however, such investments in human capital will have to generate economic and social benefits, not only for the minority groups but also for society as a whole, measured through gains in income and productivity.

A second factor has contributed to the political legitimacy of affirmative action initiatives. The leadership of the Afro-descendents movement has consistently adopted a holistic approach by tying their struggle for racial equality to the demands of the large majority of the Brazilian people for more and better education and employment opportunities (Guimarães 2007). The political relevance of this linkage between different dimensions of social justice advocacy illustrates the synergies among the various agendas that jointly constitute the cultural liberty strategy of inclusive development discussed in the previous section.

As a redistributive policy tool and an approach to the investment in human capital in a country where minorities represent about 50 percent of the population, affirmative action, however, will soon manifest its limited scope. Unless the other agendas of inclusive development–democratic consolidation, accelerated pro-poor economic growth, and effective social policies—are integrated into a common strategy, opposition will grow and undermine public support for affirmative action. The Brazilian middle- and high-income classes take for granted their privileged access to free and superior higher education at public universities after sending their children to private secondary schools and admission exams preparatory courses.

Conclusion

Available data indicate that ethnic and racialized minorities in LAC are more likely than whites to live in poverty, be illiterate, die at a younger age, and reside in substandard housing in neighborhoods with deficient infrastructure (UNDP 2004; Hall and Patrinos 2006). The economic cost of keeping Afro-descendents and indigenous peoples excluded from the benefits of development are significant. For selected countries with disaggregated income and employment information, the estimated gains from the economic inclusion of minorities are significant. Based on 1997–98 household surveys information, I estimated that the economies of Bolivia, Brazil, Guatemala, and Peru would potentially expand by 36.7, 12.8, 13.6, and 4.2 percent, respectively, as a result of ending the long-term social exclusion of Afro-descendants and indigenous peoples. Increases in gross domestic product (GDP) would result from two different sources: potential gains in aggregate production and income arising from the full use of the existing education, skills, and experience of Afro-descendant and indigenous individuals in the jobs they actually hold; and potential gains in aggregate production and income due to expanding the education and skills of Afro-descendant and indigenous individuals to levels similar to those of the white population in those countries. The joint result from these two sources is the gain that would accrue to GDP if the human capital and productivity gaps in the labor force of Afro-descendant and indigenous groups relative to whites were eliminated (Zoninsein 2004).

The current level of minority agency mobilization around the goals of multicultural policies in various countries in LAC, (Van Cott 2005; Yashar 2005; Zoninsein and Feres Jr. 2007) and the increasing convergence of LAC political and economic elites around the objectives of regional economic integration (Ocampo and Martin 2003; Ffrench-Davis 2005) suggest that the design and coordination of a common regional agenda of education reform and minority inclusion are timely. There is growing support among the region's progressive political and economic leadership for a new holistic development strategy for regional integration. Accelerated economic growth based on higher levels of production and export of commodities in the region in recent years offers the opportunity for a public policy retooling in the direction of inclusive regional development, focusing on education policy, among other priorities. This retooling should integrate multiple policy agendas in individual countries—democratic consolidation, sustainable accelerated growth policies, effective social programs, and the inclusion of minorities—to promote inclusive development.

The success of affirmative action programs in higher education in Brazil indicates a model for cooperation in regional education policy that would mobilize minority agency, civil society organizations, and nation-states. The 2002–7 Brazilian experience with affirmative action in higher education provides a template for engaging minority agency in pragmatic approaches to promote their socioeconomic inclusion. A regional conference including university authorities, faculty, researchers, and policy makers, to share experiences and evaluate best practices and institutional innovations to expand the access of Afro-descendents and indigenous peoples to higher education could become a fruitful next step in the regional mobilization of minority agency. Affirmative action in higher education also could constitute a catalyst for the regional mobilization around the various agendas of a strategy of inclusive development and cultural liberty.

NOTES

1. The construction of a South American Union, according to Ambassador Jorge d'Escragnolle Taunay Filho, secretary for South America in the Brazilian Ministry of Foreign Relations, is a recent process and constitutes one of the axes of current Brazilian foreign policy. Taunay Filho argues that such a union will demand resources, time, and a long-term strategic approach involving multiple areas of activity, well beyond a narrow focus on regional trade relations, to achieve a cohesive regional space for cultural, political, economic, and social development (Taunay Filho 2007).

2. Kymlicka (1996) differentiates two types of collective claims by ethnic and national groups: internal restrictions and external protections. The first type involves the claims of a group against its own members and seeks to protect the group from the destabilizing impact of internal dissent; the second type involves the claims of a group against the larger society, and seeks to protect the group from the effects of economic and political decisions of the larger society. Kymlicka argues that liberals should support external protections where they promote fairness and balance between groups within a nation-state, but should oppose internal restrictions that limit the agency of individuals in questioning traditional authorities and organized practices.

3. Agreed at the World Conference against Racism, Racial Discrimination, Xenophobia, and Related Intolerance, in Durban, South Africa, 31 August–7 September 2001, organized by the United Nations.

4. According to the *Human Development Report 2004*, "Cultural liberty is the freedom people have to choose their identity—to be what they are and who they want to be—and to live without being excluded from other choices that are important to them" (27). "The aim of multicultural policies is not to preserve tradition, however, but to protect cultural liberty and expand people's choice—in the way people live and identify themselves—and not to penalize them for these choices" (88).

REFERENCES

Bhaduri, Amit. 2002. "Nationalism and Economic Policy in the Era of Globalization." In Deepak Nayyar, ed., *Governing Globalization: Issues and Institutions*. New York: Oxford University Press.

Chua, Amy. 2004. *World on Fire: How Exporting Free Market Democracy Breeds Ethnic Hatred and Global Instability*. New York: Anchor Books.

Donnelly, Jack. 2003. *Universal Human Rights in Theory and Practice*. 2nd ed. Ithaca, N.Y.: Cornell University Press.

Ffrench-Davis, Ricardo. 2005. *Reforming Latin American Economies after Market Fundamentalism*. London: Palgrave MacMillan.

Guimarães, Antônio Sérgio. 2007. "Novas Inflexões Ideológicas no Estudo da Ação Afirmativa" [Ideological changes in the study of affirmative action]. In Jonas Zoninsein and João Feres Jr., eds., *A Ação Afirmativa na Universidade Brasileira* [Affirmative action in Brazilian universities]. Belo Horizonte: Federal University of Minas Gerais Press.

Hall, Gillette, and Harry A. Patrinos. 2006. *Indigenous Peoples, Poverty, and Human Development in Latin America*. New York: Palgrave MacMillan.

Ignatieff, Michael. 2001. "Human Rights as Politics and Idolatry." In Amy Gutmann, ed., *Human Rights as Politics and Idolatry*. Princeton, N.J.: Princeton University Press.

Inter-American Development Bank. 2006. *Operational Policy on Indigenous Peoples and Strategy for Indigenous Development*. Washington, D.C.: Sustainable Development Department.

Kymlicka, Will. 1996. *Multicultural Citizenship: A Liberal Theory of Minority Rights*. Oxford: Oxford University Press.

Langer, Erick D., and Elena Muñoz, eds. 2003. *Contemporary Indigenous Movements in Latin America*. New York: Rowman and Littlefield.

Ocampo, José Antonio, and Juan Martin. 2003. *Globalization and Development: A Latin American and Caribbean Perspective*. Stanford, Calif., and Washington, D.C.: Stanford University Press and World Bank.

Rao, Vijayendra, and Michael Walton. 2004. "Culture and Public Action: Relationality, Equality of Agency, and Development." In Vijayendra Rao and Michael Walton, eds., *Culture and Public Action*. Stanford, Calif.: Stanford University Press.

Sen, Amartya. 2006. *Identity and Violence: The Illusion of Destiny*. New York: W. W. Norton.

Taunay Filho, Jorge d'Escragnolle. 2007. "O Sentido da Integração Sul-Americana" [The meaning of South American integration]. *Valor Econômico*, June 27, 2007.

Telles, Edward E. 2007. "Incorporating Race and Ethnicity into the UN Millennium Development Goals." *Inter-American Dialogue.*

Turner, J. Michael. 2007. "Inclusão Social e Ações de Discriminação Positiva em Favor dos Afrodescendentes na América Latina" [Social inclusion and positive discrimination actions for Afro-descendants in Latin America]. In Jonas Zoninsein and João Feres Jr., eds., *A Ação Afirmativa na Universidade: Perspectivas Comparadas.* [Affirmative action in Brazilian universities]. Belo Horizonte: Federal University of Minas Gerais Press.

United Nations Development Programme (UNDP). 2004. *Human Development Report 2004: Cultural Liberty in Today's Diverse World.* New York: Oxford University Press.

Van Cott, Donna Lee. 2005. *From Movements to Parties in Latin America: The Evolution of Ethnic Politics.* Cambridge: Cambridge University Press.

Weisskopf, Thomas E. 2004. *Affirmative Action in the United States and India: A Comparative Perspective.* New York: Routledge.

Wimmer, Andreas. 2002. *Nationalist Exclusion and Ethnic Conflict.* Cambridge: Cambridge University Press.

World Bank. 2003. *Durban Plus One: Opportunities and Challenges for Racial and Ethnic Inclusion and Development.* Report by the Office of Diversity Programs and the Latin America and Caribbean Regional Office. Washington, D.C.

Yashar, Deborah J. 2005. *Contesting Citizenship in Latin America: The Rise of Indigenous Movements and the Postliberal Challenge.* Cambridge: Cambridge University Press.

Zoninsein, Jonas. 2004. "The Economic Case for Combating Racial and Ethnic Exclusion in Latin American Countries." In Mayra Buvinic, ed., *Social Inclusion and Economic Development in Latin America.* Baltimore: Johns Hopkins University Press.

Zoninsein, Jonas, and João Feres Jr., eds. 2007. "Introdução," [Introduction]. In Jonas Zoninsein and João Feres Jr., eds., *A Ação Afirmativa na Universidade Brasileira.* [Affirmative action in Brazilian universities]. Belo Horizonte: Federal University of Minas Gerais Press.

10

The Whitewashing of Affirmative Action

J. ANGELO CORLETT

In my book *Race, Racism, and Repara-tions*, philosophical arguments were adduced in favor of reparations to American Indians and blacks, grounding such policies in a genealogical analysis of ethnic identity in order to properly identify those who ought to receive reparations.[1] That genealogical conception of ethnicity has important normative and ethical implications for public policy administration in general, and reparations and affirmative action programs in particular. For present purposes, the argument herein assumes that reparations and affirmative action are in principle morally justified primarily on the basis of backward-looking reasons. The main focus, however, is on affirmative action. ·

It will be argued that it is morally wrong to lump together several groups into one set of "disadvantaged" or "minority" groups, just as it is wrong to not recognize other groups subsumed under the general categories we often use in shorthand: Asians, Latinos/as, and so forth.[2] Whether racist or sexist (or both), the experiences of each group are different, and the extent to which members of each group have experienced harm from racism and sexism varies widely. More-over, each of these groups has been victimized in the United States—not only by the ruling majority ethnic classes but also in some cases by members of other "disadvantaged" or "minority" groups. For instance, white women in the United States have generally served as a constant source of racist harm to folk of color, many Jewish people have often engaged in racism against certain people of color, and Latinos/as have often been a source of racism against blacks in particular. This is unsurprising when one considers the complexities and universality of racism.[3] Additionally, the discussion herein refers to various groups in terms of their behavior on average, or as a class, recognizing implicitly that there are within all such groups exceptions to general statements made about the groups.

Each of these factors seems to suggest that any public policy of compensatory or distributive justice ought to become and remain sensitive to various levels and kinds of programs and benefits of affirmative action, each targeting a different ethnic group that has, on average, experienced significant harm due to racism and/or sexism. For example, Indians and blacks are deserving of significantly greater kinds and degrees of compensatory justice than any other groups in U.S. history based on the kinds, levels, and degrees of racist oppression against them continually (even today) by the U.S. government and its non-Indian and nonblack citizenry, as a fair-minded and holistic reading of U.S. history reveals.[4] That same reading of U.S. history is likely to clarify that certain other ethnic groups have experienced greater racist and/or sexist discrimination than others. Although white women have for generations been prohibited from full participation in U.S. society, their complicity in the racism against people of color condemns them, along with their white male counterparts, as racist oppressors. And it would be an unjust policy indeed that would award white women anything akin to what it awards to, say, Latinos/as and certain other ethnic groups of color. It would be even more unjust to award compensation to Latinos/as or white women in anything akin to what such policies award to Indians and blacks.

U.S. affirmative action policies and programs were developed for the most part by many well-intentioned whites, and by some well-meaning people of color. And these policies certainly represent a measure of improvement over the then status quo in U.S. society regarding race relations. But by not seeing the complexities of ethnicity, racism, and sexism in the United States, such policies lack the specificity necessary to guide programs of affirmative action in ways that are immune from charges of unfairness. Such specificity includes a working principle that grounds affirmative action benefits on what members of racially oppressed groups *deserve* in light of the *amount* of racist harms experienced in U.S. society, all things considered. And a fair-minded and holistic study of U.S. history reveals that white women deserve far fewer benefits from affirmative action programs than do at least a few ethnic groups in U.S. society. So the very programs that were designed to level the playing field of opportunities in U.S. society against racial discrimination have the effect of improving the plight of white women undeservedly over various folk of color. The fact that white women rarely, if ever, challenge such programs along the lines mentioned here condemns them (in general) on moral grounds of egoistic self-interest. But as Angela Y. Davis reminds us, that is quite congruent with what some of the leaders of the white women's suffrage movement held from its very inception in the United States. Recall that Elizabeth Cady Stanton, in her December 26, 1865, letter to the *New York Standard*, wrote: "it becomes a serious question whether we had better stand aside and see 'Sambo' walk into the kingdom first. . . . In fact, it is better to be the slave of an educated white man, than of a degraded, ignorant black one."[5] What white women knew about being slaves is highly dubious, and for a white woman to speak of herself as even possibly being a slave to another in the face of Indian and black slavery in the United States is perhaps a form of racist insensitivity or insult (or perhaps even massive ignorance beyond comprehension).[6] But what is clear here is that even the leadership of the white women's movement in the United States was thoroughly racist and can hardly be reasonably counted among those who are oppressed in ways akin to the ways in which many folk of color have been racially oppressed in the United States. And if the (relatively enlightened) leadership of the white women suffrage movement was racist, then one can only imagine what the rank-and-file supporters were like. It is an open question precisely how racist the contemporary women's movements are in the United States. But the consistent lack of great numbers of people of color in their ranks tends to suggest that some degree of the long-standing white feminist racism is still entrenched among many white women feminists—even some of those who purport to support means of justice for addressing racist harms.

If there are to be affirmative action policies and programs, they must reflect the histories and complexities of ethnicity and racism in a particular society such as the United States. Only then will there be any reasonable hope that concerns of justice will be addressed fairly, providing Indians and blacks with the highest kinds and degrees of compensation, such as reparations and perhaps affirmative action programs, on the one hand, and Latinos/as, for instance, with significantly lower but meaningful kinds and degrees of affirmative action benefits, on the other. To do otherwise, as the United States has been doing for decades, is to not take seriously the facts of history and the complexities of ethnicity and racism in U.S. society. It is also inconsistent in that such policies and programs seek to benefit folk because of their ethnicities, yet each of the target groups is treated by the programs in "color-blind" ways. Consistency (in terms of proportional harms suffered and rectified) would require that public policies and programs targeting groups victimized by racism would retain color consciousness in the implementation of such programs.

However, public policy must not permit the influx of recent immigrants "of color" to adversely affect the genuine purpose of reparations and affirmative action programs. If the aim of such programs is to counterbalance the racist and sexist discrimination in U.S. society (a backward-looking consideration), then only those groups that have been significantly harmed by such racism and sexism in the United States ought to qualify as targets of such public policy. Thus it is morally wrong to lump together blacks, say, with Haitians, Nigerians, or Kenyans for purposes of reparative justice, as the latter groups (and several like them) were not a part of the systemic racist oppression in the United States. Ignoring this fact of history concerning ethnic relations in the United States does serious harm to those ethnic groups deserving of affirmative action programs because it depletes the always meager resources allocated to such compensation and programs, thereby cheating those most deserving of the benefits of the programs. In short, it violates principles of desert and proportionality concerning corrective justice.

My differentialist analysis of racist harms better enables public policy to include compensatory and affirmative action programs that target more precisely those oppressed ethnic groups most deserving of them. It would be a policy that sets up differential reparations and affirmative action programs. Only reparative justice via compensation can in some significant measure begin to correct the wrongs done to Indians and blacks by the U.S. government and some of its supportive businesses. As argued in *Race, Racism, and Reparations*, reparations and affirmative action are two totally separate matters. The latter is not a legitimate replacement of the former, as most seem to believe. While reparations are, among other things, compensatory, affirmative action programs are not compensatory in the normal legal sense. This implies that, while the compensatory nature of reparations awards monetary damages (either legislatively or judicially) to the oppressed with no strings attached because they are deserving of the restitution, affirmative action programs are designed, for instance, to assist oppressed peoples in matters of education and employment wherein the oppressed work to earn salaries in order to receive such benefits.

Moreover, affirmative action by its very nature and magnitude cannot begin to address or serve as adequate compensation for wrongs done to, say, the forebears of present-day Indians and blacks, as an adequate policy of reparations can. Reparations are to be awarded, when they are awarded, to groups based on the extent of the harms suffered by a particular group at the hands of, say, the state or certain businesses. So there are degrees of reparations, based on a complex array of factors: harms suffered, the *means rea* of perpetrators, and so forth. But to the extent that affirmative action programs are justified as means toward achieving justice in the face of past and current racist discrimination in U.S. society, such programs must begin to differentiate between the kinds and levels of benefits awarded to various groups: Indians, blacks, Latinos/as, Asian Americans, and so forth.

If affirmative action programs are going to evade charges of morally arbitrary and unjust (because unfair) implementation, they not only require an analysis of the nature of ethnic group membership (which is found in *Race, Racism, and Reparations*), but they also need to be sensitive to the varying degrees and levels of racist discrimination that have been and are experienced, on average, by members of various groups. One of our guiding principles here ought to be Aristotle's claim that like cases ought to be treated alike (and conversely, dissimilar cases ought to be treated dissimilarly). Once again, a fair-minded and holistic reading of U.S. history shows us that the forebears of today's Indians and blacks have experienced (and for today's Indians and blacks, *continue* to experience) by far the worst sorts of oppression. Subsequent to or simultaneous with reparative compensation to Indians and blacks, affirmative action programs ought to reflect this in the kinds and amounts of benefits awarded to members of these groups. Perhaps Latino/a and Asian groups, or certain subgroups of each, ought to be construed as the next most deserving of affirmative action programs. Again, a fair-minded and holistic reading of U.S. history is essential here. Whatever the case, neither of these ethnic groups has any rightful claim to affirmative action benefits that would even remotely match the claims of Indians or blacks, for neither has experienced genocide at the hands of the U.S. government, or the most massive land theft in human history by one country, or the brutality of race-based slavery.

While there are some who would argue that Latinos/as, more specifically Mexican Americans, are owed affirmative action—even reparations—for the lands stolen from Mexico by the United States, such claims are rendered highly dubious in light of the fact that Mexico stole the lands from Indians. The United States owes little, if anything, to Mexicans for those reasons, any more than one thief owes another for stealing property belonging to yet a third party (in this case, various Indian nations). What Mexican Americans and various other Latinos qualify for is some level of affirmative action benefits for various levels of significant and long-term racist oppression experienced in the United States, as a careful study of U.S. history reveals. But whatever Latinos deserve along these lines, it is but a drop in the proverbial bucket compared to what Indians and blacks deserve given their far worse treatment in the United States. If anything, the Mexican government owes Indians of certain nations quite a lot in terms of reparations for the losses sustained by Indians by way of Mexico's oppression of them throughout its history. But that matter must be taken up in another forum.

After Indians and blacks are awarded their due amounts and kinds of affirmative action benefits, then Latinos/as and Asians would deserve and ought to receive some amount of affirmative action. After all, they were prohibited from voting, lacked certain other employment and educational opportunities, experienced significant violence for generations, and so forth, and continue to suffer significant forms of racist discrimination. Of course, all of this and much more were withheld, and much more violently, from Indians, enslaved Africans, and "emancipated" blacks under Jim Crow, as history is clear to point out. But in light of the fact that they have already benefited most from affirmative action programs since the inception of such programs more than three decades ago, white women do not deserve even the lowest levels and kinds of affirmative action benefits. This is especially true given that white women enjoyed (and still enjoy) a high level of white privilege in U.S. society as they shared responsibility for the racist oppression of folk of color. And this white privilege was shared to some extent by all white women, regardless of socioeconomic class.

This means that there is to be a moratorium on hiring white women from affirmative action programming funds. Although many will think this is a radical proposal, it is far better (for the most deserving folk of color) than the status quo, which continues to benefit the least deserving groups targeted by affirmative action programs far greater than it benefits much more deserving groups, based on kinds and duration of harms experienced by such groups. Thus the suggested differentialist policy of affirmative action in hiring is a step in the right direction in attempting to turn the tide of a grossly unjust situation.

More specifically, the differentialist strategy of affirmative action would treat white women as it would treat white men. Moreover, based on the duration, degrees, and kinds of racist/sexist oppression experienced by Indians in U.S. society over the centuries, Indian women would enjoy the category of most highly ranked in this program because they have not only experienced the evils of racist oppression as did Indian men, but the evils of sexism also. Indian men would constitute the second most highly ranked group targeted for affirmative action programs of hiring. Black women would rank third, and black men fourth for similar reasons of racism and sexism experienced by the former, and racism experienced by the latter. Yet the differential amounts of affirmative action benefits received by each of these groups would not be tremendous, as each has experienced some of the most horrendous evils in human history. Indeed, they belong to a class of the most oppressed. Furthermore, as noted earlier, this proposed program in no way serves as a substitute for the reparations that are deserved by each of these groups. Long after these groups would rank certain other ethnic groups, including Latinos/as, Asian Americans of various groups, and some others. And in each case, as with Indians and blacks, the groups are to be categorized dualistically by gender because of the pervasiveness of sexism in U.S. society. In each case, a fair-minded and holistic reading of U.S. history is crucial for our understanding of which groups deserve what level(s) of affirmative action benefits.

The point here is that governments need to nonarbitrarily award such benefits so that those whose ancestors actually assisted in the racist oppression of various ethnic groups—for example, white women—do not end up benefiting more than other groups, which deserve more compensation by well-intentioned but wrongheaded public policy. This follows from the venerable moral and legal principle that one ought not to benefit from one's own wrongdoing or the wrongdoings of others.

Of course, Indians and blacks are not the only groups to whom the U.S. government, and certain corporations, owes reparations. The U'was in Colombia are owed reparations for their land and natural resources stolen from them by the U.S. government, Occidental Petroleum, and the Colombian government, and now Iraqis deserve reparations from the U.S., British, Danish, and coalition governments for the loss of innocent lives, land, and natural resources, not to mention human rights violations, due to the unjust military invasion and occupation of Iraq. And the list here continues almost uninterrupted throughout the history of the United States.

The time has arrived when we must cast aside the mantle of self-serving support of the well-intended programs of affirmative action that have to some extent, admittedly, improved socioeconomic power for many people of color in the United States. But much more could have been and should be accomplished along these lines if not for policies and programs that unwarrantedly assist white women when they could and should instead assist many more deserving people of color. This is a qualitative and a quantitative claim, for if not for programs of affirmative action assisting white women, those same benefits could and should have been used to provide much more deserved benefits for greater numbers of Indians and blacks, and in more profound and lasting ways.

Certainly white women, with their history of complicit racist oppression against folk of color, are *not* in a moral position to claim any right to affirmative action, unless, that is, there is such a large pool of funding for such programs that there is funding left over (a highly unlikely event) after all of the more deserving folk of color have received due support, and subsequent to adequate compensatory reparations to victims of racist oppression. So it is not that white women deserve nothing for their being discriminated against and for so long. It is that their claims to affirmative action benefits hardly "weigh in" heavily compared to the claims of various folk of color based on the history of harms against them. And this is especially true in light of how greatly white women benefited from the varieties of white privilege throughout U.S. history and from affirmative action programs since their inception. But it is also due to the fact that the amount of harm suffered by white women over the generations is counterbalanced by their oppression of others during the entirety of that same period.

Affirmative action policies and programs need not become otiose in U.S. society. Indeed, they are essential for meeting the most serious considerations of justice, especially if compensatory reparations are not forthcoming for the heirs of greatest oppression in the United States. However, as they stand, the policies supporting and defining affirmative action programs are vague and too imprecise to continue them. But I have provided a starting point for rethinking how affirmative action programs can and should be reworked so that affirmative action benefits are awarded far less arbitrarily than they are currently awarded. This revision of affirmative action programs requires numerically large political groups such as white women to support, in an unselfish manner, a system that is far more just and fair than the programs currently implemented nationwide. It requires, in short, that white women step aside and permit justice and fairness to run their proper courses in terms of affirmative action programs targeting in greater ways people of color. Where funding for such programs is always going to run short of what is needed, priorities must be established that target the most deserving. This requires, in turn, that white women support what is not in their selfish interests. It requires something that many white feminists have advocated, however hypocritically, for generations: reasonable ethnic (racial) justice and fairness in a nonideal world. It is presently time for white women in the United States to begin to walk the challenging walk, rather than merely talking the cheap talk, of racial justice. It is high time that we stop the whitewashing of affirmative action.

NOTES

This essay was originally presented at the Third Annual Conference on Race in 21st Century America, Michigan State University, April 3, 2003. The contents of this essay constitute a revised version of a section of J. Angelo Corlett, *Race, Racism, and Reparations* (Ithaca, N.Y.: Cornell University Press, 2003), chap. 7. See also J. Angelo Corlett, "Race, Ethnicity, and Public Policy," in *Race or Ethnicity?: On Black and Latino Identity*, ed. Jorge Gracia (Ithaca, N.Y.: Cornell University Press, 2007), 225–47; and J. Angelo Corlett, "Race, Racism, and Reparations," *Journal of Social Philosophy* 36 (2005): 568–85. Bill Lawson, Howard McGary, and Curtis Stokes provided very helpful comments on this paper.

1. By "Indians" is meant those whose genealogy traces to those who are indigenous to the region now occupied by the United States. By "blacks" is meant those whose genealogy traces back to slavery of Africans in the United States or those whose genealogy traces to Jim Crow.

2. By "Latinos/as" is meant that cluster of ethnic groups in the United States whose genealogies trace to Mexico, Central and South American countries, and the Caribbean countries, as well as Spain and Portugal.

3. J. Angelo Corlett, *Race, Racism, and Reparations* (Ithaca, N.Y.: Cornell University Press, 2003), chap. 5.

4. Bernard R. Boxill, *Blacks and Social Justice* (Totowa, N.J.: Rowman and Littlefield, 1984); J. Angelo Corlett, *Responsibility and Punishment*, 3rd ed. (Dordrecht: Kluwer Academic, 2006), chap. 9; Howard McGary, *Race and Social Justice* (London: Blackwell, 1999). See also *Journal of Ethics* 7 (2003): 1–160.

5. Angela Y. Davis, *Women, Race and Class* (New York: Random House, 1981), 70.

6. See bell hooks, *Ain't I a Woman* (Boston: South End Press, 1981), 121–45.

For Further Reading

Alex-Assensoh, Yvette M., and Lawrence J. Hanks, eds., *Black and Multiracial Politics in America*. New York: New York University Press, 2000.

Allegretto, Sylvia, Jared Bernstein, and Lawrence Mishel. *The State of Working America: 2006/2007*. Ithaca, N.Y.: Cornell University Press, 2007.

Anderson, Terry H. *The Pursuit of Fairness: A History of Affirmative Action*. New York: Oxford University Press, 2005.

Bean, Frank D., and Gillian Stevens. *America's Newcomers and the Dynamics of Diversity*. New York: Russell Sage Foundation, 2003.

Blauner, Bob. *Still the Big News: Racial Oppression in America*. Philadelphia: Temple University Press, 2001.

Brown, Michael K. *Whitewashing Race: The Myth of a Color-Blind Society*. Berkeley: University of California Press, 2003.

Donnelly, Jack. *The Concept of Human Rights*. London: Croom Helm, 1989.

———. *Universal Human Rights in Theory and Practice*. Ithaca, N.Y.: Cornell University Press, 1989.

Evans, Tony. *The Politics of Human Rights: A Global Perspective*. London: Pluto Press, 2005.

Graham, Hugh Davis. *The Civil Rights Era: Origins and Development of National Policy, 1960–1972*. New York: Oxford University Press, 1990.

———. *Collision Course: The Strange Convergence of Affirmative Action and Immigration Policy*. New York: Oxford University Press, 2002.

Hu-DeHart, Evelyn. *Across the Pacific: Asian Americans and Globalization*. Philadelphia: Temple University Press, 1999.

Hunt, Lynn. *Inventing Human Rights: A History*. New York: W. W. Norton, 2007.

———, ed. *The French Revolution and Human Rights: A Brief Documentary History*. New York: Bedford Book, 1996.

Ishay, Micheline R. *The History of Human Rights: From Ancient Times to the Globalization Era*. Berkeley: University of California Press, 2004.

———, ed. *The Human Rights Reader: Major Political Essays, Speeches, and Documents from Ancient Times to the Present*. 2nd ed. New York: Routledge, 2007.

Jacoby, Tamar, ed. *Reinventing the Melting Pot: The New Immigrants and What It Means to Be American*. New York: Basic Books, 2004.

Jennings, James, ed. *Blacks, Latinos, and Asians in Urban America: Status and Prospects for Politics and Activism*. Westport, Conn.: Praeger, 1994.

Jordan, Winthrop P. *White over Black: American Attitudes toward the Negro, 1550–1812*. Chapel Hill: University of North Carolina Press, 1968.

Katznelson, Ira. *When Affirmative Action Was White: An Untold History of Racial Inequality in Twentieth-Century America*. New York: W. W. Norton, 2005.

Kymlicka, Will. *Liberalism, Community, and Culture*. Oxford: Oxford University Press, 1989.

———. *Multicultural Citizenship: A Liberal Theory of Minority Rights*. Oxford: Oxford University Press, 1996.

McClain, Paula D. *"Can We All Get Along?": Racial and Ethnic Minorities in American Politics*. 4th ed. Boulder, Colo.: Westview Press, 2006.

Mills, Charles W. *Blackness Visible: Essays on Philosophy and Race*. Ithaca, N.Y.: Cornell University Press, 1998.

———. *The Racial Contract*. Ithaca, N.Y.: Cornell University Press, 1997.

Perry, Barbara A. *The Michigan Affirmative Action Cases*. Lawrence: University Press of Kansas, 2007.

Robinson, Jo Ann O., ed. *Affirmative Action: A Documentary History*. Westport, Conn.: Greenwood Press, 2001.

Rubio, Philip F. *A History of Affirmative Action: 1619–2000*. Jackson: University Press of Mississippi, 2001.

Skrentny, John D. *The Minority Rights Revolution*. Cambridge, Mass.: Belknap Press of Harvard University Press, 2007.

Smith, Rogers M. *Civic Ideals: Conflicting Visions of Citizenship in U.S. History*. New Haven, Conn.: Yale University Press, 1997.

Sowell, Thomas. *Affirmative Action around the Globe: An Empirical Study*. New Haven, Conn.: Yale University Press, 2004.

Swain, Carol M., ed. *Debating Immigration*. New York: Cambridge University Press, 2007.

Thernstrom, Abigail, and Stephan Thernstrom, eds. *Beyond the Color Line: New Perspectives on Race and Ethnicity in America*. Stanford, Calif.: Hoover Institution Press, 2002.

Vaca, Nicolas C. *The Presumed Alliance: The Unspoken Conflict between Latinos and Blacks and What It Means for America*. New York: Rayo, 2004.

Weisskopf, Thomas E. *Affirmative Action in the United States and India: A Comparative Perspective*. New York: Routledge, 2004.

Winbush, Raymond A., ed. *Should America Pay? Slavery and the Raging Debate on Reparations*. New York: Amistad, 2003.

About the Editor and Contributors

EDITOR

CURTIS STOKES is professor of political philosophy and African American politics in the James Madison College at Michigan State University. He was founding director (2002–05) of the doctoral program in African American and African Studies at Michigan State University. His publications include five books, including *The State of Black Michigan, 1967–2007* (2007), coedited with Joe T. Darden and Richard W. Thomas.

CONTRIBUTORS

ROBERT APONTE is associate professor and chairperson of the Department of Sociology at Indiana University, Indianapolis, and an affiliated scholar at the Julian Samora Research Institute at Michigan State University. He has published widely on Latino immigration, poverty, and race and ethnic relations.

WARD CHURCHILL is a former professor and chair in the Department of Ethnic Studies at the University of Colorado at Boulder. Now retired, he devotes most of his time to research and writing. Among his more than twenty books are *Act of Rebellion: The Ward Churchill Reader* (2003) and, with Jim Vander Wall, *Agents of Repression: The FBI's Secret Wars against the Black Panther Party and the American Indian Movement* (2002).

J. ANGELO CORLETT is professor in the Department of Philosophy at San Diego State University. His publications include several books, including *Race, Racism and Reparations* (2003). He is also the editor-in-chief of the *Journal of Ethics*.

PERO GAGLO DAGBOVIE is associate professor in the Department of History at Michigan State University. He is the author of several books, including *The Early Black History Movement: Carter G. Woodson, and Lorenzo Johnston Greene* (2007).

H. L. T. QUAN is assistant professor in the School of Justice and Social Inquiry at Arizona State University. She has published articles on immigration, feminism, and race and ethnic relations, and is currently working on a manuscript on development and antidemocracy.

NATSU TAYLOR SAITO is professor in the College of Law at Georgia State University. She has published extensively on race, immigration, and civil liberties. She is the author of *From Chinese Exclusion to Guantanamo Bay: Plenary Power and the Prerogative State* (2007).

ROBERT C. SMITH is professor in the Department of Political Science at San Francisco State University. He is a distinguished scholar in the field of African American politics and the author of many books, including *We Have No Leaders: African Americans in the Post–Civil Rights Era* (1996) and *American Politics and the African American Quest for Universal Freedom*, 4th ed. (2008).

DARRYL C. THOMAS is associate professor in the Department of African and African American Studies at Penn State University. He has published widely on race and ethnicity, international politics of the third world, globalization, and Africa and human rights. His most recent book is *The Theory and Practice of Third World Solidarity* (2001).

GEORGE A. YANCEY is associate professor in the Department of Sociology at the University of North Texas. An expert on race relations, he has authored several books, including *Who Is White? Latinos, Asians, and the New Black/Nonblack Divide* (2003) and *Interracial Contact and Social Change* (2007).

JONAS ZONINSEIN is professor of International Political Economy and Economics in the James Madison College at Michigan State University. His publications include articles and books on affirmative action and economic globalization, including *Monopoly Capital Theory: Hilferding and Twentieth-Century Capitalism* (1990).